THEOLOGY AND CONTEMPORARY CULTURE

LIBERATION, POSTLIBERAL AND REVISIONARY PERSPECTIVES

Drawing from postliberal, revisionary and Latin American liberation theological perspectives, David Kamitsuka offers proposals on theological method and doctrine responsive to the intellectual, pastoral and socio-political challenges of contemporary culture. He recasts intermovement polemics in order to forge a theological approach which promotes what are often considered to be competing values among these three theological movements: solidarity with the oppressed (liberationist), redescribing the Christian communal sense of scripture (postliberal), and fully critical reflection (revisionist). The author advocates an apologetic strategy entailing coherentist and consensus elements for justifying Christian claims in the pluralistic public realm. He provides a model for reading scripture theologically which addresses the challenges of poststructuralism and a globally diverse church. Kamitsuka uses rule theory to adjudicate doctrinal disputes on the relationship between salvation and political liberation, and he proposes methodological "virtues" for theological practice rooted in practical judgments concerning the vitality and fidelity of Christian communities.

DAVID G. KAMITSUKA received his doctorate in systematic theology from Yale University. He teaches modern religious thought at Oberlin College, Ohio, where he is Associate Professor of Religion. He has written articles for *Modern Theology* and the *Journal of Religion*; this is his first book.

THEOLOGY AND CONTEMPORARY CULTURE

Liberation, Postliberal and Revisionary Perspectives

DAVID G. KAMITSUKA

CAMBRIDGE
UNIVERSITY PRESS

PUBLISHED BY THE PRESS SYNDICATE OF THE UNIVERSITY OF CAMBRIDGE
The Pitt Building, Trumpington Street, Cambridge, United Kingdom

CAMBRIDGE UNIVERSITY PRESS
The Edinburgh Building, Cambridge CB2 2RU, UK http://www.cup.cam.ac.uk
40 West 20th Street, New York, NY 10011–4211, USA http://www.cup.org
10 Stamford Road, Oakleigh, Melbourne 3166, Australia

First published 1999

Printed in the United Kingdom at the University Press, Cambridge

Typeset in Baskerville

A catalogue record of this book is available from the British Library

Library of Congress cataloguing in publication data

Kamitsuka, David G.
Theology and contemporary culture: liberation, postliberal
and revisionary perspectives / David G. Kamitsuka.
p. cm.
Includes bibliographical references and index.
ISBN 0 521 65005 4 (hardback)
1. Theology–Methodology. 2. Liberation Theology.
3. Postliberal Theology. 4. Revisionary Theology
(Christian theology) I. Title
BR118.K36 1999 98-49525
230′.046–dc21 CIP

ISBN 0 521 65005 4 (hardback)

For my parents
Arthur Jun and Kazuko Lily Kamitsuka

Contents

Acknowledgments

I am most grateful to many friends and colleagues for their encouragement throughout the years of writing this book. In particular, I would like to acknowledge the invaluable assistance of those who made this book possible. I thank David H. Kelsey for his keen advice and support at key stages of this undertaking. I am also greatly indebted to Hans W. Frei (1922–1988) for inspiration on this project, on my teaching and so many other things. I very much miss his theological spirit and friendship.

For a sabbatical leave to work on this book, I am grateful to Oberlin College for the James W. and Anne F. Ford Fellowship in the Humanities. From Cambridge University Press, I would like to express my appreciation to Kevin Taylor, Senior Commissioning Editor, Religious Studies, for his support of my research and Jan Chapman for her expert copy-editing. I would also like to thank Corey L. Barnes, my former student and recent Oberlin graduate, for his painstaking work on the index.

A special word of appreciation goes to my wife, Margaret, who generously gave of her time and insight to help me bring this project to completion. Our countless discussions about drafts of these chapters were indispensable. Most especially, it is her companionship throughout this process that I will always cherish. My siblings and I continue to be blessed with the unfailing support of our parents. I dedicate this book to them as a small token of my gratitude for their love and the faith and hope which imbues their lives.

Introduction

It is my sense that I have not been alone these past several years in being deeply influenced by liberation, postliberal and revisionary movements yet puzzled also about how to bring together their best methodological and theological perspectives. These movements have drawn impressively from the powerful and forward-looking legacies of modern Christian theology. Who does not join liberation theologians in being moved by the prophetic foresight in Pope John XXIII's call for the church in the modern world to be a church of the poor? Who is unimpressed by Friedrich Schleiermacher's bold and subtle defense of religious piety in the face of religion's cultured despisers, which has inspired revisionary theology? Who does not find postliberal theology's indebtedness to Karl Barth justified in light of his masterful rendering of a strange new biblical world as a direct challenge to nationalism and other modern ills? Revisionary, postliberal and liberation theologies have been notable custodians of these modern theological legacies, precisely because of the creative ways in which they have transmuted them for the contemporary theological scene. Theology today would be well served in trying to incorporate strands of insight from these movements.

However, intermovement exchanges have not been particularly helpful to those interested in this pursuit, since theologians from these three movements have mostly squared off in ways that have produced more heat than light. For over a decade, the literature has bristled with often highly polemical comments by revisionary and postliberal theologians about each other's work. For philosophical and theological reasons, postliberals have heavily criticized revisionary strategies of making "religion experientially intelligible to the cultured and

uncultured among both its despisers and its appreciators" by attempting to secure the validity of Christian faith with problematic appeals
to foundational "universal principles or structures" of human experience.[1] Revisionary theologians, disturbed that postliberal theology
seems "too willing to leave to *ad hoc* arrangements" the task of defending Christian claims,[2] have charged them with "abandoning . . . a
public realm."[3] Latin American liberation theological writings have
come under critical scrutiny as well. Postliberal and revisionary
theologians, though appreciative of liberation theology's ethical commitments, have leveled some strong criticisms. Postliberals typically
identify liberation theology with a revisionary method which attempts
to translate the Christian faith into extratextual or "nonbiblical idioms
. . . deliberately and systematically" which they fear could jeopardize
the "biblical formation of the *sensus fidelium*."[4] Some revisionary
theologians have worried that liberation theology uses its "commitments to a particular cause [to] supply all the criteria (praxis criteria)
necessary for truth in theology" without an adequate analysis of the
"theory-laden" nature of that praxis.[5] For their part, liberation theologians have posed direct and unavoidable challenges to many of the
assumptions of those revisionary–postliberal theological debates and
have criticized their North Atlantic counterparts for applying "the
cosmetic vocabulary of 'social concern'" to their theological proposals,
"hoping to update a sluggish old inventory by slapping a new label
on obsolete goods."[6] The overall impression given to most onlookers
is that intractable differences have generated something of an
intermovement impasse.

At one level these polemics are not only understandable but fitting.
As Wesley Kort has recently observed, theologies are "bound to differ"

---

[1] George A. Lindbeck, *The Nature of Doctrine: Religion and Theology in a Postliberal Age* (Philadelphia: Westminster, 1984), p. 129.

[2] David Tracy, response to the review symposium on his *Plurality and Ambiguity* in *Theology Today* 44 (1987/88), p. 515.

[3] David Tracy, "Theology, Critical Social Theory, and the Public Realm" in *Habermas, Modernity, and Public Theology*, ed. Don S. Browning and Francis Schüssler Fiorenza (New York: Crossroad, 1992), p. 21.

[4] George A. Lindbeck, "Scripture, Consensus, and Community," *This World: A Journal of Religion and Public Life* 23 (1988), p. 14.

[5] David Tracy, "The Foundations of Practical Theology" in *Practical Theology: The Emerging Field in Theology, Church and World*, ed. Don S. Browning (San Francisco: Harper & Row, 1983), p. 61.

[6] Gustavo Gutiérrez, "Liberation Praxis and Christian Faith" in his *The Power of the Poor in History*, tr. Robert R. Barr (Maryknoll: Orbis, 1983), p. 64.

and with productive results.[7] At the risk of sacrificing nuance regarding all that is involved in the production of discourse, one might say that part of what causes a theological movement to coalesce is that theologians begin to pursue their work with the commitment to common focal values – that is, certain interests, concerns and emphases – which distinguish their approach to theology from other theologies. It is not a mischaracterization to say that revisionary theology, shaped by modernity's "turn to the subject," has confronted secularity in terms of the overarching framework of the person as *homo religiosus*. Revisionary theology's pursuit of its rightful place in the public intellectual realm by means of strategies such as mutually critical correlations between interpretations of religion and culture is driven by the focal value of promoting theology as fully critical reflection on Christian witness. Postliberal theology has emphasized the importance of an intratextual use of scripture in rendering a story which shapes Christian communal identity and has the assimilative power to absorb the world. Its focal value has been to promote the redescriptive function of theology in relation to the distinctive internal logic of Christian beliefs and practices. Liberation theology is marked by a turn not to the subject but to the subjugated. Liberation theology resists any theological strategy (correlationist or intratextually redescriptive) which might deflect from the demands of the material and spiritual needs of the oppressed. Its mode of critical reflection is concretely informed by the focal value of solidarity with the oppressed who struggle to articulate their hope in the midst of the denial of their personhood.

Given the deeply rooted differences among their paradigm-shaping theological focal values, why not let these movements go their own way, plowing their own deep furrows in roughly parallel lines? Our times require something more. The breadth of the challenges and uncertainties reflected in contemporary culture and Christian communities is simply too complex to be adequately addressed from only a single perspective. One of the ramifications of the impact of contemporary cultural plurality is that theologians, alongside other theoreticians, now face the erosion, if not deconstruction, of the categories and

---

[7] See Wesley A. Kort, *Bound to Differ: The Dynamics of Theological Discourses* (University Park, Pa.: Pennsylvania State University Press, 1992).

norms for theoretical practice which once constituted the universe
of modern scholarship. I do not want to exaggerate the situation, but
formerly reassuring beliefs about a general foundation for knowledge,
the perspicuity of texts, the objectivity of ivory-tower intellectuals,
the inevitability of social progress, and other icons of modernity can
no longer be held with the equanimity which marks the writings of
even our recent theological predecessors. More disturbing still is the
unprecedented worldwide suffering to which theology must also
respond. Our hopes for a "global village" are chastened by the urgent
voices of the truly deserted in our world who hunger for economic and
political betterment beyond the oases of the North Atlantic middle
class or even the pockets of privilege scattered throughout the world.
The demands for intelligibility in the public realm, remembering the
suffering of the victims of oppression, remaining open to plurality
within the church, and the biblical imagination necessary to form
Christian communities responsive to these challenges are simply too
great for us to continue with our isolated enclaves of theological busi-
ness as usual. More productive mutually critical conversation is needed
if theology is going to speak cogently and relevantly to the intellectual,
pastoral and socio-political challenges Christian communities face
today.

   This book pursues the contention that to begin to meet the challenges
of contemporary culture, working proposals are needed which encompass all of these movements' values: normative redescription of
Christian communal beliefs, fully critical theological reflection, and
solidarity with the oppressed. Theology must continue to serve its
redescriptive function in relation to Christian communal forms of life.
It must continue to develop as a fully critical discourse on Christian
witness, taking its proper place in the public intellectual realm. It must
continue to insist on the ethical mandate for solidarity with the
oppressed who are marginalized from dominant culture. Without
these values, theology becomes either an antiquated practice of an
intellectual elite, unable to convey the existential and social power of
the Christian story to the world; or so absorbed in the thick description
of Christian beliefs and practices that it loses all sense of accountability
to critical public dialogue; or ill-equipped vigilantly to assess ideological bias in the discourse and praxis of dominant and marginalized
Christian communities. While there are other crucial values for theo-

logical practice today, I believe any theology would do well to draw from all three of these in order to respond to the breadth of our evolving ecclesial, intellectual and political scene.

Given intermovement conflicts and criticisms, my efforts to make best use of liberation, postliberal and revisionary insights emerge in the process of recasting past misfiring conversations, clarifying differences, and pursuing common ground. These proposals and recastings of conversations are not attempts irenically to mask conflicting, at times even incommensurable, viewpoints. I merely want to propose some possibilities for promising intermovement conversation by drawing together insights from these movements in ways which may not be immediately apparent. Thus far, I have spoken of conversations among theological movements, but movements are not in conversation, theologians are. I propose, therefore, to engage the work of some key figures within these movements, in particular: revisionists Schubert Ogden and David Tracy; postliberals George Lindbeck and the late Hans Frei; and Latin American liberationists Clodovis Boff and Gustavo Gutiérrez. This strategy of addressing particular theological positions admittedly fails to do justice to the rich diversity which has emerged from within these movements, but it has the advantage of being able to correct specific misleading claims. Hence I need to make it clear that when I speak of postliberal, liberation or revisionary theology, I am making my case in light of the theologians whom I name. These theologians have been particularly influential, but I do not mean to give the impression that they represent all other theologians who associate themselves with any of these movements.[8]

Indeed, regarding revisionists, one of the arguments I will make is that there appears to be a growing divergence between some of the views of Ogden and Tracy – a divergence which coincides, not accidentally, with new areas of mutual interest among Tracy and post-liberal and liberation theologians. Postliberals have tended to gather rather closely around the fire of Lindbeck's programmatic text, *The Nature of Doctrine*, but I do not mean to imply that there are no differences or changes in thought within this movement. For example,

---

[8] For excellent introductory overviews of each of these three movements, see James J. Buckley, "Revisionists and Liberals"; Rebecca S. Chopp, "Latin American Liberation Theology"; and William C. Placher, "Postliberal Theology" in *The Modern Theologians: An Introduction to Christian Theology in the Twentieth Century*, ed. David F. Ford, 2nd edn. (Cambridge, Mass. and Oxford: Blackwell, 1997).

on issues of biblical hermeneutics, postliberals have engaged in self-critique of the postliberal platform, so to speak, which has spurred reevaluation on the issue of characterizing scripture literarily as narrative. Latin American liberation theologians, although sharing common religious and political commitments, do not make up a unified methodological approach except in the most general of senses. I have chosen to focus on Gutiérrez not only because he is one of the originators and most influential articulator of Latin American liberation theology, but also because Gutiérrez's theology is the subject matter of brief but important critical pieces by Ogden and postliberals Stanley Hauerwas and George Hunsinger.[9] My reason for choosing Boff from among the other Latin American liberation theologians, who are perhaps currently better known in North Atlantic theological circles, is that his *Theology and Praxis* has appropriately been described as "the best systematic discussion of methodological questions related to a theology of politics" which has yet emerged from Latin America.[10]

Exchange of ideas between Tracy and postliberals has been quite regular in the last decade; nevertheless, first impressions have been hard to change, necessitating a reevaluation of where Tracy and postliberals currently stand.[11] Though they have disagreed in the past, I see potential for fruitful ongoing conversation on issues as vital as apologetics and hermeneutics. There has been little actual interchange between Ogden and postliberals. Ogden has only engaged one postliberal theologian in any extended way – in his highly critical review of

[9] Schubert M. Ogden, "The Concept of a Theology of Liberation: Must Christian Theology Today Be So Conceived?" in his *On Theology* (San Francisco: Harper & Row, 1986), pp. 134–50. Stanley Hauerwas, "Some Theological Reflections on Gutierrez's Use of 'Liberation' as a Theological Concept," *Modern Theology* 3 (1986), pp. 67–76. George Hunsinger, "Karl Barth and Liberation Theology," *Journal of Religion* 63 (1983), pp. 247–63.

[10] José Míguez Bonino, *Toward a Christian Political Ethics* (Philadelphia: Fortress, 1983), p. 120 n. 3. Clodovis Boff, O.S.M., *Theology and Praxis: Epistemological Foundations*, tr. Robert R. Barr (Maryknoll: Orbis, 1987).

[11] See e.g., David Tracy, "Lindbeck's New Program for Theology: A Reflection," *Thomist* 49 (1985), pp. 460–72; "On Reading the Scriptures Theologically" in *Theology and Dialogue: Essays in Conversation with George Lindbeck*, ed. Bruce D. Marshall (University of Notre Dame Press, 1990), pp. 35–68. Hans Frei, "The 'Literal Reading' of Biblical Narrative in the Christian Tradition: Does It Stretch or Will It Break?" in *The Bible and the Narrative Tradition* (New York and Oxford: Oxford University Press, 1986), pp. 47–61. William C. Placher, "Revisionist and Postliberal Theologies and the Public Character of Theology," *Thomist* 49 (1985), pp. 392–416; *Unapologetic Theology: A Christian Voice in a Pluralistic Conversation* (Louisville: Westminster/John Knox, 1989), esp. pp. 155–60.

Frei's posthumously published *Types of Christian Theology*.[12] Likewise, postliberal theological treatments of Ogden are few and brief and nothing in-depth exists, to my knowledge, on his most recent work.[13] I intend to bring the views of Ogden and postliberals into proximity with each other in an effort to see where long-standing disagreements still hold or can give way to at least some degree of complementarity. Ogden and Tracy have addressed the work of Gutiérrez and/or Boff;[14] postliberal theologians, with the exception of Hauerwas and Hunsinger, have mentioned Gutiérrez or Boff only very briefly.[15] Notwithstanding this sparse postliberal–liberation theological interaction, I will argue at various points in this study that underexplored common ground exists between postliberal and liberation theologies on methodological and constructive theological topics.

The following three questions loosely forecast the scope of my proposals and investigations into intermovement conversation: How should one's conception of theology configure the three focal values discussed above? How should the theologian instantiate those values methodologically when defending Christian claims or using scripture theologically? How should one assess theological differences? The chapters I outline below offer responses to these questions. Chapter one serves as a general introduction to how these three movements clash or share similarities and sets the stage for the proposals which follow in subsequent chapters. This first attempt to recast conversations among

---

[12] Hans W. Frei, *Types of Christian Theology*, ed. George Hunsinger and William C. Placher (New Haven and London: Yale University Press, 1992). Ogden's review appears in *Modern Theology* 9 (1993), pp. 211–14. See also Ogden's brief comment on Lindbeck in Schubert M. Ogden, "Karl Rahner: Theologian of Open Catholicism," *Christian Advocate* (Sept. 7, 1967), p. 11.

[13] For some of these treatments, see Hans W. Frei, "Theological Reflections on the Accounts of Jesus' Death and Resurrection," *Christian Scholar* 49 (1966), pp. 303–306 and *Types*, pp. 63–64. David H. Kelsey, "Method, Theological" in *The Westminster Dictionary of Christian Theology*, ed. Alan Richardson and John Bowden (Philadelphia: Westminster, 1983), pp. 364, 365, 367. Placher, *Unapologetic Theology*, pp. 159, 171 n. 26. Ronald F. Thiemann, *Revelation and Theology: The Gospel as Narrated Promise* (University of Notre Dame Press, 1985), pp. 5–6; *Constructing a Public Theology: The Church in a Pluralistic Culture* (Louisville: Westminster/John Knox, 1991), pp. 91, 144–47, 151–53.

[14] See n. 9 above; see also Schubert M. Ogden, *Faith and Freedom: Toward a Theology of Liberation*, rev. edn. (Nashville: Abingdon, 1989), p. 77; *Is There Only One True Religion or Are There Many?* (Dallas: Southern Methodist University Press, 1992), pp. 89–91. David Tracy, *The Analogical Imagination: Christian Theology and the Culture of Pluralism* (New York: Crossroad, 1986), esp. pp. 390–91; "God of History, God of Psychology" in his *On Naming the Present: God, Hermeneutics, and Church* (Maryknoll: Orbis; London: SCM, 1994), pp. 50–53.

[15] See Kelsey, "Method, Theological," p. 364; Kathryn Tanner, *The Politics of God: Christian Theologies and Social Justice* (Minneapolis: Fortress, 1992), p. 119 n. 31.

theologians from these three movements investigates the issue of how values inform the conceptions of theology of Frei, Gutiérrez and Ogden. I argue specifically that Ogden's criticisms of how Frei and Gutiérrez conceive of theology is a factor of disagreement over the configurations of focal and unfocused values informing their conceptions. That is, what Ogden considers focal (fulfilling the task of fully critical reflection by maintaining theology's independence from the Christian witness) is also a value – albeit an unfocused and under-developed one – in Frei's and Gutiérrez's conceptions of theology. Correlatively, Ogden underappreciates how what is focally valued by Frei (theology's task of normative redescription of the Christian form of life) and Gutiérrez (theology's solidarity with the oppressed) throws a critical light on his own conception of theology. This chapter intends to clarify that while real differences exist between their configurations of focal and unfocused values, nevertheless, it is possible for all three theologians to agree in a formal way that any theology should nurture all three values. Having established this minimal ground of formal agreement, I can then move on in subsequent chapters to propose how these focal values should be instantiated methodologically. This will entail investigating the differences that arise within and between theological movements when it comes to making actual choices about specific aspects of theological practice.

Chapter two begins a two-part investigation (continued in chapter three) of what constitutes a viable approach to defending the validity of Christian claims in light of the so-called linguistic-historical turn. This issue has spawned often highly polemical debates between revisionists and postliberals, making it necessary to sift through the overstatements and understatements both groups have made about the other's views on apologetics. Chapter two highlights revisionary apologetic methods, examining how Ogden and Tracy similarly endorse fundamental theology's task of defending the theoretical credibility of Christian faith but have increasingly diverged on how to secure that credibility – due in part to the fact that each reads the demands of the current intellectual situation differently. I argue that when trying to defend the reality of God, Ogden both understates the problematic nature of his appeals to common human experience and reason and overstates the force of what his theistic arguments can establish. The effectiveness of his apologetic arguments will be tested in hypothetical exchanges with contemporary secular theorists Richard Bernstein and Richard Rorty. Tracy has significantly evolved in his stance on apologetics (originally it was quite close to Ogden's). We will trace the twists and linguistic-historical turns of his moves toward a more postmodernly sensitive, nonfoundational apologetic approach. Two elements I believe a nonfoundationalist apologetics would need are a coherentist approach to the justification of belief and a consensus approach to pluralistic public debate. Chapter three lays out a proposal for just such an apologetics.

My proposal in chapter three for a nonfoundationalist apologetic method borrows a conceptuality from recent moral philosophy called "wide reflective equilibrium," a process of bringing beliefs, principles and background theories into a coherent whole. I present this method within the polemical context of arguing that postliberals, long accused of being confessionalists, and liberationists, long accused of discarding theoretical credibility concerns for praxiological ones, do or could endorse something like this approach. From this perspective, and somewhat ironically, they are as prepared to converse in the pluralistic public realm as their revisionary colleagues. This chapter attempts to demonstrate how using a wide reflective equilibrium approach allows the theologian to defend the presuppositions as well as the constitutive claims of Christian belief via coherentist arguments during indirect and direct apologetic exchanges with proponents of competing reflective equilibria. Using critical background theories, wide reflective equilibrium tests not only the theoretical but also the practical validity of Christian claims, making it an approach that is highly compatible with liberationists' insistence on the indispensable role of the social sciences in theological practice. By promoting multifaceted, publicly intelligible argumentative strategies which move from debate to overlapping consensus with non-Christian interlocutors, wide reflective equilibrium apologetics could be seen as a method of choice for any of these theological movements.

Chapter four investigates an issue all three movements consider integral to doing Christian theology: reading the Bible theologically as the church's book – that is, as scripture in light of tradition. This entails the daunting task of adjudicating among a plurality of intracommunal and intercommunal reading practices as well as confronting the poststructuralist attack on logocentric, closed canons. My proposed approach to a scripture–tradition relationship draws from three impulses at work in revisionary, postliberal and liberationist hermeneutics: continuity, to combat textual deconstruction and communal fragmentation; plurality, to foster openness to otherness especially at the church's margins; and critique, to offset interpretive bias and textual distortions. I propose how these three hermeneutical impulses might be implemented in an approach which synthesizes methodological elements from all three movements: the functional plain sense, rule theory of doctrine, a dialectical approach to doctrinal reformulation, and critical exegetical and hermeneutical tools of analysis. I envision a hermeneutical approach where the interpretive framework is relatively stable and flexible; scripture is used normatively yet read critically; and reading practices remain dialectically open to new, especially marginalized perspectives.

Chapter five is a forward-looking thought project on an issue raised in the previous chapter: the use of rule theory for identifying inter-communal continuity among differing plain senses of scripture. In this chapter, I test that proposal specifically with a postliberal–liberationist debate initiated by Hauerwas and Hunsinger regarding the theological implications of Gutiérrez's use of the concept of liberation. I will try to demonstrate the fruitfulness of using rule theory for distinguishing between their theological "vocabularies," which differ according to context and audience, and their regulative doctrines – an exercise intended to show the kind of grammatical compatibilities and complementary differences which postliberals have previously overlooked in relation to liberation theology. This analysis is also intended to contribute to challenging a fairly widespread North Atlantic opinion that liberation theologians (and Gutiérrez, in particular) tend to conflate liberation and salvation.

Chapter six takes stock of several issues running throughout the previous chapters regarding how a theologian can effectively instantiate the three focal values analyzed in chapter one in light of practical judgments about ecclesial well being. One issue has to do with how the theologian relates the scriptural world and host culture. Another issue has to do with the kinds of obligations the theologian should fulfill when arguing for doctrinal innovation or preservation, given the diversity of Christian communities. A third has to do with how the theologian envisions the independence and connection of theology to Christian discourse and practice. Theological positions can be viewed as attempts to find the "virtuous mean" between extreme "vices" (as Aristotle might say) on each issue. I will argue for what I believe to be the virtuous mean in each case – virtuous in the sense that they uphold the focal values of all three theological movements.

The impression I wish to leave with the reader is that recasting inter-movement conversations is a fruitful way to open new methodological and constructive avenues for conversations on theology in contemporary culture. Reflecting on theology in light of these movements' values would seem to be imperative if theology is going to be able to address the deterioration of modernity's philosophical bulwarks, the weakening of Christian communal cohesion, and the irruption of the oppressed from the underside of history. This book's offerings attempt to draw from the promise of revisionary, postliberal and liberation movements to envision a theology responsive to our uncertain yet hopeful age.

CHAPTER ONE

Values informing conceptions of theology

In analyzing revisionary, postliberal and liberation conceptions of theology, we enter into the midst of intermovement polemics. This might well be expected since conceptions of theology are informed by a host of complex theological judgments and values which take shape in relation to the wide-ranging intellectual, ecclesial and socio-political exigencies confronting theology in contemporary culture. Inevitably, theologians will read those demands differently, placing greater or lesser stress on various concerns and agendas which, in turn, affects the way they orient their theologies. The opportunities for differences and disputes abound. For example, Ogden believes that any adequate conception of theology today must value theology's task of assessing critically any and all Christian claims and, to do this fully, theology must have sufficient independence from the Christian witness on which it reflects. Without this value, theology is reduced to propaganda. The academic theological guild has fought long and hard to secure its freedom from being forced to be an arm of any group's imposition of belief, and this value would promote that intellectual freedom for theology. Frei's conception of theology values theology's ecclesial function of redescribing Christian communal attempts to render a habitable scriptural world. Without this value, theology is too easily absorbed into other semiotic systems with no distinctly Christian theological perspective to offer an increasingly secular, biblically illiterate and fragmented society. For Gutiérrez, theology adequately conceived must come to terms with the call for solidarity with the oppressed by responding to their material needs and attending to their spiritual wisdom. Without this value of solidarity, theology will simply continue to instantiate the self-serving socio-political interests of the privileged – undisturbed, except in the most superficial ways, by both the suffering and the theological richness from the underside of history.

Not surprisingly, these differences have fueled intermovement polemics. Ogden wonders whether a postliberal conception of theology such as Frei's "is entirely lacking in a 'critical' aspect and, therefore, is a purely 'descriptive' activity" which is not really theology but something "that could just as well be left to the social scientist or the analytic philosopher."[1] Frei may have revisionary theologies such as Ogden's in mind when describing "the story of modern Christian theology" as "almost exclusively that of . . . apologetics"; whether or not "this development has now just about run its course," Frei believes theology should "search for alternatives."[2] Ogden suggests that what Gutiérrez proposes is not really theology at all but a form of Christian witness because it amounts to, "the mere rationalization of positions already taken."[3] Ogden, with his move "toward a theology of liberation," could be a target for Gutiérrez's charge about the "'trendiness'" of first-world academic theologians who "simply tack on the word 'liberation' to whatever they have always been saying anyway."[4]

To conclude that these are pure instances of conflict between conceptions of theology whose lines of difference are clearly understood is mistaken. I read these comments as indicative of misfiring conversations, so to speak, about configurations of focal and unfocused values informing conceptions of theology. Conflicts of these sorts can occur when theologians unduly conclude that what is focally valued in their conception of theology is completely lacking in another theologian's conception of theology. In actuality, that value may not be absent but underdeveloped or given lower priority in relation to other values. It is, one might say, an unfocused value. Furthermore, and perhaps more importantly, theologians sometimes miss the significance

[1] Schubert M. Ogden, review of *Types of Christian Theology*, by Hans W. Frei, *Modern Theology* 9 (1993), p. 212.

[2] Hans W. Frei, "Remarks in Connection with a Theological Proposal" in his *Theology and Narrative: Selected Essays*, ed. George Hunsinger and William C. Placher (New York and Oxford: Oxford University Press, 1993), p. 27.

[3] Schubert M. Ogden, "The Concept of a Theology of Liberation: Must Christian Theology Today Be So Conceived?" in his *On Theology* (San Francisco: Harper & Row, 1986), p. 143.

[4] Schubert M. Ogden, *Faith and Freedom: Toward a Theology of Liberation*, rev. edn. (Nashville: Abingdon, 1989). Gustavo Gutiérrez, "Liberation Praxis and Christian Faith" in his *The Power of the Poor in History*, tr. Robert R. Barr (Maryknoll: Orbis, 1988), p. 64. (Where I have quoted an author quoting another author's word(s) I have used two sets of inverted commas.)

of another theologian's differing focal value and how its focalness implicitly challenges weaknesses in their own conception of theology. To complicate the situation further, the apparent clash of focal values is often linked to conflict over whether to define theology strictly or broadly. A strict definition reserves the term theology for second-order discourse – that is, critical reflection *on* Christian belief and practice; whereas theology broadly defined encompasses both second-order theological reflection and first-order reflection *in* faith done within Christian communities. We will see below how conflicts over focal values intersect with clashes over applying the term theology strictly or broadly.

This chapter is by no means an exhaustive analysis of any theologian's conception of theology but, rather, is a heuristic exercise which tracks how theological values inform conceptions of theology. I also endeavor to support the claim that any adequate conception of theology today should entail some configuration of all the values which these three movements promote: fully critical reflection, normative redescription of Christian communal beliefs, and solidarity with the oppressed. I hope to demonstrate that Ogden, Frei and Gutiérrez can be shown to agree formally on this point because each one gives some explicit or implicit support for all three values. At any given time or place, theologians may have very good reasons for prioritizing one of these values over others; furthermore, there are other theological values arising from other contextual challenges not addressed within the scope of this chapter (e.g., religious plurality, ecological destruction, other systemic social evils, etc.). Nonetheless, agreement at least on the validity of these three values carves out a minimum area of formal conceptual common ground for meeting many pressing issues of contemporary culture. In subsequent chapters, we will examine what it means to translate these values methodologically into theological practice, and it will be in the process of making proposals about theology and its practice that I will try to make good on upholding all three of these values.

This chapter will proceed as follows. In the first section, I investigate two specific examples of misfiring conversations regarding how to conceive of theology – one initiated recently by Ogden with Frei regarding his *Types of Christian Theology* and another with Gutiérrez. I will argue that in both cases, Ogden rightly identifies underdeveloped

areas in Frei's and Gutiérrez's conceptions of theology, but his conclusions are misleading or unhelpful in light of their writings as a
whole. Not only does Ogden mistake the unfocused nature of certain
values for a glaring deficiency in Frei's and Gutiérrez's conceptions of
theology but, also, he underappreciates how the focal values his
postliberal and liberation theological colleagues bring to the conversation critically interrogate the configuration of focal and unfocused
values in his own conception of theology. In the second section, I will
make a case for how mutual recognition of the values informing each
one's conception of theology creates conditions for constructive intermovement challenges regarding each theologian's most unfocused
value. For example, Gutiérrez can be challenged to clarify how liberation theology can be both engaged and independently critical. Frei
can be challenged to clarify how postliberal redescriptive theology
can value the call for solidarity with the oppressed. Ogden can be
challenged to clarify how his revisionary approach can protect
theology's connection to Christian communal forms of life – which is
a crucial aspect of both normative redescription and solidarity with
the oppressed.

RECASTING MISFIRING CONVERSATIONS

Frei's theology – descriptive social science?

In a review of Frei's posthumously published *Types of Christian Theology*,
Ogden argues that he has found real conceptual inadequacies in Frei's
conception of theology. I will argue that although Ogden uncovers
underdeveloped aspects, his "misgivings" that Frei's conception of
theology is "entirely lacking in a 'critical' aspect" are challenged by a
more complete view of how Frei conceives of theology.[5] The narrowness of Ogden's emphasis on a few passages from *Types of Christian
Theology*, coupled with the roughness in Frei's manuscript and the

---

[5] Ogden, review of *Types*, p. 212. Several provisoes must be made at the start about Frei's text. As
explained by the book's editors, with the exception of Appendix C (Frei's review of Eberhard
Busch's biography of Karl Barth), this posthumously published volume is comprised largely of
lecture notes. See Hans W. Frei, *Types of Christian Theology*, ed. George Hunsinger and William
C. Placher (New Haven and London: Yale University Press, 1992), pp. ix–x. These pieces
were in various stages of transition into Frei's intended book-length study on christology which
was never completed. What is obvious, as Ogden acknowledges, is that this is not the book
Frei envisioned, and it is not free from problems of inconsistency, repetition and lack of overall
cohesion.

zealousness of Ogden's own point of view regarding what needs to be corrected in it, gives too skewed a picture of Frei's conception of theology and theological values. Therefore I will also refer to texts other than *Types of Christian Theology* where he addresses issues pertinent to Ogden's criticisms. This will give us a more balanced picture of the focal and unfocused values informing Frei's conception of theology. It is my contention that Ogden's critique is a factor of differing configurations of focal and unfocused values. Therefore, allowing a fuller presentation of Frei's conception of theology to form the backdrop to Ogden's critique will, I believe, move the conversation forward by putting the differences between Frei's postliberal and Ogden's revisionary orientations into a more useful perspective.

Frei envisions theology as a vocation in which the theologian does not speak for him or herself "without first speaking for the community." This claim is at the heart of his focal value of normative theological redescription of the Christian form of life and shapes his conception of theology. What does it mean to speak "for" the community? It has nothing to do with either an exaggerated sense of the authority of the theologian in matters ecclesial or an expectation that the theologian should uncritically promulgate the church's beliefs. The theologian's most pressing objective is (as Clifford Geertz would say) to redescribe thickly the internal logic of the faith which is displayed in the community's speech and action, particularly in its reading of scripture. This means that theology must not only think *about* but *with* the community – that is, with "the cumulative tradition and the most supple and sensitive minds and consciences in the community past and present." Thus, while many of Frei's texts precede the development of certain postliberal terms (indeed, the term "postliberal" itself), his work as a whole supports directly or indirectly the postliberal focal value of the theological thick description of Christian communal discourse and practice.[6]

A very particular issue stands at the heart of this theological value

---

[6] Hans W. Frei, "Theology and the Interpretation of Narrative: Some Hermeneutical Considerations" in his *Theology and Narrative*, p. 100. In characteristically cultural-linguistic, postliberal fashion, Frei believes that this redescriptive task is enhanced by Geertzian and Wittgensteinian notions of religion viewed as a cultural and "semiotic system within which we . . . orient ourselves [and] . . . become native" by learning to use its grammar as in a "language game." Frei, *Types*, p. 13. On thick description, see George A. Lindbeck, *The Nature of Doctrine: Religion and Theology in a Postliberal Age* (Philadelphia: Westminster, 1984), p. 115.

for Frei: the status of the historically normative Christian communal *sensus literalis* of scripture. As we will see in chapter four, postliberal theologians speak more and more of the literal sense as the traditional "plain sense" of scripture – a functional term designating the Christian community's use of the Bible as authoritative, but they draw from Frei's research to assert that historically the plain sense has largely been the literal, history-like reading of the story. Most of his writings have addressed, from one angle or another – historical, dogmatic, hermeneutical, ecclesial – what has followed from the eclipse of the literal sense in the modern era: a lack of religious sensitivity to the biblical narrative structure, a dissolving of the ascriptive identity of Jesus, a loss of common interpretive ground with Jewish midrashic traditions, and so on.[7] In addition to a plethora of historical-critical approaches, a growing number of hermeneutical alternatives in the modern and postmodern periods compete with the church's literal sense. There are interpretations which take scripture as: prefiguring "'a new eternal gospel'" (Lessing); moral allegory within the limits of reason alone, so to speak (Kant); "haunting" us with its "foreclosing secrecy" (Kermode); disappearing in an "'intertextual' network" (deconstructionists); disclosing "the 'religious dimension of common human experience'" (Ricoeur); even exemplifying the genre of realistic narrative (New Criticism).[8]

The value Frei places on the church's historically normative plain sense of scripture is not meant to preclude the theologian from borrowing from various hermeneutical approaches, including those listed above. Rather, he sets the first-order theological discourse of the church, rooted in the plain sense, in a certain position of high visibility within the conversation of the Bible's various interpreters. In this way, the "implicit logic governing the sensus literalis," as articulated in first-order discourse, asserts itself as a plumbline for the theologian's use of

---

[7] These and other themes are discussed throughout Frei's writings but chiefly and most fully in *The Eclipse of Biblical Narrative: A Study in Eighteenth and Nineteenth Century Hermeneutics* (New Haven and London: Yale University Press, 1974) and "The 'Literal Reading' of Biblical Narrative in the Christian Tradition: Does It Stretch or Will It Break?" in *The Bible and the Narrative Tradition*, ed. Frank McConnell (New York and Oxford: Oxford University Press, 1986), pp. 36–77. One could say that Frei's *Types of Christian Theology* is a long commentary on how the literal sense stretches or breaks in various ways. Or we could look at his mapping of the different types of modern theology in this book as a kind of synchronic presentation of the status of the literal sense which complements the diachronic presentation in *The Eclipse of Biblical Narrative*.

[8] Frei, "Literal Reading," pp. 42–43, 48, 63; *Types*, p. 59.

other hermeneutical tools.[9] Without this plumbline, theology may come under the influence of any number of alternative hermeneutical or historical-critical readings of the Bible, which may or may not have anything relevant or constructive to contribute to the role Christian scripture has played historically as "a guide to life, an inspiration to heart and mind, a norm for believing."[10] For Frei, privileging Christian communal readings of scripture goes hand in hand with recognizing that first-order Christian discourse is a kind of theology and that the term should not be restricted to the second-order theological discourses of professional theologians.[11] In other words, he uses the term theology broadly rather than strictly, which reflects postliberal theology's focal value about (professional) theology's redescriptive task involving reflection with the Christian community.

Theology thus defined attempts to identify the "interpretive pattern" instantiated in the Christian communal use of scripture through which "*all* of reality is experienced and read" by the Christian believer.[12] To my mind, if theology were to devalue the task of identifying the implicit logic of scripture with which Christians can interpret their world, it would compromise one of its most important ecclesial, cultural and political functions. In an age where texts are losing their intrinsic meaning, to be able to use scripture to construct a habitable world could be decisive for vital Christian communities in the future. Frei intuitively recognizes that the existential power and social relevance of the Christian story is more likely to come from the biblically and ecclesially formed community of believers than from the academic theological guild. His focal value of thickly redescribing a scriptural world may seem unduly inward-looking to some especially in our pluralistic age; however, he reads the contribution of theology in our historical moment differently. For Frei, modern theology has often been distracted from its distinctive vocation as rigorous redescriber of the internal logic or grammar of Christian communal discourse; it has so accommodated to modern culture for apologetic purposes that it no longer brings its particular word to the world but simply reinforces secular culture by providing it with a balm of transcendent security.

9 Frei, *Types*, p. 44.
10 Frei, "Literal Reading," p. 68.
11 See Frei, *Types*, pp. 20–21, 40.
12 Frei, "Literal Reading," p. 72.

His focal value is meant to nurture the community's Christian identity, and a community that knows its own identity "might then contribute once again to [Western] culture or its residues, including its political life, its quest for justice and freedom."[13]

Ogden does not address any of these issues related to Frei's focal value. Instead he turns his attention to analyzing Frei's conception of theology in terms of the value Ogden has brought into the sharpest focus in his own conception of theology – that is, maintaining theology's capacity to reflect critically on the Christian witness. For Ogden, Christian theology is defined as "deliberate, methodical, and reasoned . . . reflection on the claims expressed or implied by . . . the Christian witness of faith."[14] This definition is derived from what he believes constitutes critical reflection generally in any liberal arts discipline in the academy: answering the twofold question of meaning and truth without special pleading. To reflect critically, the theologian must hold that "the thought and speech distinctive to the Christian religion are privileged data only with respect to the *meaning* of what is thought and said, not with respect to its truth" which must be validated according to general (not religion-specific) criteria.[15] A Christian claim is appropriate when congruent with the normative witness of faith and credible when congruent with scholarly general criteria for truth.[16] These are what Ogden takes to be the formal defining tasks and criteria of theology as fully critical reflection, and they remain the constant demand which must be met for discourse to be genuinely theological.

While theology's task of validating the appropriateness and credibility of the Christian witness is preeminent for Ogden, theology is meant to serve more than the demands of the critically reflective process in and of itself. Christian theological reflection has "goals . . . [which] cannot be limited simply to the advancement of theology itself as a distinct form of theoretical reflection." The goal of theology is linked to its reason for existing at all – that is, the prior existence of the Christian witness of faith. "Were it not for this witness, theological

[13] Ibid., p. 74.
[14] Schubert M. Ogden, "Theology and Religious Studies: Their Difference and the Difference It Makes" in his *On Theology*, p. 116.
[15] Schubert M. Ogden, "Theology in the University" in his *On Theology*, p. 127.
[16] See Ogden, *On Theology*, pp. 139, 140. Ogden claims that the "ultimate criteria for the truth . . . can only be our common human experience and reason" (p. 140). This claim will be evaluated in ch. 2.

reflection as such would have neither object nor data; and there certainly would be no need for it without the continuing praxis of witness that it exists to serve."[17] Given then that theological reflection depends on the prior existence of the Christian witness, what is the nature of the service theology exists to provide to the church? Here Ogden is adamant. In order for the service rendered by theology to be fully critical, the service must be indirect and comprehensive. It must be indirect, because theology cannot assume the validity of any Christian claim. Theology, like any critical reflection, "can validate the claims on which it reflects only insofar as it is sufficiently independent also to invalidate them."[18] The service theology provides must also be comprehensive – that is, no aspect of the Christian witness can be exempt from theology's critical purview – "including not least those [aspects] comprising the official teaching or doctrine of the church."[19] If theology's service to the church were to be direct or restricted in its scope, it would become a "mere rationalization of positions already taken."[20] When Ogden calls for the emancipation of theology from any such rationalizing function, he raises a vitally important issue. To conceive of theology as under pressure simply to approve existing church doctrine (or conversely not to see theology as obligated to assess any religious belief or practice) would certainly call into question its status as fully critical reflection. Whether one's theological vocation is situated primarily in the academy or the church, Ogden is surely right in valuing a conception of theology which strives to be fully critical.

My endorsement of his focal value notwithstanding, I dispute the way Ogden brings these concerns to his reading of Frei's *Types of Christian Theology* and sees a conception of theology so devoid of this kind of critical function that it appears to be "a purely 'descriptive' activity of the sort that could just as well be left to the social scientist or the analytic philosopher."[21] More precisely stated, Ogden is not

[17] Schubert M. Ogden, "On Teaching Theology," *Criterion* 25 (1986), p. 14. See also Schubert M. Ogden, "The Nature and State of Theological Scholarship and Research," *Theological Education* 24 (1987–88), p. 126.

[18] Schubert M. Ogden, "The Service of Theology to the Servant Task of Pastoral Ministry" in *The Pastor as Servant*, ed. Earl E. Shelp and Ronald H. Sutherland (New York: Pilgrim, 1986), p. 97. See also Ogden, "Theological Scholarship," p. 127 and "Theology in the University: The Question of Integrity" in his *Doing Theology Today* (Valley Forge, Pa.: Trinity, 1996), p. 90.

[19] Schubert M. Ogden, "Toward Doing Theology," *Journal of Religion* 75 (1995), p. 10.

[20] Ogden, *On Theology*, p. 143.

[21] Ogden, review of *Types*, p. 212.

suggesting that Frei makes faith a precondition for doing theology (a charge he levels at Gutiérrez); rather he faults Frei with failing to specify the necessity of testing the validity of Christian claims and, hence, resting content with a purely descriptive endeavor. I believe his critique is a function of a conflict over configurations of focal and unfocused values, complicated by a clash over whether to define theology strictly or broadly.

Following from his insistence on the indirect service of theology for the Christian witness, Ogden advocates that the term "theology" is best used strictly and not broadly. While he affirms that "all Christians simply as such share in the common responsibility" of "critically reflecting on the validity of the Christian witness," nevertheless, the reflection in which most Christians engage cannot be called theology in the proper sense of the word at all. Although he has at times conceded that "there is clear precedent in tradition for using 'theology' in . . . a broad sense, and I have no objection to its still being so used," he harbors serious worries about continuing to promote anything other than a strict usage of the term. He feels that the need for doing fully critical reflection today is so "urgent" that "there are the best of reasons why the word 'theology' should have come to have the much stricter sense."[22] Ogden believes that not defining theology strictly leads to: (1) a failure in "clearly and consistently distinguish[ing] the secondary praxis of doing theology from the primary praxis of bearing witness"; and (2) theology "concerned solely with explicating the *meaning* of the Christian witness and not also with establishing its *truth*."[23] Proponents of a strict definition of theology, such as Ogden, are wary that proponents of a broad definition, such as Frei, will fail on both counts.

On the first point, Frei, in principle, maintains a distinction between theology and witness (as Ogden would put it) by specifying that while the term theology covers first- and second-order discourse, these two discourses are not the same. The church's first-order "self-involving" theological discourse, including the communal plain sense of scripture – important as it is from Frei's perspective – is not all of theology. He maintains that just as first-order theological discourse is vital, so also is second-order redescription and critical "appraisal"; theologies that do

[22] Ogden, "Service of Theology," p. 90; "Toward Doing Theology," pp. 2, 5.
[23] Ogden, "Toward Doing Theology," pp. 9, 8.

not maintain this distinction result in "a muddle."[24] He is clear on the aspect of appraisal which Ogden associates with appropriateness issues. Frei specifies that after theology (descriptively) articulates the internal logic or grammar of first-order Christian speech, it critically assesses "any given articulation of Christian language" according to "norms governing Christian use."[25] In light of these points, we can safely say that Frei's broad definition of theology is not without the necessary distinctions that make critical appraisal possible. Nevertheless, does second-order theology include a *fully* critical task, validating not just the appropriateness but also the theoretical credibility of Christian beliefs?

Theoretical credibility, which traditionally has been central to Christian apologetics, is a less-than-clear aspect in Frei's manuscript (thus irking Ogden). He does speak of a "quasi-philosophical or philosophical activity . . . which consists of trying to tell others, perhaps outsiders of how [Christian-specific discourse would] . . . compare and contrast with their kinds of ruled discourse." Elsewhere, he states that this activity is meant to "show us why or how it is the case that statements within a religious context are not the same as apparently similar or identical statements made outside the religious contexts."[26] Frei does not follow with a proposal for how he would carry out this apologetic endeavor; however, he does speak approvingly of how Karl Barth does "*ad hoc* apologetics, in order to throw into relief particular features of . . . [the biblical] world by distancing them from or approximating them to . . . descriptions of . . . other linguistic worlds."[27] He suggests that Barth's apologetics are *ad hoc* precisely in order to resist giving external description of Christianity (e.g., a general phenomenology of religious experience or a general hermeneutic of religious texts) the upper hand over Christian self-description in theological method. He attributes to Barth the view that while theology makes indispensable use of general philosophical concepts, redescriptive theology grounded in internal Christian norms "takes absolute priority over theology as an academic discipline," with its concern for rendering positive religion intelligible according to universal

---

[24] Frei, *Types*, pp. 26, 124, 49.
[25] Ibid., p. 2.
[26] Ibid., pp. 21, 48.
[27] Ibid., p. 161.

categories.[28] However, Frei is quick to qualify Barth's rather unyielding stance, explaining that Barth's methodological rule for this "subordination" of external philosophical concepts to Christian self-description "cannot be stated abstractly but must be worked in specific application." In practice, Frei points out, Barth's position on the absolute priority of Christian self-description was "a *pragmatic* priority choice" in light of "the theological [and one might also say political] *situation* of his day."[29] Barth's theological and methodological stance may have continuing application outside the German confessing church, but it was inspired and crafted within that particular context. This historical observation about Barth leaves Frei open to deciding what kind of "priority" should be accorded to Christian self-description in his context.

Frei gives only indications in *Types of Christian Theology* about just what kind of relationship he would want to see obtain between internal Christian self-description and external description regarding *ad hoc* apologetics. The indications are woven throughout his typing of modern theology and must be limned from his assessments of the various types – not an easy task given that Frei, it seems to me, was grappling with many issues in this not fully formulated typology.[30] I am interested in finding out what the typology (its incompleteness aside) can tell us about the kind of quasi-philosophical or philosophical activity he envisioned as useful and the extent of his interest in pursuing theoretical credibility questions. I would argue that his stance emerges from the way he grapples with Barth and Schleiermacher in his typology. Is Frei a Barthian "Type Four," where apologetics are *ad hoc* because Christian self-description takes absolute priority over external

---

[28] Ibid., p. 40. The term academic, in Barth's day, referred to that "untranslatable German word *Wissenschaft*" with its "general criteria of intelligibility, coherence, and truth" (pp. 97, 2). Academic theology adopted a theological method which was subsumed under *wissenschaftlich* criteria.

[29] Ibid., pp. 42, 43. Frei discusses how Barth sought to counteract the theological and political consequences of certain liberal German theologies which compromised this priority by seeking to correlate Christian self-description with concepts drawn from the culture of German national renewal in the 1930s (see pp. 154ff.).

[30] He was clearly trying to hold many variables and issues in play – perhaps more than can be done on a single axis typology. One of the editors of *Types of Christian Theology*, George Hunsinger, identifies several polar themes Frei was tracing, all at the same time, including: general or Christian-specific criteria; external or internal modes of describing the Christian religion; symbolic vs. literal interpretations of Jesus. See George Hunsinger, "Afterword: Hans Frei as Theologian" in Frei, *Theology and Narrative*, pp. 259ff.

philosophical description which employs generally applicable criteria? (Ogden assumes so.[31]) Or is there anything in Schleiermacher's brand of "Type Three" correlational theology which would bear on Frei's view of how to render the Christian faith publicly credible?

Frei recognizes that his interpretation of Schleiermacher might be contested because he is "a controversial case," but we can pass over this historical theology controversy. My concern here is solely with Frei's interest in "the direction of the endeavor" of Type Three.[32] What fascinated him about Schleiermacher was his commitment (at least with regard to his reading of the story of Jesus) both to maintain "genuine continuity" with "the Church's understanding of scripture" and to correlate external description and internal description in light of the cultured despisers of religion (thus irking Barth).[33] Schleiermacher's method of correlation, in Frei's view, "proposes no supertheory or comprehensive structure" for bringing external and internal description together but rather appeals to "an ad hoc conceptual instrument," namely, "'a little introspection.'"[34] Thus, Schleiermacher had his own kind of *ad hoc* apologetics which caught Frei's eye. Whether Schleiermacher succeeded in his day on the tasks of both appropriateness and credibility we can leave aside (Frei himself was "not sure"[35]). My question is whether Frei was interested in pursuing anything in the spirit of Schleiermacher's theological approach for his own intellectual context.

A hermeneutical key is needed to read Frei's unfinished assessments of Types Three and Four correctly – a key which I believe is found in his article "Barth and Schleiermacher: Divergence and Convergence." By the end of this essay, notwithstanding his Barthian affinities, Frei seems to speak as much through Schleiermacher as through Barth! It is the voice of what Frei calls his "hypothetical Schleiermacher" which points out the risk of conceiving of theology as a purely internally ruled descriptive undertaking. Frei's Schleiermacher wonders (with Frei

---

[31] Ogden, review of *Types*, p. 214.

[32] Frei, *Types*, pp. 70, 38.

[33] Ibid., p. 66.

[34] Ibid., pp. 3, 71. Frei is quoting from Friedrich Schleiermacher, *The Christian Faith*, tr. H. R. MacKintosh and J. S. Stewart (Edinburgh: T. & T. Clark, 1928), p. 13. As Frei states: "It's as though the principle of correlation *could* have been something else if he hadn't lived in Prussia when he did and experienced the philosophical possibilities of his time" (p. 71).

[35] Ibid., p. 36.

adding parenthetical comments): "Without the constant, continuing *practice* of correlation (although surely it must be without a comprehensive principle of correlation), do not all criteria for intelligibility . . . go out the window . . . ? . . . Does not Christian theology threaten to turn into the in-group talk of one isolated community among others, with no ground rules for mutual discourse among them all?"[36] Frei's Schleiermacher sees the slippery slope one ventures out on with a strict Barthian method. When Frei concludes in *Types of Christian Theology* that for theologians such as Schleiermacher and Barth, "[a]t *some* point, though not too quickly, *philosophical* agnosticism has to set in in the interest of full-blooded Christian theology," one has the sense that the phrase "though not too quickly" is directed pointedly at Barth (and Barthians).[37] Hence it would be misleading to speak too blithely of Frei as a Type Four theologian after the model of Barth. Doing so obscures how Frei, who found a way to see through both Schleiermacher's and Barth's eyes, was oscillating somewhere between Types Three and Four.[38] He could see that each type has its own slippery slope. Type Three risks being pulled toward a position reductive of Christian-specific meaning; Type Four risks being pulled toward in-group talk, eschewing concerns for public defenses of the Christian faith. Even without having fleshed out a method for how to do theology in a way that maintains firm footing on both slippery slopes, Frei can be read as endorsing the importance of validating the theoretical credibility of Christian claims with some kind of accountability to public criteria of intelligibility.

If the above recast conversation between Ogden and Frei has rendered a plausible interpretation of Frei's conception of theology, then it would be accurate to say that fully critical reflection is a value for him, albeit an unfocused one. While theology's redescriptive, ecclesially oriented task is focal for Frei, he is also concerned with what is focal for Ogden's conception of theology. The issue is one of priorities

---

[36] In *Barth and Schleiermacher: Beyond the Impasse*, ed James O. Duke and Robert F. Streetman (Philadelphia: Fortress, 1988), p. 85.

[37] Frei, *Types*, p. 91.

[38] This interpretation is supported by David Ford's observation that after one of the Cadbury lectures (from which some of the material in *Types of Christian Theology* is taken), Frei commented "that he would probably place himself between Types 3 and 4." David F. Ford, "On Being Theologically Hospitable to Jesus Christ: Hans Frei's Achievement," *Journal of Theological Studies* 46 (1995), p. 538.

given historical contingencies. The modulation of Frei's priorities is nicely summarized when he states that the theologian's "first task is . . . to give a normative description rather than positioning himself [or herself] to set forth or argue Christian truth claims."[39] This position is surely informed by his reading of how tempting it has been in the modern and contemporary periods to eclipse the plain sense of scripture for the expedience of apologetics. Without a doubt, he was struggling to bring into focus for himself a postliberal approach for publicly validating Christian discourse in a way that would not eclipse the role of the plain sense of scripture in theological redescription. However, it would be inaccurate to conclude that Frei's focus on redescription means he conceives of theology as merely descriptive social science, entirely lacking in a formal endorsement of the value of theology as fully critical reflection. What is at issue is the configuration of focal and unfocused values.

Gutiérrez's theology – Christian ideology?

Gutiérrez, as one of the original articulators of an innovative theological movement, has concentrated less on defining theology systematically and more on the overall paradigm shift theology needs to make in light of the challenges from the underside of history. As with many a "revolutionary" theological thinker, the precision of method arises after the theological challenge is nailed to the church door. Yet, to characterize Gutiérrez's thought as theologically "revolutionary" is itself misleading because his theological approach is to a great extent one of retrieving for his Latin American context many aspects of traditional Christian theology and spirituality – always with the intent of empowering the church of the poor. In contrast to Ogden, Gutiérrez would find it constraining to define theology currently being done in Latin America by the particular sets of questions and criteria of adequacy which Ogden uses to secure theology's legitimacy as a form of inquiry in the academy. For Gutiérrez, liberation theology is not defined as a particular form of inquiry (e.g., a specific case of generic critical reflection). Rather, liberation theology encompasses all reflection about God which functions in various ways in the service of the church's worship and God's liberating activity in the world. He maintains the "deep and irreversible

[39] Frei, *Theology and Narrative*, p. 100.

conviction that we must avoid an academic theology disassociated from grassroots . . . theology" and popular piety.[40] For Gutiérrez (as for Frei), the term theology is not restricted to (academically oriented) critical reflection on the various forms of Christian witness but includes all forms of the church's reflective activity. This broad conception of theology goes hand in hand with his attempt to implement his focal value of solidarity by affirming the "'theologising' potential" of the church of the poor, which "needs to understand itself, for its own sake." It is incumbent on the professional theologian to listen not only to the questions arising from the grassroots context but also to the "answers which these Christians are discovering for themselves" as they reflect on their life and faith.[41]

With this value in mind, the forms of service theological reflection performs are broad ranging: both direct and indirect, in faith and on it. Gutiérrez's exposition of these forms (or as he calls them, theological "functions") are sparse and scattered throughout his writings, leaving himself open for misinterpretation. He says that "[c]ritical reflection 'in light of the word' is only one function of theology (the others are theology as wisdom and theology as rationally organized knowledge)";[42] or "[t]heology as critical reflection on Christian praxis in light of the Word does not replace the other functions of theology, such as wisdom and rational knowledge; rather it presupposes and needs them";[43] or "[t]heology will be reflection in and

[40] Gustavo Gutiérrez, "Reflections from a Latin American Perspective: Finding Our Way to Talk about God," tr. John Drury, in *Irruption of the Third World*, ed. Virginia Fabella and Sergio Torres (Maryknoll: Orbis, 1983), p. 224. See, José Míguez Bonino, "Popular Piety in Latin America," tr. J. P. Donnelly, in *The Mystical and Political Dimensions of the Christian Faith*, ed. Claude Geffré and Gustavo Gutiérrez (New York: Herder & Herder, 1974), pp. 148–57.

[41] Gustavo Gutiérrez, "The Task of Theology and Ecclesial Experience," tr. Dinah Livingston, in *La Iglesia Popular: Between Fear and Hope*, Concilium 176, ed. Leonardo Boff and Virgil Elizondo (Edinburgh: T. & T. Clark, 1984), pp. 62, 63. This broad use of the term theology can have institutional ramifications. For example, Gutiérrez describes how an EATWOT (Ecumenical Association of Third World Theologians) conference decided not to restrict participation to professional theologians but to include nonacademically trained people working at the base Christian community level. Dialogue such as this among a diversity of theological voices leads inevitably to certain "tensions" and "confrontations," which are, Gutiérrez affirms, "very beneficial and enriching" and which strengthen both Christian activity and critical reflection (Gutiérrez, "Reflections from a Latin American," p. 225).

[42] Gustavo Gutiérrez, *The Truth Shall Make You Free: Confrontations*, tr. Matthew J. O'Connell (Maryknoll: Orbis, 1990), p. 103.

[43] Gustavo Gutiérrez, *A Theology of Liberation: History, Politics, and Salvation*, tr. and ed. Sister Caridad Inda and John Eagleson; author's new introduction and revisions, tr. Matthew J. O'Connell (Maryknoll: Orbis, 1988), p. 11. See Gutiérrez, *Truth*, p. 182 n. 50.

on faith."[44] I read Gutiérrez's theology as a threefold, differentiated but interrelated reflective activity whose elements or functions may be labeled: spiritual theology (or theology as wisdom), theology as rational knowledge, and theology as critical reflection on Christian praxis.

Spiritual theology is reflection from within the Christian community which expresses the Christian form of life in its various dimensions. Historically, Gutiérrez explains, spiritual theology has entailed "meditation on the Bible, geared toward spiritual growth" which took any number of oral or written forms.[45] Whatever the form, it usually consisted of some pastoral attempt to organize the "fundamental foci of Christian life" in a way that would be "communicable to others."[46] As such, spiritual theology is always particular and directed to the specific times and contexts in which Christians live their faith. Gutiérrez's own *We Drink from Our Own Wells* is an illustration of this spiritual function of theology. As theological reflection in the classic tradition of Anselm's *"credo ut intelligam,"* spiritual theology is reflection *in* faith.[47]

What Gutiérrez calls theology as "rationally organized knowledge" or simply theology as "rational knowledge" may or may not be an academic endeavor, but it is distinguished from spiritual theology as "an intellectual discipline." Theology as rational knowledge is more than "systematization and clear exposition," since it is "born of the meeting of faith and reason" (including but extending beyond philosophy).[48] As distinct as it is from spiritual theology, Gutiérrez conceives of both theological functions in practice as being vitally related, a viewpoint apparently informed by his reading of the historical development of theology as a scientific discipline. He notes that a fourteenth-century rift appeared between theology and contemplative spirituality that was largely unknown to earlier Christian thinkers and to the "masters of the spiritual life." Contributing to this split was the "degradation of the Thomistic concept of theology" in late-medieval Scholasticism and following. Aquinas's view, says Gutiérrez, originally had been "broad

[44] Gustavo Gutiérrez, "Faith as Freedom: Solidarity with the Alienated and Confidence in the Future" in *Living with Change, Experience, Faith,* ed. Francis A. Eigo, O.S.A. (Villanova University Press, 1976), p. 40.

[45] Gutiérrez, *Theology of Liberation,* p. 4; see Gustavo Gutiérrez, *We Drink from Our Own Wells: The Spiritual Journey of a People,* tr. Matthew J. O'Connell (Maryknoll: Orbis, 1985), p. 54.

[46] Gutiérrez, *Our Own Wells,* pp. 89, 37.

[47] Gutiérrez, *Theology of Liberation,* p. xxxiii.

[48] Gutiérrez, *Truth,* p. 103; *Theology of Liberation,* pp. 11, 5.

and synthetical: theology is not only a science, but also wisdom flowing from the charity which unites a person to God."[49] He hails Aquinas as a theologian committed to establishing "a solid foundation for theology as a rationally organized body of knowledge" without, however, separating it from spirituality and charity.[50] I read Gutiérrez as endeavoring to approximate (for his context) this kind of classically integrated theological approach by including Christian spiritual discourse and professional theology within a broad definition of theology.

In keeping with this broad definition of theology, Gutiérrez emphasizes that all theological discourse should take "its bearings from . . . the Christian life of the community . . . This fact does not weaken the rigorously scientific character of the theology; it does, however, properly situate it."[51] In other words, by remaining connected to the life of the church, both forms of theological discourse find their locus for reintegration. According to Gutiérrez, it is the third function of theology – theology as critical reflection on Christian praxis – which guides the other two dimensions of theology "more explicitly [to] have ecclesial praxis" as a unifying common "point of departure and . . . context." He wants to effect this reintegration not only to ensure that theology will be rigorously scientific – that is "a serious discourse, aware of itself, in full possession of its conceptual elements"[52] – but also because he is concerned with complex pastoral and ecclesial challenges which require a combined response from theology as rational knowledge and spiritual theology. Theology as critical reflection on Christian praxis integrates and draws upon the insights of spiritual theology and theology as rational knowledge to help put, for example, politically intensive "pastoral activity . . . in a wider context."[53] It is not an abstract or hypothetical issue Gutiérrez has in mind when he reflects on the church of the poor in Latin America and the problem of Christian community workers engaged in praxis at the grassroots

---

[49] Gutiérrez, *Theology of Liberation*, pp. 4, 5. Gutiérrez notes that in Scholastic theology, "the scientific character of theology . . . [consisted of] systematization"; theology was "confined to clarity of exposition" (pp. 178–79 n. 16). Theology thus defined, especially after the Council of Trent, was largely reduced to the status of an "ancillary discipline of the magisterium of the Church" and restricted primarily to the tasks of defending and teaching the church's authorized version of the divinely revealed truths (p. 5). Gutiérrez conceives of theology much more fully.

[50] Gutiérrez, *Our Own Wells*, p. 36.

[51] Ibid., p. 37.

[52] Gutiérrez, *Theology of Liberation*, p. 9.

[53] Ibid., p. 10.

level "who run the risk of forgetting central aspects of Christian life, because they are caught up in the demands of immediate political activity."[54] The Christian community needs the theoretical and spiritual resources of these two forms of theological discourse for guiding and assessing its thought and praxis, since the criteria for assessment of Christian praxis cannot derive "from praxis itself."[55] In order to address the pastoral challenges arising from grassroots Christian praxis in Latin America, the liberation theologian must develop not only theological criteria of assessment in relation to scripture and tradition but "a clear and critical attitude regarding economic and socio-cultural issues in the life and reflection of the Christian community." The use of social scientific theories is a necessary methodological component entailed in a commitment to making society's oppressed the focus of liberation theology.[56]

This outline of the interrelationships within Gutiérrez's threefold conception of theology may appear to some as an overschematization of his views. However, if I have erred on the side of overschematizing, I believe my identification of the impact of his focal value on his conception of theology is on the mark. He pursues the focal value of solidarity with the oppressed by: (1) encouraging the theologizing potential of oppressed Christians (which a broad conception of theology reenforces); (2) insisting that theology as rational knowledge attend to grassroots theological discourse and praxis; and (3) analyzing the socio-political realities affecting the poor by methodologically specifying the use of the social sciences in theology's critical reflection. Gutiérrez's threefold conception of theology is informed by a focal value which renders the theological project extremely difficult to carry out since the demands of solidarity with the oppressed are so vast; yet, he insists on it not only for the sake of the poor but for the sake of the future of Christian theology which has, in many ways, become so remote from the face of suffering. Professional theological writings are more a reflection of elite academic preoccupations than the interests of the "nonperson" in the global Christian community.[57] Academic

---

54 Ibid., p. xxxiii.
55 Gutiérrez, *Truth*, p. 101. "It is meaningless . . . to say that praxis is to be criticized 'in the light of praxis'" (ibid.). See *Theology of Liberation*, p. 180 n. 34.
56 Gutiérrez, *Theology of Liberation*, p. 9. See Gustavo Gutiérrez, "Theology and the Social Sciences," in his *Truth*, pp. 53–84.
57 Gustavo Gutiérrez, "Theology from the Underside of History" in his *Power of the Poor*, p. 213.

theology has become small in its vision of what it would mean to cultivate the theological virtues of faith, hope and love, because of its almost exclusive focus on the angst of the North Atlantic middle class. Gutiérrez seeks a revitalized theology – with a heart that is not estranged from the joy and pain of the poor; with a soul that lives and breathes the prophetic hope of the oppressed; and with a passion to be accountable to the God of grace, mercy and justice. Academic theology has been notoriously adept at fending off this challenge, embarrassed by the intimacy of Gutiérrez's language about God's preferential love for the downtrodden. But the truth of the matter (which we all know but avoid because of the discomfort of the challenge) is that we need serious reflection which can articulate the breadth and depth of this type of theological heart, soul and passion. If any focal value emerging from these three movements stands out as the most difficult to undertake yet the most pristine in terms of its biblical mandate, it is the liberation theological value of solidarity with the oppressed.

In his essay, "The Concept of a Theology of Liberation," Ogden wishes to "confront the challenge of liberation theology" as exemplified by Gutiérrez.[58] His opening remarks are collegially appreciative. He views Gutiérrez and other liberation theologians as part of the venerable revisionary stream of modern theology and credits them with making a genuine attempt to establish the practical credibility of the Christian faith today.[59] Within the course of Ogden's own writings one finds him responding to developments from Latin American liberation theology and expanding what he had previously deemed to be adequate criteria of credibility. In his earlier works he focused almost exclusively on the theoretical aspects of the credibility of the Christian witness of faith. In more recent works, he acknowledges that "Gutiérrez and other liberation theologians" helped him to recognize that the challenge of theoretical credibility vis-à-vis "the nonbeliever can no longer be the only challenge" to which the Christian theologian must respond.[60] It is Ogden's judgment that for theology currently to be adequate, it must address two dimensions of credibility – namely, the theoretical "quest for truth in the sense of freedom from ignorance

---

[58] Ogden, *On Theology*, p. 135.
[59] See Ogden, *Faith and Freedom*, p. 20.
[60] Schubert M. Ogden, *The Point of Christology* (San Francisco: Harper & Row, 1982), pp. 91–92.

and error" and the practical "quest for justice in the sense of freedom from want and oppression." In fact, he once described the question of practical credibility as an "even more urgent question" than that of theoretical credibility.[61]

Ogden's admiration for the "outstanding" nature of Gutiérrez's contributions gives way, nonetheless, to a fundamental critique so that, in the end, Gutiérrez's theological project appears as a deeply flawed attempt at revisionary theology. According to Ogden, Gutiérrez promotes the notion that theology is "not only contingently but necessarily an expression of faith" and "is not really possible at all unless it arises out of the theologian's own prior commitment as a Christian believer."[62] Ogden rejects this conception of theology because it collapses the distinction between theology "as critical reflection on the Christian witness, and theology undertaken as a Christian vocation," thus confusing "a contingent connection for a necessary one." As noted above, he insists that theology must be independent enough from Christian faith claims to be able to validate as well as to invalidate them. By methodologically specifying that theology starts with "the prior commitment of faith," Gutiérrez's theology not only does not assess the theoretical credibility of the Christian witness of faith but, in principle, cannot fully assess it.[63] From Ogden's perspective, if Gutiérrez's theology is to serve the church adequately as fully critical reflection, its formal defining characteristic would need to be relinquished so that it could assume its proper status independent from witness. Otherwise, Gutiérrez's theology will "remain bound so closely to the faith on which it is supposed to reflect that, while it may indeed be a reflection *in* faith, it cannot be a reflection *on* faith."[64] As it is presently conceived, Gutiérrez's theology, from Ogden's point of view, would have to be judged to be one among many Christian witnesses or "Christian ideologies," not fully critical theological reflection.[65] To the extent that the problems he detects in Gutiérrez's definition of theology typify liberation theology generally, Ogden concludes that the problem of the "collapse of the difference between theology and witness is a defining characteristic" of liberation

[61] Ibid., pp. 93, 147.
[62] Ogden, *On Theology*, pp. 134, 138.
[63] Ibid., pp. 142, 137.
[64] Ibid., p. 143.
[65] Ogden, *Faith and Freedom*, p. 31.

theology.[66] There may be conversation – even challenging exchange – between Ogden and Gutiérrez, but they are seemingly unequal partners in dialogue since, from Ogden's perspective, Gutiérrez's writings are a kind of liberationist Christian ideology.

There is some textual basis for Ogden's claim that Gutiérrez makes faith a necessary precondition for doing theology; I will address how to interpret those texts below. Nevertheless, Ogden's conclusion that Gutiérrez's writings are Christian ideology is not an adequate representation of his conception of theology when one looks at his writings as a whole.[67] Moreover, Ogden's critique is (again) an instance of conflicting configurations of focal and unfocused values – complicated by a clash over whether to define theology broadly or strictly. Recall that he finds two problems endemic to broad definitions of theology: a sole concern with meaning to the exclusion of truth questions and a failure to distinguish theology from witness. I suggest that Gutiérrez can be read as affirming Ogden's focal value, insofar as there are resources in his theology (specifically the function of theology as rational knowledge) both to be able to pursue the task of assessing theoretical credibility and to develop the sorts of distinctions necessary to ensure a sufficiently independent function of theology in relation to Christian belief and praxis. Although Gutiérrez does not explicitly give an inventory of the range of tasks of theology as rational knowledge, it is reasonable to say it would include developing the proper "criteria for discernment" with recourse to the "'deposit of faith'" for assessing Christian speech and action.[68] I take him to mean that theology turns to scripture and tradition for criteria regarding the appropriateness (to borrow Ogden's term) of Christian claims and practice. As with Frei, the task of assessing appropriateness questions seems relatively clear; however, it is more difficult to determine whether Gutiérrez envisions theology as rational knowledge as making fully critical determinations regarding the theoretical credibility of

66 Ogden, "Theological Scholarship," p. 131.
67 Ogden cites two articles by Gutiérrez: "Liberation Praxis and Christian Faith," originally published in 1979, and "Faith as Freedom," originally published in 1976 (see Ogden, *On Theology*, p. 152). I will be referring as well to numerous other texts, some of which postdate the original version of Ogden's article (in *The Challenge of Liberation Theology: A First World Response*, ed. Brian J. Mahan and L. Dale Richesin [Maryknoll: Orbis, 1981]) and others which postdate its reprint in *On Theology* (1986).
68 Gutiérrez, *Truth*, p. 102; *Theology of Liberation*, p. xxxiv.

Christian witness. I believe he gives more attention to this issue than Ogden suggests.

Gutiérrez implies that theology may entail critical reinterpretations of the tradition so that its meaning will be intelligible in light "of the problems faced by men and women of our time." Furthermore, "a theology that does not take into account the shifts in rational categories that are occurring in today's world runs the risk of expressing itself in a language alien to its age and of thereby failing in its duty of presenting the message to that age."[69] Gutiérrez remains vague, however, on the precise nature of such a critical and reconstructive task. The most he says is that theology must strive for "rationality and disinterestedness" and that "critical reflection ... by definition should not be simply a Christian justification a posteriori."[70] This presumably means that theology must have some moment of significant critical independence from the faith on which it reflects in order to assess its validity. (This would also seem to explain his comments that a "critical perspective makes [theology as] rational knowledge a necessity.") While he evinces a concern for rendering the Christian faith credible by engaging in disinterested, critical reflection of some kind, he does not commit himself to any particular method or criteria for doing so.[71] Hence we can say that what Ogden calls theoretical credibility is for Gutiérrez a value, but only an unfocused one.

The fact that this value is unfocused should not, however, be interpreted as a rejection on Gutiérrez's part of the task of securing theology's public credibility according to the best scholarly standards. Leaving this value unfocused reflects his assessment that in today's world, the make-up of the apologete's audience is changing. Apologetics are changing as well. While Gutiérrez looks favorably on aspects of modern theology's sensitivity to the challenge of scientific consciousness ushered in by the European Enlightenment, he suggests that theology today may need to be less focused apologetically on the nonbeliever and more on the believer struggling to understand the liberating "mission of the Church in the world." Gutiérrez affirms Johann

---

69 Gutiérrez, *Power of the Poor*, p. 56; *Truth*, p. 90.
70 Gutiérrez, *Theology of Liberation*, pp. 5, 81.
71 Gutiérrez, *Truth*, p. 182 n. 50. While he does not articulate what criteria would be involved, Gutiérrez does indicate that he would be opposed to criteria entailing "false universalisms" or liberal theological efforts focused exclusively on demonstrating "the essential religious dimension of every human being" (*Power of the Poor*, pp. 213, 179).

Baptist Metz's point: "'Today it is more the person of faith who lives within the Church than [she or] he who lives outside it to whom the faith must be justified.'"[72] Moreover, for the Latin American context in particular, the church's apologetic efforts must be directed first and foremost not to modernity's crises but to the "'nonmodern' . . . underside of history"; not to the nonbeliever but the "nonperson." This is the "cultural universe" to which Gutiérrez estimates he is accountable (both theoretically and practically) since "[e]very theology asks itself the meaning of the word of God for its contemporaries, at a certain moment of history."[73]

Ogden might simply construe this as an example of liberation theology's efforts at practical credibility which would bolster his point that liberation theology pursues practical credibility to the exclusion of theoretical credibility. I would argue that to see practical and theoretical credibility issues as competing in Gutiérrez's conception of theology is to misread Gutiérrez, who nowhere says that the concerns of the nonbeliever are unimportant or that scholarly efforts to address them are invalid in principle. As mentioned above, he appreciates the sensitivity of modern theology's interrogation of the modern secular mind. The only negative observation he makes is that first-world theology's focus on the cultured despisers of religion typically has obscured the realities of social conflict, and this theological obscuring of social realities has proved disastrous when applied in the Latin American context. Strictly speaking, however, it does not follow that his emphasis on the concerns of the oppressed precludes apologetic engagement with the concerns of the nonbeliever. Indeed, he predicts that if the church in Latin America does not effectively address the pressing social problems in its hemisphere, the challenge of unbelief or antagonistic alternative belief may prove as pernicious as it is in North Atlantic cultures.[74] Gutiérrez values, but in an unfocused way, the task of rendering the Christian faith theoretically credible, especially to the modern nonbeliever.

While Gutiérrez gives undeniable (if methodologically undeveloped) support to theology's task regarding theoretical credibility questions, it

---

[72] Gutiérrez, *Theology of Liberation*, p. 79.

[73] Gutiérrez, *Truth*, p. 25; *Power of the Poor*, pp. 57, 56.

[74] See Gutiérrez, *Truth*, p. 26. I will discuss liberation theology's apologetic engagement with, for example, Marxism in ch. 3.

must be noted that he has not been entirely consistent or forthcoming on the crucial point regarding how theology as rational knowledge remains sufficiently distinct and independent from spiritual theology for the politically engaged liberation theologian. An important exception is one passage where he states quite plainly that sharing the "sufferings and joys . . . as well as the faith and hope" of those who "live as a Christian community . . . all this is not a formality required if one is to do theology; it is a requirement for being a Christian."[75] By definition, he could only be referring here to theology as rational knowledge. While this statement is clear enough, it stands alone and cannot be easily reconciled with numerous other formulations throughout Gutiérrez's writings which make his position on this point appear ambiguous. Take for example his following statements: the "presence [of theologians] in . . . the 'first act'" of Christian praxis "is a necessary precondition for their reflection in the second. What comes second is theology, not the theologian"; "the theologian must be personally involved in the liberation process";[76] "Belief and understanding have an annular relationship"; "All theology is rooted in the act of faith";[77] or "Christian truths need to be lived if they are to be stated correctly and in a more than superficial way."[78] If these passages are taken at face value as methodological principles, they seemingly license the conclusion to be drawn by readers such as Ogden that Gutiérrez understands all theological reflection to be "not only contingently but necessarily an expression of faith," arising out of the theologian's own personal beliefs and actions.[79]

Ogden is correct in strongly rejecting any claim for the annular relationship between Christian belief and theological understanding as burdened with practical and theoretical difficulties. Practically, the work of theology might never begin if belief is made a condition for

---

[75] Gutiérrez, *Theology of Liberation*, p. xxxiii. The original Spanish is equally clear: " . . . *compartir sus sufrimientos y alegrías . . . así como su fe y su esperanza vividas en comunidad cristiana, no es una formalidad necesaria para hacer teología, es una condición para ser cristiano.*" Gustavo Gutiérrez, "*Mirar lejos,*" *Paginas* 93 (1988), p. 81.

[76] Gutiérrez, *Power of the Poor*, pp. 103, 73 n. 23.

[77] Ibid., pp. 56, 55.

[78] Gutiérrez, *Truth*, p. 103.

[79] Ogden, *On Theology*, p. 138. Ogden is aware that Gutiérrez defines faith as a rich concept, meaning "more than . . . believing certain things *about* God . . . because it is the eminently practical matter of believing *in* God" which includes "practical faith that works through love" (135). Thus his dispute with Gutiérrez is not over the nature of faith; rather, he questions what he sees as Gutiérrez's position that faith (in all its dimensions) is a requirement for theology.

all theological work, since "how could I or anyone else ever know when I was in a position to undertake it?" And theoretically, linking understanding and belief renders the concept of disbelief incoherent: "If in order to understand the Christian witness one must first believe it, under what conditions could one ever possibly disbelieve it," since disbelief is a decision based not on ignorance but on some degree of understanding?[80]

I believe that Gutiérrez's statements regarding the theologian's personal involvement, or the annular relationship between belief and understanding, or theology rooted in the act of faith should not be interpreted as undermining the distinction in his broad definition between the fully critical function of theology as rational knowledge and spiritual theology. Rather, these statements should be taken as part of his effort to attack forcefully "the intellectualizing of the intellectual who has no ties with the life and struggle of the poor" and to prevent schisms between academic theology and grassroots theology.[81] Gutiérrez, it seems to me, presupposes that the liberation theologian will undertake both theological functions. To be sure, he has been and still is insistent (and rightly so) in stating that the heart and soul of Latin American liberation theology is its spiritual theology.[82] However, one need not sacrifice the disinterestedness of theology as rational knowledge in order for the theologian to undertake a spiritual theology that cultivates solidarity with the liberating praxis of the Christian community. Nevertheless, much rides on how one interprets the meaning of the theologian's personal involvement (or the like), which is by no means clearly spelled out by Gutiérrez; this remains an undeveloped aspect of his thought (which I will comment on in the next section). The way in which he continues to sharpen his conception of theology will have a direct impact on the degree to which he can bring into focus the value of maintaining what Ogden would call theology's independent status as fully critical reflection; yet, as I have argued, even within the parameters of his current threefold conception of theology, Gutiérrez has in theory the resources to maintain the requisite

[80] Ibid., pp. 17, 18.
[81] Gutiérrez, *Power of the Poor*, p. 103.
[82] See Gustavo Gutiérrez, "Theology, Spirituality, and Historical Praxis," tr. Robert R. Barr, in *The Future of Theology: Essays in Honor of Jürgen Moltmann*, ed. Miroslav Volf, et al. (Grand Rapids, Mich.: William B. Eerdmans, 1996), p. 184. See also *Our Own Wells*, p. 37 and "Faith as Freedom," p. 36.

distinctions between what Ogden would call theology (strictly understood) and Christian witness. Thus, although Ogden's focal value is
currently unfocused for Gutiérrez, his broad definition of theology still
formally endorses it.

FROM CLASHING VALUES TO CONSTRUCTIVE CHALLENGES

Ogden's focal value of maintaining theology's task of fully critical
reflection on the Christian witness according to the best standards of
academe not only informs his conception of theology but also his criticisms of Frei and Gutiérrez. Ogden argues strenuously that theology
should be defined strictly as a fully critical form of inquiry which must
be sufficiently independent from the Christian witness so as to be able
to invalidate it. He finds that Frei's broad definition of theology, though
scholarly in a descriptive social scientific sort of way, does not include
a process of critically assessing the theoretical credibility of religious
discourse and is therefore inadequate. In the case of Gutiérrez, Ogden's
criticism goes further. He argues that Gutiérrez's conception of theology
completely collapses the distinction between theology and witness by
insisting that theological reflection, by definition, requires a prior commitment of faith. Working with the premise that these conversations
have misfired in large measure due to conflict over configurations of
focal and unfocused values, I attempted to recast them. I endeavored
to show how Frei and Gutiérrez can be read as affirming in unfocused
ways the value Ogden holds as focal by: (1) maintaining the logical distinction between first- and second-order theological discourse (Frei)
and between theology as rational knowledge and spiritual theology
(Gutiérrez); and (2) by valuing theoretical credibility as well as appropriateness questions. I attempted to put into perspective Frei's and
Gutiérrez's decision about leaving theoretical credibility issues unfocused in practice by suggesting that both of them give compelling
reasons for why it may be imperative to focus attention on other
values.

Nevertheless, while it is legitimate to leave unfocused certain values
in light of an overall vision of theology guided by another important
value, it is incumbent upon any theologian to give some account of
those unfocused values (at least so as not to mislead) – if the theologian
wishes to speak relevantly to contemporary culture in all its facets.

Thus, we can recast Ogden's critiques as challenges to Frei and Gutiérrez to clarify the values each only formally endorses. In so doing, we move from misfiring conversation to useful, constructive criticism. Frei and Gutiérrez are thereby seen as espousing a valid conception of theology which is marked by some areas of inadequacy as well. The same goes for Ogden. Let me give one brief example from each.

To continue a moment longer on the topic of theology as fully critical reflection, I suggested above that Gutiérrez leaves unarticulated how theology as rational knowledge can be sufficiently independent, given that he calls for the theologian to be "personally involved" in the grassroots church's discourse and praxis.[83] An important clarification is needed here regarding the nature of, and difference between, the personal involvement required of the theologian *qua* believer and that required of the theologian *qua* critical theorist. Gutiérrez is clear that the theologian doing spiritual theology must be personally involved in all ways. That is, the believing theologian must be involved in the "lived" nature of Christian truths which are seen in light of (to use the Johannine metaphor) "the Truth which is also the Way."[84] This "saving truth" is found in the way of life Christians are called to follow which includes fighting injustice and befriending the poor (and all of this rooted in prayer).[85] On theological grounds, Gutiérrez argues that the believing theologian who is not personally involved is not living the saving truth. This call to engagement, incumbent on all Christians, is to the point and does not require conceptual clarification.

Regarding the personal involvement of the theologian as critical theorist, Gutiérrez is less than clear. This has led some (e.g., Ogden) to conclude that he does view personal faith involvement as a condition of all theological understanding, making it a formal defining characteristic of even theology as rational knowledge. He came the closest to suggesting this when he stated: "theology is in fact a reflection that, even in its rational aspect, moves entirely within the confines of faith." Yet, even here, it is not at all clear whether he is being methodologically prescriptive or whether he is merely descriptively observing that for Christian theologians, "[t]he level of the experience of the faith supports a particular level of the understanding of the faith." In any

[83] Gutiérrez, *Power of the Poor*, p. 73 n. 23.
[84] Gutiérrez, *Truth*, p. 103; *Theology of Liberation*, p. 10.
[85] Gutiérrez, *Truth*, p. 181 n. 41.

case, I take his more recent statement about faith not being a formal condition for theology (quoted above) as his more authoritative and carefully articulated methodological position on this issue.[86] What he means by strongly associating personal experiential involvement in faith and theological understanding of faith may be related to the idea he also entertains that "human beings know well only what they do."[87] This remark suggests that the theologian as critical theorist who is not personally involved in Christian communal practice cannot understand that practice well. This would be a very different sort of claim than his assertion about the personal involvement incumbent upon the believing theologian. The philosophical underpinnings of this kind of relationship between involvement and understanding are not spelled out by Gutiérrez, but there are resources for approaching this epistemological issue in ways that do not collapse belief and understanding.

Gutiérrez could argue that certain kinds of learning or understanding (including theological understanding) have an unavoidable practical, or one might say, "self-involving" aspect. Charles Wood, for example, explains that the theologian often must be personally engaged in the religious subject matter because "so many of the concepts used in Christian witness – 'creation,' 'sin,' 'grace,' 'hope,' and so forth – are what we might call *existential* concepts, i.e., concepts which are instruments for self-understanding." This sort of understanding does not require faith or commitment *per se* on the part of the theologian, but since the subject matter uses self-involving concepts, "a grasp of them requires (or, perhaps better: amounts to) a certain capacity to understand *oneself* by them."[88] Wood's clarification could provide Gutiérrez with some of the conceptual precision he needs to sharpen his position. What could Gutiérrez gain if he were to explain the relationship between personal involvement and genuine understanding as "understanding by means of a self-involving extension of one's experience as learner" and not "understanding necessarily by means of personal

---

[86] Gutiérrez, *Our Own Wells*, p. 36; cf. *Theology of Liberation*, p. xxxiii. See also n. 75 above.

[87] Gutiérrez, *Power of the Poor*, p. 59.

[88] Charles M. Wood, *Vision and Discernment: An Orientation in Theological Study* (Atlanta: Scholars, 1985), p. 86. Wood observes that this requisite involvement on the part of the learner is not unique to the theologian but may also apply to other theorists of other subject matters (see pp. 87f.). Wood also notes that "various theologians of liberation" promote self-involving theological understanding ("The Knowledge Born of Obedience," *Anglican Theological Review* 61 [1979], p. 332; cf. pp. 334, 338f.).

faith"? He would be able to emphasize (as insistently as he clearly wishes) that the theologian must be personally involved in concrete Christian communal life, without contradicting the distinction (he also wishes to maintain) between the kind of engagement required of the believing theologian and that required of the theologian as critical theorist (particularly in relation to theology as rational knowledge). Furthermore he could argue that the existentially gripping and politically urgent nature of certain objects of theological reflection in Latin America (e.g., the suffering and Christian hope of the poor) makes this particular kind of self-involving theological understanding fitting and even imperative.

Since one agenda in chapter three is to propose how postliberals might make good on their endorsement of *ad hoc* apologetics, I will not dwell here on what Frei leaves underdeveloped regarding theoretical credibility questions; rather, I will comment briefly on how he leaves unfocused the value of solidarity with the oppressed. Postliberal theology has not been known for its discussions of this issue. Were it to be found that solidarity with the needs and theologizing of oppressed Christian communities is not even an unfocused value, then postliberal theology would, in my opinion, have a seriously deficient conception of theology, exemplifying self-serving interests of the privileged Ivy League. One must be careful, however, not to make this an issue of political or religious rhetoric. A critical attitude toward or lack of appeals to metaphors of liberation, for example, does not mean a lack of theological interest in the church's accountability to God's call for preferential love for the poor.

Given what we know of Frei's conception of theology, it is to be expected that his views on Gutiérrez's value would be intertwined with the postliberal focal value of normative theological redescription which fosters Christian communal identity in relation to the plain sense of the identity of Jesus. Socio-political justice issues such as "[s]lavery, the ordination of women, the institutional rigidification of the ownership-wage earner structure of ... postindustrial capitalism," and so on, are assessed, Frei implies, in terms of "the ongoing tradition of an appropriate service of a Lord who would be a servant."[89] Frei's primary christological text, *The Identity of Jesus Christ*, does not focus on

[89] Frei, *Types*, pp. 126–27.

the issue of how the nature of Jesus' servanthood bears on social issues
such as these;[90] however, in Frei's *Types of Christian Theology*, one finds
an intriguing passage: "Perhaps the most haunting identity statement
. . . of Jesus in the New Testament is Matt. 25:40 . . . Who is the Jesus
of this text? He is that Messiah, that Son of Man, who is not *identical*
but *identified* with the poor, the undeserving, the spiritual and economic
underclass."[91] Frei does not elaborate further, so it would be a stretch to
conclude from a statement such as this that his conception of theology
focuses on the theological value of solidarity with the oppressed (over
and above its clear religious importance). However, one can say that his
interest in christologically based Christian character formation is poised
to begin such reflection and certainly does not inhibit it. Liberation
theologians especially could appreciate a theological approach which
begins with the question of the identity of Jesus in relation to the poor,
although they would insist on some intentional use of the social
sciences for this reflection to be fully critical. Postliberal views on
theological uses of the social sciences will be addressed in later chapters, but suffice it to say here that in Frei's conception of theology,
attending to the social needs and theological reflection of the
oppressed is an unfocused value, but the impetus for it is so deeply
imbedded in the plain sense of the identity of Jesus as to be unavoidable – even if this impetus is methodologically underdeveloped.

   I have endorsed Ogden's formal claim that for reflection on faith to
be fully critical, it must have at least a moment of sufficient independence from Christian witness to be able to evaluate critically any and
all Christian beliefs. This is not an endorsement, however, of Ogden's
material criterion of theoretical credibility. Ogden's contention that
the Christian witness can be determined to be theoretically credible
only if it is found to be confirmed by common human experience and
reason will be examined in the following chapter. Here I want to dwell
for a moment on one value which is underdeveloped in Ogden's conception of theology. Just as some of the underdeveloped values of
Frei's and Gutiérrez's conceptions of theology turned out to be what
Ogden holds as most focal, similarly, an underdeveloped aspect of
Ogden's conception of theology is an aspect central of each of his inter-

90 Hans W. Frei, *The Identity of Jesus Christ: The Hermeneutical Bases of Dogmatic Theology* (Philadelphia: Fortress, 1975).
91 Frei, *Types*, p. 136.

locutors' focal values: second-order theology's interactive relationship with first-order discourse is central to Frei's focal value of normative redescription; attentiveness to the theologizing of the grassroots Christian community is central to Gutiérrez's focal value of solidarity with the oppressed.

In keeping with Ogden's strict definition, theology must maintain the proper relatedness to and distinction from religious discourse and praxis. The reason for this is that any theology suffers distortions when it either becomes too dependent on the Christian community's "practical aims and interests" or when it becomes "so estranged" from the witness on which it is reflecting that it appears "to be only apparently engaging in validating [it]."[92] Ogden directs most of his comments to specifying how theology (strictly defined) should remain independent from witness. His writings, to my knowledge, do not develop how theology and witness could avoid estrangement. When what one wishes to highlight is theology's fully critical distance from Christian witness, Ogden's definition seems appropriate since a strict definition enhances theology's independence. However, Frei's focal value of thick description requires maintaining theology's close connection with what Lindbeck has called the Christian community's connatural sense of "the interior rule of faith."[93] Without that connection, the subtly encoded "informal set of rules under which [scripture] has customarily been read in community" may well be eclipsed.[94] The full import of being able to identify such rules will not become apparent until chapter four, but we can make a similar point using Gutiérrez's theological orientation. Ogden can be challenged to clarify how his strict definition of theology is able not only to reflect critically upon the Christian witness but also is open to critical correctives from the theologizing of the grassroots church.

Ogden does not dwell on theology's connection to the Christian witness – other than to state the self-evident: Christian theology would not exist if not for the prior existence of the Christian witness as its object of study. He leaves unquestioned whether this is enough of a connection (or a sufficiently elaborated connection) in order to undertake what Frei would call thinking *with* the Christian community and

---

[92] Ogden, "Theological Scholarship," p. 128.
[93] Lindbeck, *Nature of Doctrine*, p. 79.
[94] Frei, "Literal Reading," p. 68.

what Gutiérrez would consider necessary for solidarity with the oppressed. Ironically, Ogden's acknowledgment of how he critically revised his own conception of theology and theological method, based on what he would call the "witness" of liberationist writings such as Gutiérrez's, would indicate that he sees the importance in remaining open to correctives from the church's witness. The reality of Ogden's own theological development would seem to be a step ahead of his elaboration on this unfocused aspect of his conception of theology.

If the underdeveloped aspects of a theologian's conception of theology can be construed as unfocused but still real values needing further clarification and development, then conflict over configurations of values can be recast into a constructive challenge to bring certain values into clearer focus. Furthermore, if one can encompass the three values I have been advocating with either a strict or a broad approach (and I believe in principle one can), then there is good reason to conclude that theology may appropriately be formally defined either broadly or strictly. Both ways of using the term theology have legitimacy, though it may be difficult for theologians with a strict definition to appreciate the strengths of a broad definition of theology, and vice versa. While Ogden may differ with Frei's or Gutiérrez's configuration of focal and unfocused values, he would not be justified in concluding that their respective broad definitions of theology are illegitimate. The same is true for Ogden's conception of theology. Frei or Gutiérrez might disapprove of Ogden's configuration of values, but they would not be justified (were they ever to do so) in deeming his strict definition of theology as illegitimate.

This does not mean, however, that strict or broad definitions of theology are equally appropriate in all circumstances. Practically speaking, each tends to reinforce certain risks or challenges. A broad conception of theology such as Frei's or Gutiérrez's risks losing an essential element of what theology has to contribute to Christian communities – that is, the independence it needs to assess fully critically all aspects of Christian communal beliefs and practices. A strict definition such as Ogden's risks becoming so remote from Christian communal beliefs and practices that it is only apparently assessing them or being challenged by them. Given that any conception of theology will entail some risks, the theologian must calculate the risks and benefits of a strict or broad approach in light of the context in which she or he is situated. I give my own contextually informed judgment on this question in chapter six, but for my present purposes, I want to insist that there is no reason why both approaches cannot remain on the table, so to speak, as valid options – as long as all the values I have been speaking of receive at least formal endorsement.

There can be no theological synthesis of Ogden's, Frei's and Gutiérrez's conceptions of theology; nevertheless, it is fair to say that these revisionary, postliberal and liberation theological players formally endorse all three values as vital for theology. Differences in configurations of focal and unfocused values or differences between strict and broad approaches to defining theology are not grounds enough for deeming anyone's conception of theology illegitimate. The formal conditions for theological conversation having been thus established, the question becomes this: at the concrete level of theological practice, how does one make good on a formal endorsement of these three values? Here we enter into the methodological realm of making actual choices about material criteria of credibility and appropriateness, modes of argumentation, how to relate theory and praxis, and so on. Opportunities for intermovement disagreement, critique and mischaracterization proliferate. The twofold issue which emerged with some prominence in this chapter is how to pursue what Ogden calls theoretical and practical credibility. The next two chapters address this complex issue, first by examining revisionary approaches in light of the linguistic-historical turn in philosophy and then by proposing an approach for a public accounting of Christian faith and practice which I believe is more intelligible and relevant for contemporary culture – in part because it reflects all three of the focal values presented here.

CHAPTER TWO

Apologetics and the linguistic-historical turn

One of the findings from chapter one is that theologians from revisionary, postliberal and liberation theological movements can all be construed as affirming, to varying degrees, the value of theology assessing the validity of Christian belief in a fully critical manner. Having established this formal common ground, we are now in a position to discuss how this value is instantiated methodologically in relation to apologetics or, more generally, any publicly intelligible attempt to redeem the theoretical credibility of Christian belief. My proposal on this theological task developed partly out of an attempt to untangle the especially robust intermovement polemics between revisionary and postliberal theologians on this issue. Theologians from each movement have made accusations that theologians from the other are failing to appreciate the demands of public accountability in the current intellectual climate and failing to appreciate what kind of apologetic approach is best suited to defend Christian claims in that context.

David Tracy says that he is "unpersuaded" that Lindbeck's theological method "is other than confessionalism with occasional 'ad hoc' apologetic skirmishes."[1] Tracy has even described Lindbeck as holding the view that theology should "not engage in a deliberately apologetic task at all."[2] Tracy implicates proponents of a cultural-linguistic theory of religion (i.e., postliberal theologians) of "abandoning" any notion of a "shared rational space," which Tracy believes must be affirmed in order for theologians (or anyone) to redeem their claims to validity rationally and publicly. He suggests that (postliberal theologians not-

---

[1] David Tracy, "Lindbeck's New Program for Theology: A Reflection," *Thomist* 49 (1985), pp. 469, 470.

[2] David Tracy, "The Uneasy Alliance Reconceived: Catholic Theological Method, Modernity, and Postmodernity," *Theological Studies* 50 (1989), p. 555.

withstanding) there is broad philosophical support, even from neo-pragmatists such as Richard Rorty, for the necessity of the notion of a "shared rationality" – at least minimally defined.[3] This estimation of postliberal theology may in part be due to the fact that postliberals have disparaged past revisionary theological attempts to find putatively neutral norms for fully critical discourse common to Christian and non-Christian worldviews. By judging those attempts to be "either wholly vacuous . . . or already slanted toward one system or another,"[4] postliberals have perhaps provoked Tracy and others to view them as abandoning concern for *any* kind of shared rational space and, thus, as taking a position even more extreme than Rorty on this point. Moreover, Lindbeck appears at times to set his postliberal approach in opposition to apologetics when, for example, he states that "[p]ost-liberals are bound to be skeptical . . . about apologetics."[5]

Revisionists have been criticized by postliberals for attempting to justify interpretations of Christian beliefs on the basis of some universal, framework-independent standard of rationality. According to William Werpehowski, revisionary attempts to correlate "Christian claims and practices to representations of some general basic . . . 'faith'" constitute ineffective apologetics, because the exact "connection" of this general basic faith to particular Christian claims "remains indeterminate at both cognitive and practical levels."[6] Ogden says that the claims of Christian witness "'are true . . . only because they meet the requirements of completely general criteria'"; William Placher sums up the postliberal viewpoint when he responds that Ogden's stance simply misses the mark in today's philosophical milieu and is

[3] David Tracy, "Theology, Critical Social Theory, and the Public Realm" in *Habermas, Modernity and Public Theology*, ed. Don S. Browning and Francis Schüssler Fiorenza (New York: Crossroad, 1992), pp. 21, 19. Richard Rorty would have no problem with Tracy attributing to him a prag-matic commitment to the necessity of "a public realm . . . (as a kind of heuristic fiction) for any modern democratic society." Tracy, however, goes beyond Rorty to argue for "a shared concept of reason" along the lines of Habermas's theory of "communicative rationality" (pp. 19, 22).

[4] Bruce D. Marshall, "Absorbing the World: Christianity and the Universe of Truths" in *Theology and Dialogue: Essays in Conversation with George Lindbeck*, ed. Bruce D. Marshall (University of Notre Dame Press, 1990), p. 86.

[5] George A. Lindbeck, *The Nature of Doctrine: Religion and Theology in a Postliberal Age* (Philadelphia: Westminster, 1984), p. 129. In a similar vein, William Placher notes: "postliberals can *appear to be* in full retreat from the intellectual debates of the modern world." William C. Placher, *Unapologetic Theology: A Christian Voice in a Pluralistic Conversation* (Louisville: Westminster/John Knox, 1989), p. 20.

[6] William Werpehowski, "Ad Hoc Apologetics," *Journal of Religion* 66 (1986), p. 285.

tantamount to playing by "a set of rules that have already become obsolete."[7]

These are sweeping and unyielding accusations from each side. It may seem therefore that the revisionary–postliberal conversation has come to an impasse, since each side accuses the other basically of having illegitimate views on what constitutes valid and effective apologetics in today's pluralistic community of inquiry. Furthermore, these accusations do not seem to be coming completely out of the blue. They could be seen, even if at times unfairly inflated, as not completely unprovoked reactions to overstatements and understatements made by each side. On the revisionary side, there has been the tendency to understate the difficulties entailed in employing general criteria for credibility in light of the linguistic and historical character of experience and reason and to overstate the apologetic force of their metaphysical arguments. On the postliberal side, there has been a tendency to understate the importance of defending Christian claims in the public realm and to overstate their criticisms of some revisionary apologetics in such a way that all apologetic arguments are seemingly thereby indicted.

I have spoken thus far only of revisionary and postliberal inter-movement polemics on apologetics. Indeed, the bulk of the debate on apologetic strategies has taken place among the North American players. Latin American liberation theological contributions to the kinds of methodological disagreements in which revisionists and postliberals are embroiled has been limited, due in part to the choice of liberation theologians to focus on other theological concerns. However, as illustrated with Gutiérrez in chapter one, the notion that Latin American liberation theologians are uninterested and unconcerned with rebutting public challenges to the credibility of Christian belief is misleading. In chapter three, I will argue that Boff not only insists on the value of theoretical credibility (often to the point of endorsing the kinds of revisionary metaphysical apologetics I will assess critically in this chapter), but he also has in place many of the elements necessary for the type of approach I believe is a better option for doing apologetics, given the linguistic-historical turn.

The linguistic-historical turn is not one thing but a series of philo-

---

[7] Placher, *Unapologetic Theology*, p. 159. Placher is quoting Schubert M. Ogden, *On Theology* (San Francisco: Harper & Row, 1986), p. 20.

sophical "revolutions" (in Thomas Kuhn's sense of the word[8]) which have slowly eroded the classical metaphysical presupposition that philosophical knowledge is about a search for truth as something necessary, universal and extrahistorical which language reflects. There have been contributors to the linguistic-historical turn of contemporary thought from many sectors: linguistic philosophy, pragmatism, post-structuralism, to name a few. The proponents of these and other various disciplines and schools of thought may not see eye-to-eye on many issues, but all share the notion that philosophy should no longer be spoken of as a "spectatorial" science seeking to discover the Nature of Things. Indeed, philosophy since the 1960s has challenged an account of knowledge unmediated by language, throwing the door open for new ways to think about what one is doing with words when one is doing philosophy (e.g., solving problems by proposing "new, interesting and fruitful ways of thinking about things").[9]

Thinkers who have brought these philosophical issues to bear on religious thought range from Cornel West to Jeffrey Stout to post-liberals.[10] West eschews metaphysics in order to embrace critical and pragmatic thought in the mode of Gramscian intellectuals who "combine theory and action, and relate popular culture and religion to structural social change." West's critical reflection is grounded in his reading of African American cultural experience and, particularly, prophetic thought and practice in the African American church, signaling how current distrust with philosophical abstraction is being replaced with reflection rooted in particular communities.[11] Stout, an iconoclast of philosophical and theological symbols of authority, traces the demise of foundationalism in the history of philosophy and its impact on classical theism. He proposes an approach to religious

---

[8] See Thomas S. Kuhn, *The Structures of Scientific Revolutions*, 2nd edn. (University of Chicago Press, 1974).

[9] Richard Rorty, "Metaphilosophical Difficulties of Linguistic Philosophy" in *The Linguistic Turn: Recent Essays in Philosophical Method*, ed. Richard Rorty (University of Chicago Press, 1967), pp. 39 n. 75, 34. Rorty's essay in this volume foreshadows his exposition on the demise of metaphysical philosophy a decade later in *Philosophy and the Mirror of Nature* (Princeton University Press, 1979).

[10] For a survey of religious thinkers on this topic see William Dean, *History Making History: The New Historicism in American Religious Thought* (Albany: State University of New York, 1988).

[11] Cornel West, *Prophesy Deliverance! An Afro-American Revolutionary Christianity* (Philadelphia: Westminster Press, 1982), p. 121. West distinguishes his pragmatism from Rorty's, claiming that "Rorty is highly suspicious of thick historical accounts." Cornel West, "Afterword: The Politics of American Neo-Pragmatism" in *Post-Analytic Philosophy*, ed. John Rajchman and Cornel West (New York: Columbia University Press, 1985), p. 269.

moral philosophy with the ethicist functioning as "*bricoleur*," pragmatically using whatever religious or secular resources that work.[12]
Postliberal theologians reject ahistorical metaphysical realist assumptions of propositionalist theories of religion and the assumptions of
experiential-expressive theories about prelinguistic foundational
religious experience. The postliberal cultural-linguistic approach to
thick description of the Christian grammar can, despite what some
would call its premodern theological conservatism, arguably be classified as postmodern.[13] Even this cursory glance at these three projects
in religious thought shows how diverse the application of aspects of the
linguistic-historical turn can be. By endorsing the validity of the
changes the linguistic-historical turn has wrought in philosophy and
theology, I am not endorsing everything done in its name. I am simply
arguing that theologians who have not taken seriously at least some
dimensions of its critique of modernist ways of approaching knowledge, language, power, and experience are in a dubious position of trying to address today's challenges to the credibility of religious belief with
problematic and outmoded categories from modernity's golden past.

The objective of much of this and the next chapter is to clear conceptual ground for rethinking how we might more effectively undertake the apologetic task in light of the linguistic-historical turn. My
hope is that this will help move the discussion beyond the impasse of
the now familiar revisionary–postliberal criticisms mentioned above.
Before making any methodological proposal, it is necessary to work
through the tangle of overstatements and understatements surround-
ing intermovement disputes. Doing so will make it possible to construe
revisionary, postliberal and liberation theologians as being on a more
or less level playing field, so to speak, on the issue of apologetic argumentation. What levels the playing field is that it is not credible to
promote an apologetic approach that (1) tries to secure anything more
or less than what a coherentist argument can do, and that (2) depends
on anything more or less than a provisional consensus within the shared

[12] For Jeffrey Stout's critique of foundationalism, see his *The Flight from Authority: Religion, Morality, and the Quest for Autonomy* (University of Notre Dame Press, 1981); for the notion of moral *bricolage*, see his *Ethics After Babel: The Language of Morals and Their Discontents* (Boston: Beacon, 1988), pp. 74ff. and *passim*.
[13] Nancey Murphy and James Wm. McClendon, Jr., classify postliberalism as a postmodern theology ("Distinguishing Modern and Postmodern Theologies," *Modern Theology* 5 [1989], pp. 191–214).

rational space of the pluralistic public realm. Revisionists may try to overshoot these goals and postliberals and liberationists may appear to be unwilling to pursue them. I believe that for the time being at least, any theologian who voices concern about the public credibility of Christian claims in today's intellectual context must eventually play on this field.

When I discuss postliberal and liberationist apologetics in the next chapter, I will make a proposal for a particular approach to pursuing credibility which combines coherentist and consensus elements, based on a form of argumentation known in philosophical circles as "wide reflective equilibrium." For purposes of evaluating revisionary apologetics here, all the reader need have in mind are some formal aspects of coherence and consensus. A coherence approach to the justification of belief establishes some fit between the belief in question and the wider web of beliefs and theories which one holds as secure at a given time. This approach, as philosopher Michael Williams observes, is (1) nonfoundational because it rejects the possibility of finding "a privileged class of beliefs . . . which are 'intrinsically credible' or 'directly evident'" which can "serve as ultimate terminating points for chains of justification"; (2) nonskeptical because it presupposes that in order to think at all, "we must have some beliefs not thought open to doubt" – at least for the time being; and (3) fallibilistic, not because one is skeptical that the web of beliefs on which one is depending may be completely false, but because it is reasonable to "allow for a measure of fallibilism" in one's thinking – even about those beliefs one is justified in holding firmly in the present context.[14] The presupposition which is entailed in this fallibilism point is that the justification of a belief must be held separate from its truth. This point is philosophically complex, but there is a certain commonsensicalness to it as well: "we all want to allow for the possibility that even very strongly justified beliefs [could] . . . turn out, in the light of further evidence, to be false."[15]

The consensus approach to apologetics depends on the notion of contextually shared rational space where debates among advocates of competing positions can take place. The assumption here is that while

[14] Michael Williams, "Coherence, Justification, and Truth," *Review of Metaphysics* 34 (1980), pp. 243, 253, 269.

[15] Ibid., p. 268. A further reason to hold justification and truth separate is so as not to give the impression that a coherentist mode of justification necessarily entails a coherence theory of truth. Indeed, theological views on what is an adequate theory of truth are in flux, which to some extent reflects the current philosophical climate where many proposals are being debated.

it is no longer credible to speak of universal, framework-independent criteria of rationality, nonetheless, this does not mean that all we are left with is radical incommensurability. We can assume that we have *some* beliefs held in common with our conversation partners by making "maximum sense of the words and thoughts of others" in a way that charitably "optimizes agreement." As a methodological principle for debate in a postmodern context, this kind of "charity," notes Donald Davidson, "is forced on us, whether we like it or not, if we want to understand others."[16] When this principle is extended communally, it becomes reasonable to speak not simply of a rational space shared between two conversation partners, but a rational space shared in a broad context of inquiry where participants are attempting to engage each other in good-faith critical dialogue toward the goal of points of provisional consensus.

I think it is safe to say that Ogden's and at least the early Tracy's arguments for theoretical credibility seem ill-suited to being directed toward coherentist justification or pluralistic public consensus. Indeed Ogden's apologetic method seems to be a rather pure instance of an approach which continues a problematic turn to the modern subject as a framework-independent experiencer and reasoner. While Ogden believes he is appealing to universal philosophical criteria (via phenomenological and transcendental methods), his arguments have, in effect, no more potential justificatory force than what coherence or consensus approaches can muster. Regarding Tracy, I will argue that he has made more of a linguistic-historical turn than Ogden and, thus, has made notable movement toward coherentist and consensus methods of apologetic argumentation – though some ambiguities remain.

The process of focusing critical light on revisionary apologetics clears ground for new thinking about credibility issues. I question the philosophical presuppositions grounding the distinction (which Ogden relies on heavily) between theoretical and practical credibility. This distinction depends on the notion that theoretical credibility entails redeeming the metaphysical implications of the Christian witness and practical credibility entails redeeming its moral and political demands.

[16] Donald Davidson, "On the Very Idea of a Conceptual Scheme" in Rajchman and West, eds., *Post-Analytic Philosophy*, p. 142. In some cases, one may conclude that another person's set of beliefs is, in most important ways, incommensurable with one's own. However, as Davidson observes, "we improve the clarity and bite of declarations of difference . . . by enlarging the basis of shared (translatable) language or of shared opinion" (p. 142).

Simply put, the former has to do with the structures of ultimate reality which are universal and "*necessary* in our experience" and the latter has to do with the structures of human culture "that are merely *contingent* relative to our own existence" because they have to do with human action."[17] Because the linguistic-historical turn renders this theoretical–practical distinction problematic, my proposal for a wide reflective equilibrium apologetics in chapter three navigates a different route to redeeming the credibility of Christian claims. Furthermore, this approach sustains the focal values of all three theological movements, making the wide reflective equilibrium playing field potentially amenable to revisionary, postliberal and liberation theologies.

UNDERSTATING THE PROBLEMS OF PRIMORDIAL EXPERIENCE

It is to the credit of revisionary theologians for pressing the point that Christian theology has as one of its tasks to defend the credibility of the Christian witness according to the best standards of judgment of the day. Ogden has consistently stressed throughout his career that common human experience and reason should be accepted as the material criteria of theoretical credibility today, voicing confidence that "these criteria are not in serious question."[18] Even in today's "anti-Enlightenment" intellectual milieu, Ogden still promotes defending religious claims on the basis of common human experience and reason, and he is not alone in his endorsement of this approach.[19] He insists that the Christian religion, like any religion, has as its primary function to meet "above all the need for 'a metaphysical grounding for values.'"[20] One must show that what the claims of the Christian witness imply

[17] Schubert M. Ogden, "The Metaphysics of Faith and Justice," *Process Studies* 14 (1985), p. 93.
[18] Schubert M. Ogden, *Faith and Freedom: Toward a Theology of Liberation*, rev. edn. (Nashville: Abingdon, 1989), p. 123.
[19] Schubert M. Ogden, "The Enlightenment Is Not Over" in *Knowledge and Belief in America: Enlightenment Traditions and Modern Religious Thought*, ed. William M. Shea and Peter A. Huff (Cambridge University Press, 1995), p. 324. See Pamela Dickey Young, *Christ in a Post-Christian World* (Minneapolis: Fortress, 1995), esp. pp. 74–82.
[20] Schubert M. Ogden, *The Point of Christology* (San Francisco: Harper & Row, 1982), p. 33. Ogden is quoting anthropologist Clifford Geertz. I believe he misrepresents Geertz when he attributes to him the view that religions meet "*above all* the need for 'a metaphysical grounding for values'" (p. 33; emphasis added). Geertz nuances his point by saying that this need "seems to vary quite widely in intensity from culture to culture" (*The Interpretation of Cultures* [New York: Basic, 1973], p. 131.

metaphysically can be "shown to refer through *all* possible experience"
and be shown not to be falsified by the "constant structure" of experience.[21] Until recently, Tracy also has been as firm as Ogden in his
theological conviction that for the "objective referent" of the cognitive
claims of Christianity to be validated, those claims must be investi-
gated "by an explicitly metaphysical inquiry."[22]

Revisionists such as Ogden and the early Tracy employ a very particular view of human experience to make this point apologetically.
Their apologetic efforts have revolved around appeals to the notion
of some type of primordial experience of basic faith which religious
language re-presents. Lindbeck calls this a hybrid or "two-dimensional"
experiential-expressive and propositionalist theory of religion because
it appeals to (1) "a common core experience" of basic faith "present in
all human beings" which all religions attempt to express in religious
symbols and (2) which imply "informative propositions or truth claims
about objective realities."[23] Ogden and (the early) Tracy define religious
language as expressive discourse which attempts to answer reflectively
the "limiting" or existential question of human existence, a classic
example of which was penned by Pascal as he contemplated his
existence vis-à-vis eternity: " 'Who has set me here? By whose order
and arrangement have this place and this time been allotted me?' "[24]
Religious re-presentative language is distinctive because "it not only
implies an answer to the question, but also *explicates* such an answer," in
diverse ways and often with differing degrees of adequacy.[25] Whatever
the diversity or adequacy of the answer, the limiting or existential
question remains basic. The question is never "*whether* life is ultimately

---

[21] Ogden, *On Theology*, p. 91; Schubert M. Ogden, "Myth and Truth" in his *The Reality of God* (San Francisco: Harper & Row, 1963), p. 117.

[22] David Tracy, *Blessed Rage for Order: The New Pluralism in Theology* (New York: Seabury, 1978), p. 155.

[23] Lindbeck, *Nature of Doctrine*, pp. 16 (twice), 31.

[24] Schubert M. Ogden, "The Reality of God" in his *Reality of God*, pp. 30, 31; see *Point of Christology*, pp. 30f. and Tracy, *Blessed Rage*, pp. 132ff.

[25] Schubert M. Ogden, "Concerning Belief in God" in *Faith and Creativity: Essays in Honor of Eugene H. Peters*, ed. George Nordgulen and George W. Shields (St. Louis: CBP, 1987), p. 88. The notion of religions having differing degrees of adequacy raises the question of whether there are many true religions or only one. Ogden argues against the Christian exclusivist position (Christianity alone is true), the Christian inclusivist position (there can be anonymous Christians), and the pluralist position (all world religions are valid paths to the truth). He proposes a fourth option: If one religion is shown to be true, then there "*can be*" other true religions – but only if the others are shown to "give expression to substantially the same truth." Schubert M. Ogden, *Is There Only One True Religion or Are There Many?* (Dallas: Southern Methodist University Press, 1992), pp. 83, 103.

meaningful" but "always only *how* the meaning that we are sure life finally has can be so conceived and symbolized that we can continue to be assured of it."[26] Religious language is thus the attempt to "'*re*assure'" by re-presenting the "basic confidence and trust in existence which *is* our fundamental faith, our basic authentic mode of being in the world."[27]

While the answer that religion gives is certainly primarily existential (e.g., having to do with "the meaning of ultimate reality for us"), it is also by implication metaphysical (e.g., having to do with "the structure of ultimate reality in itself"). Currently, Ogden stresses that the answer religion gives has socio-political implications as well. My point here is that, for Ogden, faith and "the justice that faith demands" necessarily imply metaphysical claims.[28] Following from this existential–metaphysical distinction are two different kinds of metaphysical arguments for the reality of God – phenomenological types of arguments for the reality of God which analyze the structures of our primordial experience and transcendental arguments for God as the necessary condition of all we believe and do. As we will see, Tracy has made attempts to revise his position on both types of apologetic arguments, with some uneven results. In this section, I will focus on Ogden's apologetic use of Whiteheadian phenomenology and Tracy's phenomenological hermeneutics of the truth of the biblical classic.

Employing a phenomenology developed by process philosopher Alfred North Whitehead, Ogden argues that one can make the case for theism by appealing to a certain kind of "empirical" analysis of human experience (not any kind will do). Most empirical or experiential analyses are based on the "assumption that the sole realities present in our experience, and therefore the only objects of our certain knowledge, are ourselves and the other creatures that constitute the world."[29]

---

26 Ogden, "Concerning Belief," p. 89. Delwin Brown, for one, is unconvinced by Ogden's claim that the presupposition of the religious question is basic *faith*. Brown argues that the genuine question religious language generates "admits of two answers – faith and unfaith" ("God's Reality and Life's Meaning," *Encounter* 28 [1967], p. 259). Ronald Thiemann also argues that to take seriously cultural pluralism and "the full radicality of atheism's challenge," one must "acknowledge at least the possibility that atheism may be the truth about reality." Ronald F. Thiemann, *Constructing a Public Theology: The Church in a Pluralistic Culture* (Louisville: Westminster/John Knox, 1991), p. 91.

27 Ogden, *Reality of God*, p. 32. See Tracy, *Blessed Rage*, p. 103.

28 Ogden, "Metaphysics of Faith and Justice," p. 88; see "Concerning Belief," p. 90.

29 Schubert M. Ogden, "Present Prospects for Empirical Theology" in *The Future of Empirical Theology*, ed. Bernard E. Meland (University of Chicago Press, 1969), p. 79.

Hence, if one tried to defend theism on these empirical grounds, one would face two unsatisfactory possibilities. Either one would have to "refer the word 'God' to some merely creaturely reality or process of interaction, or else . . . deny it all reference whatever by construing its meaning as wholly noncognitive."[30] That is, "God" would either be reductively construed as a functional placeholder for what I project onto (experienced) reality, or the term "God" would be retained but would be construed in "noncognitive terms as expressing a '*blik*.'"[31] Such approaches offer few methodological resources for the theologian attempting phenomenologically to justify, as Ogden wishes to do, the objective reality of God as the ground of all human experience.

Ogden believes Whitehead's theory of nonsensuous perception supplies an analysis of "the most basic mode of experience" which can serve as the empirical foundation for assertions about the reality of God.[32] Whitehead distinguishes between two different modes of human experience. One mode is objective or reflexive and refers to the "outer perceptions through our senses whereby we discriminate the behavior of all the different beings of which we are originally aware." The other more primary mode is existential or intuitive and refers to "our inner nonsensuous perception of our selves and the world as parts of an encompassing whole."[33] At the level of primitive, nonsensuous experience, there is what Whitehead calls a "'dim and, all but, subconscious'" awareness of value and worth and "of the infinite whole in which we are all included as somehow one."[34] This experience, Ogden asserts, compels one to recognize that this immediate sense of value or worth is called forth or "evoke[d]" by something greater than our reflexive experience of self and world.[35] Whitehead calls this "'the sense of Deity'" or "'the intuition of holiness.'" For Ogden, if one begins with this kind of Whiteheadian empiricism, one is justified in concluding that "the assertion of God as transcendent personal reality is far from

30 Ibid., p. 80.
31 Ogden, *Point of Christology*, p. 132. Ogden describes a "blik" (R. M. Hare's term) as "a 'historical perspective' or 'an intention to behave in a certain way'" (ibid.) or simply "a basic attitude toward life and experience." Schubert M. Ogden, "Linguistic Analysis and Theology," *Theologische Zeitschrift* 33 (1977), p. 319; see also *Reality of God*, p. 84.
32 Ogden, "Present Prospects," p. 81.
33 Ogden, *Reality of God*, p. 105.
34 Ogden, "Present Prospects," pp. 84, 85.
35 Ogden, *Reality of God*, p. 37.

a mere speculation which is empirically groundless." The Whiteheadian understanding of God is neither a projection of an idea nor a blik. Ogden appears at points to concede that this phenomenological argument for theism is not indubitable. It is based on "'an appeal to the self-evidence of experience,'" and that appeal takes place "within a hermeneutical circle which excludes any simple resolution of fundamental differences" on this subject. He maintains, nevertheless, "that the type of empiricism Whitehead elaborates remains sufficiently close to essential features of our experience which everyone must recognize that no one can simply dismiss it."[36]

Taken alone, this is a rather modest phenomenological claim; however, Ogden has a more ambitious agenda which requires a less modest claim. For one, he wants to refute that atheism undermines claims about this universal primordial sense of deity. He insists that because this experience of God is on the nonsensuous level, it need not be thought of at the reflexive level of consciousness where it is often seemingly absent and therefore often denied. Thus, "the assertion that God is directly experienced by every human being as such is in no way incompatible with the existence of non- or even a-theistic modes of thought."[37] Ogden's point is not merely that it is possible to deny reflectively but still have basic faith; rather he argues that such denial is a serious misunderstanding of human existence, indicative of a not "fully self-conscious" understanding of the "experiences in which we all inescapably share."[38] I will return to the overstatement in this argument against atheism in the next section. Suffice it to say here that in comments such as these, Ogden is no longer clearing space for a "hermeneutical circle which excludes any simple resolution of fundamental differences" regarding the "self-evidence of experience"; rather, by making the pull of this phenomenological analysis unavoidable he vastly understates the difficulties of appealing to primordial experience – difficulties which he himself has more recently recognized, as we will see.

Ogden's indebtedness to a Whiteheadian phenomenology has persisted even when he has broken with other process thinkers on certain

---

[36] Ogden, "Present Prospects," pp. 86, 87.

[37] Schubert M. Ogden, "The Experience of God: Critical Reflections on Hartshorne's Theory of Analogy" in *Existence and Actuality: Conversations with Charles Hartshorne*," ed. John B. Cobb, Jr., and Franklin I. Gamwell (University of Chicago Press, 1984).

[38] Ogden, *Reality of God*, p. 20.

conceptual issues. In early years, Ogden promoted, along with Charles Hartshorne, "an analogical [approach to] speaking of God and his actions."[39] That is, God-talk is based on "man's immediate encounter with reality" where "he is able to grasp the *logos* of reality as such and to represent it" in theological terms (e.g., God as "pure unbounded love").[40] Later, Ogden abandoned this approach because of the difficulties entailed in basing a theistic analogy on some kind of immediate knowledge of God. Claiming that something is understandingly experienced at the nonsensuous level seemed to invest the dim experience of value with more cognitive content than it could logically carry. Needless to say, philosophical pressures have taken their toll on claims such as this. Since *The Point of Christology* (1982), Ogden has become firm in his judgment that in light of current philosophical analysis about the linguistically mediate nature of all knowledge, "the whole idea of 'immediate knowledge,' whether of God or of anything else, is radically problematic." Knowledge is by definition mediate in that it involves the use of concepts and language; in short, it is "'essentially linguistic.'" The "immediate experience of God can become knowledge of God, or even experience of God *as* God, only through the mediation of concepts and terms."[41] His point here would seem to signal a shift from the reliance he had in earlier writings on what one could know, albeit dimly, about the nature of deity based on the self-evidence of nonsensuous experience. He recognizes that if one depends (as he sees Hartshorne needing to do in order to ground analogical talk of God) on asserting that the immediate experience of God is a cognitively meaningful encounter, one runs headlong into the objections of the linguistic philosophers who insist that knowledge is mediate. (And Ogden has come to agree with their point.) Hence he argues against Hartshorne's (and, by implication, his own previous) attempt to establish analogical talk about God because it is fatally dependent on the self-contradictory notion of immediate knowledge.

Curiously, however, this has not caused Ogden to abandon the

---

[39] Schubert M. Ogden, "What Sense Does It Make to Say, 'God Acts in History'?" in his *Reality of God*, p. 179.

[40] Ibid., pp. 183, 181, 178. Elsewhere Ogden makes a similar claim when he writes that "the apparent universality of religion in some form throughout all human culture is evidence that human beings generally have somehow understood reflectively as well as existentially the gift and demand of God's original self-presentation to their existence" (*On Theology*, p. 39).

[41] Ogden, *Point of Christology*, p. 137; "Experience of God," pp. 32, 36.

Whiteheadian category of primordial nonsensuous experience; thus, significant ambiguity continues to surround his apologetics. While he now clearly is opposed to any position (such as Hartshorne's) which trades on the notion of nonsensuous immediate *knowledge*, Ogden argues strongly that "one may, and even must, speak of 'an immediate *experience* of God,'" or at least an "unavoidable experience of 'the inclusive something.'"[42] Furthermore, he seems unwilling to deny that this experience is "the *noetic* source of all our thought and speech about God."[43] Despite Ogden's retreat from "immediate knowledge of God" and change to "immediate experience of 'the inclusive something,'" he does not seem to have fully circumvented the problem of reconciling claims to immediacy and linguistic mediation. If, as he describes it, this experience is intentional (i.e., an experience *of* something), then it is by definition mediate and cannot be called *immediate* experience.[44] By continuing to understate the problem of the immediate experience of God, Ogden undermines the credibility of his phenomenological apologetics.

In *Blessed Rage for Order*, Tracy also depends on the notion of "pre-reflective, pre-conceptual, pre-thematic" common human experience and makes reference to Hartshorne's view that "we have direct awareness of God."[45] However, by the time of his 1985 review essay on Lindbeck's *The Nature of Doctrine*, Tracy asserts that he has distanced himself from theological methods that appeal to "inner-pre-reflective experience." He concedes that making appeals of this kind *was* one of the "real problems" within the revisionary theological paradigm. He argues that he and other revisionists have made "the turn to an explicitly hermeneutical position" which attempts "to address both the 'linguistic' . . . and the 'cultural' . . . issues which Lindbeck announces as news." Tracy asks the reader to consider his "own explicitly hermeneutical turn in *The Analogical Imagination* in contrast to the hermeneutically informed but underdeveloped position on 'common human experience'

---

[42] Ogden, *Point of Christology*, p. 138; "Experience of God," p. 34.

[43] Schubert M. Ogden, "Process Theology and Wesleyan Witness" in *Wesleyan Theology Today*, ed. Theodore Runyan (Nashville: Kingswood, 1985), p. 71.

[44] I am using the term intentional in a way similar to Wayne Proudfoot who defines an intentional mental state as that which "can be specified only by reference to an object" as opposed to the putative notion (how could we know of it?) of a mental state preceding and "unstructured by the distinction between subject and object" (*Religious Experience* [Berkeley: University of California Press, 1985], pp. 237 n. 7, 12).

[45] Tracy, *Blessed Rage*, pp. 47, 201 n. 95.

in *Blessed Rage for Order*."[46] I agree that Tracy's writings since the mid 1980s have been marked by linguistic-historical turnings but one can still detect troubling experiential-expressive echoes whose problematic aspects Tracy sometimes appears to understate.

At the heart of Tracy's analysis in *The Analogical Imagination* of systematic theology's approach to publicness is the notion of the religious classic's disclosure of truth. It seems to me that the religious classic – a concept which one intuitively wants to embrace because it is so, well, classic – is a terribly slippery concept whose possible problematic philosophical entailments (e.g., experiential-expressivism) Tracy does not consistently weed out. He defines a classic as any artistic or cultural expression which "discloses permanent possibilities for human existence both personal and communal" and therefore is a part of the "public heritage of our common human experience of the truth." Those who seriously engage a classic will "recognize nothing less than the disclosure of a reality we cannot but name truth."[47] A religious classic also carries this kind of disclosive power, provoking a claim to attention for "some sense of recognition . . . of the whole as radical mystery." Bringing a religious classic such as the Bible into public conversation can serve an apologetic function because its truth is "available, in principle, to all human beings."[48] Tracy's views on the interpreter's engagement with the meaning and truth of the biblical text will be discussed further in chapter four, but suffice it to say here that "true" has various related technical hermeneutical meanings. It can mean quasi-aesthetically, "the beautiful *as true*." It can also mean a dialogical event of manifestation (Gadamer) or, more complexly, the truth can be both a disclosure and a concealment (Heidegger).[49] By appealing to a hermeneutically accessed notion of the disclosive truth

---

[46] Tracy, "Lindbeck's New Program," pp. 462, 463, 464. Tracy does not cite specific evidence of this hermeneutical turn, but we can observe it in the way he relates basic faith and concrete Christian faith. In *Blessed Rage for Order*, Tracy argues that what is re-presented in concrete Christian language "*is* the basic faith [which] . . . all humanity experiences" (p. 223; emphasis added). Later, Tracy nuances this point by emphasizing that Christian-specific religious experience is not reducible to the common human experience of basic faith which "is itself constantly transformed by, even as it informs" concrete Christian religious experience. David Tracy, *The Analogical Imagination: Christian Theology and the Culture of Pluralism* (New York: Crossroad, 1986), p. 379.

[47] Tracy, *Analogical Imagination*, pp. 14, 115, 108.

[48] Ibid., pp. 169, 133.

[49] Ibid., p. 85 n. 31. David Tracy, *Plurality and Ambiguity: Hermeneutics, Religion, Hope* (San Francisco: Harper & Row, 1987), p. 121 n. 1.

of the biblical classic, Tracy differentiates himself from Ogden;[50] yet he still seems to rely on the kind of prethematic experience Ogden promotes. For example, Tracy explicates an existential condition for entering into serious conversation with (and resonating with the truth of) the religious classic by appealing to Ogden's notion of "fundamental trust and wonder in the very meaningfulness of existence" which is "*directly* experienced in . . . common human experience." The concrete disclosure of the Christian classic (i.e., the event of Jesus Christ) is spoken of as "re-presenting" this "always-already . . . event experienced, even if not named."[51] In passages such as these (from *The Analogical Imagination*), it is difficult not to conclude that Tracy was, in his essay on Lindbeck, overstating the extent or clarity of his linguistic-historical turn. If he wishes to trade heavily on such experiential-expressive entailments of the classic's disclosure of truth, he risks provoking charges that he has reneged on the linguistic-historical turn by understating the problematic nature of primordial experience.

Tracy himself is not averse to abandoning technical language and simply explaining the phenomenon of the experience of the truth of a classic in a commonsensical way: "Any one who has experienced even one such moment [of manifestation] – in watching a film, in listening to music, in looking at a painting, in participating in a religious ritual, in reading a classic text, in conversation with friends, or in finding oneself in love – knows that truth as manifestation is real."[52] Furthermore, Tracy takes a more postmodern stance when he observes that we must leave behind "any belief in the transparency of consciousness to itself" because "all experience and all understanding is hermeneutical."[53] His writings have only increased their postmodern provisoes about how disruptive historical consciousness and "self-interrupting" language have called into question the modern *logos* on *theos* with "its own self-presence and self-grounding."[54] Appealing less and less to common

50 See David Tracy, "Argument, Dialogue, and the Soul in Plato" in *Witness and Existence: Essays in Honor of Schubert Ogden*, ed. Philip E. Devenish and George L. Goodwin (University of Chicago Press, 1989), pp. 91–105; see also *Analogical Imagination*, p. 86 n. 34.

51 Tracy, *Analogical Imagination*, pp. 164, 184 n. 29, 424. This is the "phenomenological moment" of systematic theology's analysis of the Bible's truth. Tracy specifies that there is also a "transcendental moment" which I will address below (p. 183 n. 26).

52 Tracy, *Plurality and Ambiguity*, p. 29.

53 Ibid., pp. 78, 77.

54 David Tracy, "The Return of God in Contemporary Theology" in his *On Naming the Present: God, Hermeneutics, and Church* (Maryknoll: Orbis; London: SCM, 1994), p. 44.

human experience, Tracy now prefers to appeal to the "game" of conversation with the classic which explores "possibilities in the search for truth."[55] This dialogic search for truth entails an openness to difference, otherness and mutual transformation. The correlations which follow from the interpreter's dialogic encounter with the Christian classic will not focus on "harmony, convergence or sameness"; indeed, the correlational theologian "must be not only wary but downright suspicious of how easily claims to analogy or similarity can become subtle evasions of the other and the different." Tracy, in an effort to foster dialogic exchange which acknowledges the other disclosed in the "world of meaning" of the Bible, promotes what he calls the recognition of "similarities-in-difference."[56] In these textual encounters, what is disclosed as other may be recognized as "possibility" – presumably the possibly true. Reading him charitably, one can translate the rather coy language of possibility and similarities-in-difference into Davidsonian terms and conclude that he is just talking about how outsiders could make sense of the Bible which confronts them as other.[57] Nevertheless, categories such as similarities-in-difference could covertly carry with them the underlying philosophical assumption about a primordial similarity of human experience. Such categories, left uninterrogated, would call into question the consistency of the linguistic-historical turn which Tracy otherwise increasingly endorses. To let slip by even an innuendo of a primordial similarity in human experience is to understate how such a category is a nostalgic return to a modernist era undisturbed by the other and the different.

OVERSTATING THE FORCE OF TRANSCENDENTAL ARGUMENTS

Many revisionary theologians view transcendental arguments as a vital apologetic tool because the logic of any monotheistic religion demands philosophical defenses of the "universality and necessity of . . . God."[58] Transcendental arguments allow the theologian to deduce basic faith and its objective grounding in God as "the necessary conditions of our

---

55 Tracy, *Plurality and Ambiguity*, pp. 19, 20.

56 Tracy, "Uneasy Alliance," p. 562; see *Plurality and Ambiguity*, pp. 20f.

57 Tracy notes Davidson's category of conversation; see *Plurality and Ambiguity*, pp. 93, 138 n. 30. See n. 16 above.

58 Tracy, "Uneasy Alliance," p. 559 n. 42.

existence as selves."[59] In his early essay "The Reality of God," Ogden speaks of demonstrating that God is necessarily presupposed by "all we think and do"; in fact, however, he never actually argues the case for this general claim. Rather, he limits his efforts to an argument for God as the necessary condition for the possibility of moral activity – "a so-called 'moral proof' for the existence of God.'"[60] This "proof" is an argument to the effect that necessarily implied by any moral activity or claim to moral truth "is the unconditioned meaningfulness of our life" and the objective ground of our basic faith in that meaningfulness, which we properly mean by "God."[61] The appeal to an experience of basic faith links this type of apologetic argument to the same experiential-expressivism discussed above; hence revisionary uses of transcendental arguments for God entail the same problematic understatements. In addition, with the transcendental form of argumentation, we have a new set of problems. Transcendental arguments for theism overstate what they can "prove" metaphysically.

A form of this critique has come from a number of philosophical voices in recent years. Stephan Körner challenges the validity of transcendental deductions because one precondition for the success of the deduction is that the framework (to be necessary) must be shown to be unique – that is *"the only* available, or possible, categorial framework." The problem is that this "uniqueness demonstration" would be "difficult, if not impossible" since one could never know whether one had eliminated "all possible competitors" – even if one had eliminated all the alternative frameworks one could conceive of at the time. Without the ability to say when one had finished considering all competing frameworks, one cannot lay claim to have identified the necessary conditions for the possibility of something.[62] A. Phillips Griffiths concurs that strict "transcendental arguments are impossible" because an examination of all possible alternative conditions is "a humanly impossible task."[63] To rule out logically in advance the possibility of alternative schemes "would be to be able to do in philosophy," Richard Rorty says sardonically, "what nobody dreams we can do in

[59] Ogden, *Reality of God*, p. 43; see also *On Theology*, p. 77.
[60] Ogden, *Reality of God*, pp. 40, 43.
[61] Ibid., p. 140; see p. 37.
[62] Stephan Körner, *What Is Philosophy? One Philosopher's Answer* (London: Penguin, 1969), p. 215.
[63] A. Phillips Griffiths, "Transcendental Arguments," *Proceedings of the Aristotelian Society* 43, suppl. (1969), p. 171.

science – predict that any new theory to come along will merely be a disguised version of our present theory" (i.e., the supposedly unique and necessary one).[64] In light of these difficulties, Körner proposes a qualified or "revised notion" of philosophical argumentation which "relativizes" transcendental deductions in some way, thus correcting the overstated character of such arguments.[65]

Given the transcendental mode of argumentation Ogden chooses to employ, he cannot but fail to establish that which he sets out to do – namely, to show that moral activity necessarily presupposes basic faith and its transcendent ground. His claim about the necessary conditions for morality faces the very problems raised above about why any transcendental argument fails. He could never say that he had exhaustively considered all possible competing theories for what grounds morality, even if he had eliminated all the alternatives he could imagine. The question then arises, would Ogden be open to using revised or qualified forms of transcendental argumentation – given that to do so would significantly reduce the force of his moral proof for the existence of God?

In some writings, Ogden gives no indication that he considers the validity of deductive arguments to be weakening in any way. For example, he states that he understands "[t]he burden of theistic argument" to be that of explicating the concept of God as "not only *a* way of conceptualizing the ground of our faith in the worth of life but also the *only* way."[66] In one article at least, however, Ogden nuances this statement somewhat. He observes that the force of a deductive argument comes from the way in which the various assertions can be shown to be "necessarily interconnected." That supposed strength is also a potential weakness of a deductive argument in "that one can always rightly refuse to accept its conclusion by successfully questioning either its formal validity or the material truth of one or more of its premises." When Ogden goes on to say that "the most that any such argument can ever achieve is so to connect various assertions that one more fully grasps their meaning by understanding the price one has to pay for asserting or denying anyone of them,"[67] he appears to be entertaining

64 Richard Rorty, "Transcendental Arguments, Self-Reference, and Pragmatism" in *Transcendental Arguments and Science: Essays in Epistemology*, ed. Peter Bieri, et al. (Dordrecht: D. Reidel, 1979), p. 82.
65 Stephan Körner, "The Impossibility of Transcendental Deductions," *Monist* 51 (1967), p. 329.
66 Ogden, *Reality of God*, p. xi.
67 Ogden, "Concerning Belief," p. 93.

the possibility that the justificatory force of deductive arguments resides in their coherence and their ability to build consensus, not in their demonstration of putatively necessary conditions. Currently, however, no such explicit concession has, to my knowledge, been made by Ogden. He apparently remains committed to transcendental deductive defenses of theism which, in their current form, can only be called overstated. No doubt his apologetics will continue to provoke accusations of being "obsolete" from postliberals who debate with him on strategies for apologetics in today's intellectual situation.

Does Tracy wish to continue to defend (as Ogden apparently does) the use of transcendental arguments? Not surprisingly, we find an evolution in thought over the years – namely, a discernible linguistic-historical turn evidenced in part by his qualifications on the force of transcendental arguments. For example, in *Blessed Rage for Order*, Tracy states that the mode of analysis proper to establishing the credibility of Christianity's cognitive claims is fundamental to theology's transcendental analyses which explicate "the true conditions of possibility of" religious claims. His position here is very close to Ogden's and indeed he endorses Ogden's "'strong' argument for the use of metaphysics in theology."[68] Tracy reaffirms this position in *The Analogical Imagination* and, moreover, develops a transcendental mode of analysis proper to systematic theology (i.e., abstracting a common human experience as "the necessary . . . conditions of possibility" for recognizing the classic's concrete "uncommon or paradigmatic" disclosure of truth.[69]

Currently, we find Tracy alerting his readers to the fact that, although he continues "to believe in the aim of transcendental reflection proposed in *Blessed Rage for Order*, the need for more careful attention to the linguistic-historical character of all such claims seems far more urgent to me now than it did then (1975)."[70] He argues that revisionary theology, in order "to prove adequate to the contemporary postmodern situation," will need to develop modes of inquiry that are more attentive "to the questions of language (and thereby plurality and historicity) and questions of history (and thereby ambiguity and

---

[68] Tracy, *Blessed Rage*, pp. 69, 153.
[69] Tracy, *Analogical Imagination*, pp. 183 n. 26, 185 n. 35. See David Tracy, response to the review symposium on his *The Analogical Imagination* in *Horizons* 8 (1981), p. 334.
[70] Tracy, "Uneasy Alliance," pp. 558–59 n. 40.

postmodern suspicion)." He seems now to believe that even though a
theologian sees the need to defend Christian God-talk metaphysically,
"to have this insight is not necessarily to be able to redeem it."[71]
Admitting the need theologically to render Christian belief in God's
necessary and universal existence credible to all reasonable persons is
not to say that the means to do so are readily available. Tracy implies
that transcendental arguments – as he had thought of them in earlier
writings – might not be usable in today's postmodern intellectual
milieu. Along these lines, Tracy shows interest in reformulating (not
abandoning) his "earlier transcendental analyses" (e.g., as described in
Blessed Rage for Order).[72] He recommends that transcendental arguments be seen as having "relative, never absolute, adequacy"[73] and
states that transcendental arguments, as used in theology today, cannot be taken to be "deductive proofs *sensu stricto*." Rather they are
"reflective attempts to show to any reasonable person the intelligibility"
of the Christian claim being defended.[74] This can be done, for example,
by showing how a Christian belief claim "coheres or does not cohere
with what we otherwise consider reasonable"[75] – in short, a coherentist
not a transcendental argument. Furthermore, he argues that, to the
extent that communities of inquiry today show interest in conceiving
of rationality as historically situated and hermeneutical, then theologians and philosophers can pursue coherence arguments for "warranted
belief."[76] Given these comments, Tracy would seem to have corrected
his overstatements about transcendental arguments establishing
necessary conditions for the objective truth of Christian claims.
Postliberals need not criticize the kind of coherence and consensus
Tracy implies here as playing by rules that do not apply in today's
intellectual milieu.

A final aspect of revisionary apologetics related to transcendental

---

[71] Ibid., pp. 560, 559.

[72] Tracy, *Plurality and Ambiguity*, p. 134 n. 40.

[73] David Tracy, "Religious Studies and Its Community of Inquiry," *Criterion* 25 (1986), p. 24.

[74] David Tracy, "Approaching the Christian Understanding of God" in *Systematic Theology: Roman
Catholic Perspectives*, vol. 1, ed. Francis Schüssler Fiorenza and John P. Galvin (Minneapolis:
Fortress, 1991), p. 142.

[75] Tracy, "Uneasy Alliance," p. 561.

[76] Tracy, *Plurality and Ambiguity*, p. 29. However, Tracy warns that coherence arguments (or any kind
of argument) must not "take over" theological conversation since genuine dialogue is more than
argumentation. For Tracy, an experience of manifestation or disclosure-concealment would act
as a check and balance to prevent this from happening, because it is less a form of argumentation and more like (to return to his commonsensical definition) "finding oneself in love" (ibid.).

arguments, such as a moral proof for the reality of God, is the attempt to undermine alternative moral outlooks – a task Ogden undertakes by arguing that nontheistic moral outlooks are "essentially fragmentary" and that atheistic moral outlooks are "shot through with self-contradiction."[77] I have already cited various philosophers who call into question any claim to have eliminated all alternative frameworks in a transcendental argument. Hence, I rule out in advance that Ogden could have success in that endeavor; nevertheless, what deserves investigation is whether the arguments he puts forth against nontheistic or atheistic morality could have some apologetic force in today's cultural climate. As we will see, they are not completely without merit – if their overstatements are corrected.

Ogden wishes to demonstrate to nontheistic moral philosophers that what makes for the adequate treatment of moral experience is the view that the "necessary condition of all our moral action" is basic faith and its theistic ground. If he can establish that this condition is in fact necessary for moral activity, then nontheistic moral outlooks (i.e., those remaining silent or agnostic about God) will appear to be fragmentary accounts of moral experience. However, if Ogden fails to establish this necessity (and I will indicate below how he does fail), then the force of his argument is greatly reduced. He argues that the necessary condition for moral activity is having the motivation to "put our hearts into" our moral choices and "not succumb to cynicism or despair." Having heart means having confidence (reflective or primordial) in the "long-term significance" of our moral choices. Those moral choices must be experienced, at some level, as making "a difference which no turn of events in the future has the power to annul."[78] Because of the contingency of our existence, "the difference that we as creatures can make to one another is always limited . . . which keeps any of us from making more than an extremely limited and short-term difference to those who come after us." Ogden believes that if the only contribution our lives could make was the short-term difference we make to other contingent creatures such as ourselves, such a contribution "would make no abiding difference and, in that sense, would be meaningless." Thus, the necessary condition for putting our hearts into moral activity is that our activity be experienced as meaningful in the sense of making

[77] Ogden, *Reality of God*, p. 42.
[78] Ibid., pp. 35, 36.

an abiding or everlasting difference. Suffice it to say that he claims that God is the objective basis for our confidence in the abiding difference of our moral choices.[79]

One might wonder, as many nontheistic thinkers do, why, for life to be adequately meaningful, must it be meaningful in an everlasting sense? For even without such an ultimate conception of things, one could (as many people who do not believe in God claim they do) lead a life filled with creative activity and motivated by a sense of human moral purposefulness.[80] To my knowledge, Ogden nowhere argues the case that the meaning in life derived from making a short-term difference (as nontheists might speak of it) is not sufficient for one to put one's heart into moral activity and avoid cynicism and despair. Given that he has not demonstrated the necessity of his own proposed theistic condition for moral activity, he fails to show anything more than a possible connection between having a sense of everlasting significance and meaningful moral activity. Hence, it is difficult to conclude that he has done anything more than suggest that nontheistic positions might be fragmentary. To claim that they are "essentially fragmentary" is an undemonstrated overstatement.

Overstatement is also a problem with Ogden's argument that atheistic moral outlooks are "shot through with self-contradiction." Here it will be illuminating to examine his straightforwardly apologetic essay "The Strange Witness of Unbelief" in which he engages a classic expression of modern atheism in Jean-Paul Sartre's lecture, "Existentialism is a Humanism." Ogden wishes to demonstrate by means of an *ad hominem* argument that Sartre, to be consistent with his own premise, must reject atheism and concede to theism. Specifically, according to Ogden, the premise of Sartre's argument for atheistic existentialism is at odds with the way Sartre refutes the charge that atheism engenders "complete moral relativism."[81] Ogden argues that this refutation necessarily presupposes theism. The initial premise in

[79] Ogden, *Faith and Freedom*, p. 70. That Ogden further argues for a neoclassical theism which connects our existence with God's own process of self-creative becoming is a subject that takes us too far afield from the methodological issues I am discussing here (see, pp. 62ff.).

[80] See for example, *The Meaning of Life*, ed. E. D. Klemke (New York and Oxford: Oxford University Press, 1981); Gerald McCarthy, "Meaning, Morals and the Existence of God," *Horizons* 9 (1982), pp. 288–301 and Winfred G. Phillips, "Schubert Ogden's Transcendental Strategy Against Secularism," *Harvard Theological Review* 82 (1989), pp. 447–66.

[81] Schubert M. Ogden, "The Strange Witness of Unbelief" in his *Reality of God*, p. 127.

Sartre's defense of atheism is: "If God does not exist . . . to have a conception of human nature and so to think a good *a priori*, [then] everything is permitted . . . [and] there is no human nature and so also no *a priori* good." Ogden then interprets this premise contrapositively, arguing that Sartre implicitly concedes that God is "the necessary implication of any talk of a universal human nature or *a priori* moral values."[82] Second, Sartre refutes charges that his atheistic existentialism entails despair and relativism by conceding that in atheism "absolute moral judgments" are possible and that there is a "universal human condition."[83] Ogden then argues that in making this claim, Sartre is caught in the contradiction of: (1) arguing from an atheistic premise that if there is no God, there is no absolute moral standard (and therefore, according to Ogden, contrapositively, if there is an absolute moral standard, then there is a God); and (2) attempting to refute charges of atheism's "unmitigated relativism" by invoking the notion of an *a priori* moral standard.[84] If Sartre does not want to abandon what he needs (e.g., the principle of an *a priori* absolute standard) in order to refute the charges that his atheism entails complete moral relativism, then he must accept theism which is implicitly conceded in Sartre's own invocation of such a standard.

Even if we grant that in this debate Ogden has bested Sartre here, the question still remains: is there a route Sartre or other atheists might take which would enable them to avoid complete moral relativism but also avoid being drawn into the concession about an absolute moral standard – and hence theism? In other words, is it possible to resist the premise that absolute, objective moral standards are the necessary condition for refuting unmitigated relativism? If one can resist this premise, then one need not worry about any theistic implications which may follow. Analytic philosophers have long resisted this premise; philosophers of many sorts continue to add additional arguments for how to move beyond the objectivism and relativism (as Richard Bernstein puts it) of the issue of moral standards. Bernstein envisions secular humanistic moral communities cultivating practices of dialogue, communal judgment, and solidarity guided by *phronesis*, or practical

82 Ibid., p. 129.
83 Ibid., p. 131. Sartre's universal human condition, as Ogden observes, is that "man *qua* man shares . . . radical freedom and responsibility for himself and his fellow men" (p. 131).
84 Ibid., p. 134.

wisdom. No absolute standards for morality or truth are invoked. When debate takes place, reasons and arguments may (and should) be given in communicative exchange, but they "are of course fallible and . . . anticipatory, in the sense that they can be challenged and criticized by future argumentation."[85] To want more is a Cartesian dream of objectivism; correlatively, to claim that this much is not possible is an unnecessary nihilistic conclusion. Bernstein is unpersuaded by claims that theistic belief is necessary to ground a moral position. His response to David Tracy's apology in *Plurality and Ambiguity* for transcendent reality as a source of "resistance and hope" is instructive. Bernstein writes that while he agrees that religious traditions have at times been "witnesses" of resistance and hope, this does not make their theistic-based practices "*distinctive.*" According to Bernstein, "we might even claim that . . . the most fundamental insights of religious discourse, the truth it manifests, are more powerfully expressed in non-religious discourses."[86]

Richard Rorty offers a neopragmatic atheistic alternative to Ogden. Rorty would agree with Ogden that moral action is not compatible with complete moral relativism, but he would point out that there are several versions of relativism. The first two would probably approximate what Ogden calls unmitigated relativism, but the last, which applies to the neopragmatist position Rorty espouses, does not. "The first is the view that every belief is as good as every other. The second is the view that 'true' is an equivocal term . . . The third is the view that there is nothing to be said about either truth or rationality apart from descriptions . . . which a given society – *ours* – uses in one or another area of inquiry." The third type of relativism acknowledges that rational and moral norms are local, culture-specific ways of commending certain beliefs and practices. "True" or "good" is a functional term meaning, contingently commendable by some particular communities (but always referring to "us").[87] Such a view is contextually

[85] See Richard J. Bernstein, *Beyond Objectivism and Relativism: Science, Hermeneutics, and Praxis* (Philadelphia: University of Pennsylvania Press, 1983), p. 154.
[86] Richard J. Bernstein, "Radical Plurality, Fearful Ambiguity, and Engaged Hope," *Journal of Religion* 69 (1989), p. 91.
[87] Richard Rorty, "Solidarity or Objectivity" in his *Objectivity, Relativism and Truth: Philosophical Papers*, vol. 1 (Cambridge University Press, 1991), p. 23. Rorty claims that the third position may not even be properly termed relativistic, which is a term the objectivist, looking for a "universal standpoint," projects onto the pragmatist (p. 30).

relative but perhaps not unmitigatedly so. Morality or rationality proper to contextual relativism is a process of a "continual reweaving of a web of beliefs" in an effort to reap "practical advantages" for our society. The desire for objectivity, on the other hand, impels people "to describe themselves as standing in immediate relation to a nonhuman reality."[88] Morality or rationality proper to objectivity is the process of applying criteria which are thought to transcend the community ahistorically. Rorty considers those enamored with objectivity to be demonstrating a lingering modernist fear that the moral practices of Western liberal democracies will crumble without "buttresses which include an account of 'rationality' and 'morality' as transcultural and ahistorical."[89] Rorty is not saying that there are no valid moral standards which most communities share – even transhistorically; rather, he is saying that the standards we choose are not transcendent or ahistorical but turn out to be, to use Neurath's metaphor, merely "those planks in the boat which are at the moment not being moved about" during our voyage.[90] According to Rorty, that is all we need for rational discourse and, furthermore, turns out to be "just the way *we* live now."[91]

Bernstein and Rorty might urge the Sartre of Ogden's "The Strange Witness of Unbelief" to consider abandoning the attempt to stave off complete moral relativism by means of an appeal to an objective *a priori* moral standard. If Sartre still demurs, he might be shaken out of his apparently objectivist slumber by Rorty's polemical statement that positing any absolute criterion "seems merely a way of telling ourselves that a nonexistent God would, if he did exist, be pleased with us."[92] Ironically, this statement could be taken as confirming that a pull (whether logical or rhetorical, he does not say) toward theism does occur once an appeal is made to absolute standards. This

---

[88] Ibid., pp. 26, 29, 21.

[89] Richard Rorty, "Postmodernist Bourgeois Liberalism" in his *Objectivity, Relativism*, p. 198.

[90] Richard Rorty, "The World Well Lost" in his *Consequences of Pragmatism* (University of Minneapolis Press, 1982), p. 15. To extend the metaphor, Rorty also argues that, in fact, not that many of the planks in the boat have shifted since, say Aristotle: "*many* more of our beliefs are the same as Greek beliefs than are different (e.g. our belief that barley is better than nettles and freedom than slavery, that red is a color, and that lightning often precedes thunder" (p. 8). I find Rorty to be too sanguine about this consensus; much suffering has ensued because societies did not agree on issues of freedom and human subjugation. Rorty's general point, however, is well taken.

[91] Rorty, *Objectivity, Relativism*, p. 29.

[92] Ibid., p. 27.

indicates that a qualified apology for theism could well have a place even in today's postmodern world where argumentative persuasion and conversation take the place of strict deductive metaphysical argumentation. For those who grant Ogden's point about the need for setting moral activity within the most all-encompassing meaning-context possible, his argument for a transcendent ground to moral activity (if it is purged of its overstatements) may in fact be more apologetically persuasive than Bernstein's or Rorty's liberal democratic, atheistic approaches to communicative or pragmatically based moral activity. Nevertheless, Ogden's argument – however much it undermines Sartre – simply cannot undermine Bernstein's or Rorty's positions (the reverse is true as well). Rather, all three positions (and others besides) compete for the hearts and minds of moral agents in today's pluralistic intellectual milieu.

When Tracy writes in 1989 "[t]hat some form of transcendental reflection is needed by theology seems as clear now as it was 20 years ago,"[93] he is speaking for Ogden as well as himself. They both remain committed to this form of reflective inquiry within fundamental theology. The differences between Ogden and Tracy are as follows. For Ogden, theology cannot attain its goal of securing "the demand for a *general justification* of religious or theological statements" if it neglects metaphysical inquiry into the necessary condition for all we say and do.[94] I do not think Tracy could endorse such a blanket statement anymore, given his sensitivity to the linguistic and historical character of all rationality. Although Tracy continues to insist that theological interpretations of the Christian tradition must be correlated with interpretations of the situation, he now seems to reject that it is possible to find the kind of transparently intelligible criteria (e.g., common human experience and framework-independent rationality) he used to speak of more sanguinely. This marks a divergence between him and Ogden who continues to hold that fully critical theological reflection must be shown to cohere with common human experience and reason. Tracy has demonstrated an openness to validating Christian claims by means of coherence arguments and a consensus of warranted belief. He even admits that he sees "some truth in Barth's typically extrava-

---

93 Tracy, "Uneasy Alliance," p. 559.
94 Ogden, "Linguistic Analysis," p. 324.

gant and nicely provocative statement, 'The best apologetics is a good dogmatics.'"[95]

Postliberals try to adhere to this Barthian dictum and liberationists implicitly endorse it, but neither movement has pursued in much depth the methodology that follows from this aphorism. In my view, at least three things would have to be in place for dogmatics to have an effective apologetic thrust. There would have to be: (1) a demonstration of intelligible dogmatic coherence among first-order beliefs and second-order regulative principles; (2) a use of a breadth of non-theological tools (e.g., philosophy, the social sciences, etc.) in some mutually critical relation to the theological sources of scripture and tradition; and (3) a willingness to defend publicly the intelligibility of the dogmatic exposition to a critical interlocutor whose own position is taken seriously. Only an apologetics encompassing all three elements would be able to begin making good on the focal values of normative redescription, solidarity with the oppressed and fully critical reflection. In the chapter which follows, I will argue how employing a wide reflective equilibrium approach promotes all three of these elements and, in the process, promises to make good on all three focal values. To the extent that a wide reflective equilibrium apologetics accomplishes this, it could bring postliberal, revisionary and liberation theologians together on the same field, enriching the conversation on apologetics in today's pluralistic public realm.

[95] Tracy, *Analogical Imagination*, p. 132.

CHAPTER THREE

Credibility in the pluralistic public realm

One cannot read revisionists such as Ogden and Tracy seriously and not feel the proddings of the charge that any "theology that refuses its own need for a fundamental theology is a truncated vision of the fuller task of theology."[1] Finding problematic understatements and over-statements in the way revisionists construct arguments for the theoretical credibility of Christian beliefs does not relieve critics such as myself from addressing this issue methodologically. New ways are needed to conceptualize what credibility amounts to in today's pluralistic and postmodern public realm. In this chapter, I offer a proposal for this apologetic task based on what has come to be known in philosophical circles as wide reflective equilibrium. This approach brings together the kinds of coherentist and consensus elements outlined in chapter two in an attempt to avoid the understatements about the problematic nature of primordial experience and overstatements about deductive "proofs" which have plagued revisionary apologetics. A wide reflective equilibrium apologetics weaves together a normative presentation of Christian beliefs with a broad range of critical disciplines which test the theoretical and practical validity of those beliefs in light of the changes wrought by the linguistic-historical turn. As such, this apolo-getic method addresses theoretical and practical concerns under one argumentative umbrella. I contend that this approach, while no panacea for challenges to Christianity from the secular and religiously plural-istic realm, is as rational and practical an approach as one can have in any nonfoundationalist attempt to redeem the credibility of Christian

[1] David Tracy, "The Uneasy Alliance Reconceived: Catholic Theological Method, Modernity, and Postmodernity," *Theological Studies* 50 (1989), p. 568. An earlier and narrower treatment of some of the issues in this chapter is found in David G. Kamitsuka, "The Justification of Religious Belief in the Pluralistic Public Realm: Another Look at Postliberal Apologetics," *Journal of Religion* 79 (1996), pp. 588–606.

belief and praxis. Furthermore, it is an apologetic method which I believe postliberals and liberationists could – and in some respects already do – endorse. To the extent that their theological views can be judged to be consistent with a wide reflective equilibrium approach, they stand on the same playing field as those revisionary theologians (e.g., Tracy) who have begun to nuance and qualify their claims about what their methods can achieve. Not surprisingly, this approach, which potentially can bring postliberal, liberation and revisionary theologians together in this way, helps sustain the values each of these movements holds as focal.

A point that must be addressed at the start is whether it makes sense to speak of postliberal or liberationist apologetics, which would seem oxymoronic to some. I have already noted in the previous chapter how Tracy criticizes postliberal theologians such as Lindbeck for confessionalism and abandoning any pursuit of a shared rational space necessary for public conversation. Revisionists are not alone in this estimation of postliberal theology. It has become commonplace in many theological circles to view postliberal theology as uninterested or even opposed to engaging in apologetics in the pluralistic public realm. A recent article by Richard Lints, drawing a sharp contrast between Tracy and Lindbeck, illustrates this point. Lints attributes to Tracy an apologetic stance strongly affirming the notion of defending Christian claims according to "publicly acceptable criteria" and attributes to Lindbeck, by contrast, a stance rejecting any such notion. According to Lints, postliberal theologians remain within the confines of a particular socio-linguistic framework, apparently eschewing any attempt "to offer reasons and warrants for their claims . . . aimed at public intelligibility and acceptance."[2]

Liberation theologians, as I noted in chapter one, have been characterized by Ogden as, in a way, confessionalist as well because of their supposed lack of concern for theoretical credibility. Their focus on shared public space is, from an Ogdenian perspective, restricted to practical credibility concerns. The notion of liberation theological apologetics seems an even bigger stretch of the imagination when one takes into account the fact that revisionists and postliberals alike tend to characterize liberation theologians as neglecting theory in favor of

---

[2] Richard Lints, "The Postpositivist Choice: Tracy or Lindbeck?" *Journal of the American Academy of Religion* 61 (1993), pp. 658, 673.

praxis. Tracy suggests that the liberation theological "primacy-of-praxis position,"[3] while a positive corrective for much first-world theology today, could become "an attempt to free interpreters from the demands of theory"[4] or even "sublate" or negate theory altogether.[5] Frei likewise says that he sees in liberation theology "a relation between theory and practice under the priority of the latter."[6] These kinds of characterizations have become commonplace in North Atlantic theology.[7] A conclusion these comments point to is that liberation theologians' interest in praxiological assessments of theological claims has eclipsed any role for the so-called theoretical credibility of theological claims.

Are postliberals and liberationists retreating from doing apologetics in the pluralistic public realm in what amounts to a confessionalist move? Does liberation theology's concern with praxis negate the demands of so-called theoretical credibility? I believe that neither of these accusations fits the best of these theologies, although influential postliberal and liberation writings touching on these issues have not been sufficient yet to dissuade critics. Perhaps part of the reason for this is that postliberals and liberationists have not emphasized explicitly enough the extent to which they already do or could (and I believe should) engage in apologetic arguments. In making my case for a wide reflective equilibrium apologetics, I will address, first, what the theory is and how it has or could have application in postliberal and liberation theologies. Second, I propose how Boff's strategy for employing the social sciences in theology can have apologetic usefulness for testing the assimilative power (to use Lindbeck's term) of a Christian wide reflective equilibrium.

---

[3] David Tracy, "The Foundations of Practical Theology" in *Practical Theology: The Emerging Field in Theology, Church and World*, ed. Don S. Browning (San Francisco: Harper & Row, 1983), p. 61.

[4] David Tracy, *Plurality and Ambiguity: Hermeneutics, Religion, Hope* (San Francisco: Harper & Row, 1987), p. 101. Tracy directs this concern to a number of praxis-oriented theologies ranging from "street theologies" to liberation theologies (p. 102).

[5] Tracy, "Practical Theology," p. 61.

[6] Hans W. Frei, *Types of Christian Theology*, ed. George Hunsinger and William C. Placher (New Haven and London: Yale University Press, 1992), p. 120.

[7] Francis Schüssler Fiorenza associates Clodovis Boff with the view that praxis is "not just a goal but also a criterion of theological method." Francis Schüssler Fiorenza, "Systematic Theology: Task and Methods" in *Systematic Theology: Roman Catholic Perspectives*, vol. 1, ed. Francis Schüssler Fiorenza and John P. Galvin (Minneapolis: Fortress, 1991), p. 64. I take a different view on Boff but share other aspects in common with Fiorenza's theological approach which also promotes a version of wide reflective equilibrium. See Francis Schüssler Fiorenza, *Foundational Theology: Jesus and the Church* (New York: Crossroad, 1986) and "Theology as Responsible Valuation or Reflective Equilibrium: The Legacy of H. Richard Niebuhr" in *The Legacy of H. Richard Niebuhr*, ed. Ronald F. Thiemann (Minneapolis: Fortress, 1991).

WIDE REFLECTIVE EQUILIBRIUM

Wide reflective equilibrium has numerous proponents, each adding different nuances to the theory and adapting it to particular fields of inquiry. Were one to investigate the theory's origins (which I will not), John Rawls's *A Theory of Justice* would immediately surface.[8] I will borrow loosely from later developments of the theory advanced by Norman Daniels and Kai Nielsen (as well as Rawls himself), who have argued for why a *wide* approach to reflective equilibrium offers better resources for justificatory arguments than a *narrow* approach. As we will see, wide reflective equilibrium covers a range of theoretical and practical concerns which makes it particularly well suited for public reasoned debate after the linguistic-historical turn.

Daniels and Nielsen both point out the difference between narrow and wide reflective equilibria for use in moral theory. Narrow reflective equilibrium, stated abstractly, "consists of an ordered pair of (a) a set of considered moral judgments acceptable to a given person P at a given time, and (b) a set of general moral principles that economically systematizes (a)." Daniels points out that Rawls's original exposition of reflective equilibrium suggests an analogy to linguistic method. That is, just as grammatical principles or rules systematize linguistic intuitions implicit in the way we actually speak, so moral principles systematize ethical intuitions implicit in the moral lives we lead. Daniels argues that narrow reflective equilibrium, especially as viewed under the linguistic metaphor, is inadequate for ethical debate. "Narrow equilibrium leaves us in the position of the descriptive linguist" in the sense that no "*justificatory* and *prescriptive*" arguments are advanced for "why one descriptively . . . adequate grammar is to be preferred over another."[9] Nielsen presents the coherentist aspects of narrow reflective equilibrium similarly. This type of "partial" reflective equilibrium "consists in getting a match between our considered particular moral convictions (judgments) and a moral principle or cluster of moral principles"

[8] See John Rawls, *A Theory of Justice* (Cambridge, Mass.: Harvard University Press, 1971), pp. 19–21, 48–51.
[9] Norman Daniels, "On Some Methods of Ethics and Linguistics," *Philosophical Studies* 37 (1980), pp. 22, 25. This essay is reprinted in Norman Daniels, *Justice and Justification: Reflective Equilibrium in Theory and Practice* (Cambridge University Press, 1996), pp. 66–80. The linguistic analogy will become important when we view postliberal and liberationist approaches to apologetics in terms of reflective equilibrium.

such that the convictions and principles "form a consistent whole perspicuously displayed."[10] The danger of pursuing a narrow reflective
equilibrium kind of coherence is a tendency toward conservatism or
even ethnocentrism, since one may merely be content to find the convenient principle or set of principles to match the convictions one
already holds.

Wide reflective equilibrium, on the other hand, "casts a wider net
than narrow reflective equilibrium."[11] Not only does it entail categories
(a) and (b), as mentioned above, but also "(c) a set of relevant background theories" (moral, social, political, empirical, etc.). Daniels indicates why this third element is needed. The point of wide reflective equilibrium is to move beyond merely settling for the immediate, simple
coherence of narrow reflective equilibrium's "best fit of principles with
judgments." The argumentative use of background theories can help
"to bring out the relative strengths and weaknesses" of alternative judgments and principles and contribute to testing their "feasibility."[12] In
other words, background theories (c) can spur the wide reflective equi-
libriumist to consider competing sets of principles and judgments. To
the extent that these background theories entail independent assumptions – that is, assumptions to some nontrivial extent different from those
entailed by the judgments and principles in question – these theories
can inject a wider, self-critical perspective into the reflective process.
This use of background theories exerts a critical force on one's considered judgments and principles. "Wide reflective equilibrium does
not merely systematize some determinate set of judgments. Rather it
permits" or may even "compel" revisions of (a) and (b).[13] Changes in
judgments and principles in turn may cause the background theories
to be adjusted or jettisoned and new ones used. Equilibrium (which is
always provisional) among all three elements is achieved by making

[10] Kai Nielsen, *After the Demise of the Tradition: Rorty, Critical Theory and the Fate of Philosophy* (Boulder, Co.: Westview, 1991), p. 199.

[11] Ibid., p. 200.

[12] Norman Daniels, "Wide Reflective Equilibrium and Theory Acceptance in Ethics," *Journal of Philosophy* 76 (1979), pp. 258, 260 (reprinted in his *Justice and Justification*, pp. 21–46). Daniels only speaks of one type of feasibility test related to Rawls's proposal about justice. Background theories of the person, procedural justice, and the ideal society are used to test whether his proposal will "yield a feasible, stable, well-ordered society " (p. 260). I assume, however, that feasibility testing is not restricted to criteria derived from these theories but formally can be as diverse as the background theories employed. I will say more about this below.

[13] Ibid., p. 266.

ongoing adjustments to considered judgments, moral principles and background theories. This is why Nielsen thinks of wide reflective equilibrium as a kind of "philosophy-as-critical-theory."[14] Furthermore, when conflicts between two agents' reflective equilibria arise, it may be that workable debate can begin at the level of background theories, even in the face of serious disagreements regarding (a) and (b). Since this approach attempts to achieve wide, provisional equilibrium, it is a coherentist approach. Since it attempts to adjudicate among competing reflective equilibria, it is a consensus approach.

The issue of pluralism poses a challenge to any type of justificatory strategy. The way in which proponents of wide reflective equilibrium have responded to this challenge is crucial for my attempt to formulate an apologetic method suited for the pluralistic public realm. Rawls has increasingly become preoccupied with the question: "how is it possible that there can be a stable and just society whose free and equal citizens are deeply divided by conflicting and even incommensurable [though perhaps coherent in their own right] religious, philosophical, and moral doctrines?" To address this issue, Rawls proposes pursuing what he calls "overlapping consensus" within pluralistic public debate.[15] For example, for a diverse society to agree on a concept of justice, its citizens may have to come to consensus about it for very different reasons. Their respective moral wide reflective equilibria will have to overlap on this political issue which affects them all as citizens.

Daniels worries that this concession to pluralism might entail certain philosophical losses, since he envisions the task of wide reflective equilibrium as attempting to move "everyone who can think clearly and rationally about matters, regardless of their starting beliefs, to convergence." Having voiced this concern, though, he admits somewhat sheepishly that his expectations about a wide reflective equilibrium convergence of rational persons may be "a philosopher's dream" from which he is reluctant to be "wakened."[16] Nielsen's sympathies, I suspect, would be with Rawls on this point. He would remind us that a wide reflective equilibrium position is not unassailable or indubitable but is fallibilistic and contextual; therefore consensus may remain partial. This in no way constitutes a philosophical loss for wide reflective

---

[14] Nielsen, *After the Demise*, p. 11.

[15] John Rawls, *Political Liberalism* (New York: Columbia University Press, 1993), p. 133.

[16] Daniels, *Justice and Justification*, pp. 160–61; see pp. 151f.

equilibrium as a kind of critical theory. Nielsen gives this point
rhetorical flourish: "If a consensus rooted in such a wide reflective
equilibrium is not a rational consensus, what, then, would a rational
consensus look like?"[17]

Theological applications

Having reviewed briefly the wide reflective equilibrium conceptuality
in moral theory, we can now turn to the question of its postliberal and
liberation theological application. The correlation emerges most
strongly with category (b), which in moral theory is the set of moral
principles which systematizes the stable judgments held by the agent
or community. The closest postliberal theological equivalent to this
category would be "regulative" doctrinal principles. As is now widely
known, Lindbeck proposes a theory of doctrines as "communally
authoritative rules of discourse, attitude and action."[18] This theory
specifies that the proper task of Christian doctrines is as second-order
rules governing Christian beliefs and practices, not as first-order faith
claims. From a postliberal rule theory (and cultural-linguistic) perspective, the "relatively fixed core of lexical elements" in the beliefs
and practices of any Christian community is ruled by "the grammar
of the religion which church doctrines chiefly reflect."[19] (As we saw in
chapter one, a central element of postliberal theological method entails
identifying the internal logic or grammar of the Christian semiotic
system which guides the linguistic practices of believing communities.)
When one looks for analogues to category (b) in Boff's writings, we find
marked similarities to postliberal rule theory. For Boff, theology is
"discourse built upon a particular established grammar" which is "the
conjunct of rules organizing [Christian] discourse."[20] Theology's task
is to render explicit this "code of faith" and use it to assess the Christian
"pertinency" of religious and theological practices.[21]

[17] Nielsen, *After the Demise*, p. 224.
[18] George A. Lindbeck, *The Nature of Doctrine: Religion and Theology in a Postliberal Age* (Philadelphia: Westminster, 1984), p. 18.
[19] Ibid., p. 81.
[20] Clodovis Boff, O.S.M., *Theology and Praxis: Epistemological Foundations*, tr. Robert R. Barr (Maryknoll: Orbis, 1987), pp. 10, 15.
[21] Ibid., pp. 124, 67. Others have noted Boff's Lindbeckian orientation to theology's grammar. See David S. Cunningham, "Clodovis Boff on the Discipline of Theology," *Modern Theology* 6 (1990), p. 139.

The way category (a) follows accordingly for Lindbeck and Boff is in line with wide reflective equilibrium theory where the currently stable judgments an individual or community holds are correlated with category (b). In moral theory, judgments made in altered states (e.g., of passion) or as passing fancies are not deemed considered judgments. Nielsen avoids the psychologizing criterion and simply says that considered judgments are the "norms . . . we would most resist abandoning – the ones that humanly speaking are bedrock for us."[22] In postliberal theology, the stable judgments of the individual or community would be described cultural-linguistically in the context of religion viewed as an all-encompassing idiom or "language game." Beliefs are articulated in terms of the "vocabulary of symbols" and the "set of skills" which the believer learns to use.[23] Boff similarly situates belief (in a cultural-linguistic manner) at the level of religious "performative" discourse which is marked by a specific "vocabulary." For Lindbeck and Boff, these Christian performative beliefs are ordered not by the religion's vocabulary but its grammatical logic or "syntax."[24]

Because of the similar use of linguistic metaphors by Lindbeck and Boff, the resemblance to what Daniels labels narrow reflective equilibrium is striking. If all postliberals, such as Lindbeck, and liberationists, such as Boff, are doing is describing some convenient set of regulative principles to match what Christians already believe, then the label "narrow reflective equilibrium" would fit and the charges of confessionalism leveled by Tracy and Ogden could be apt. To demonstrate that this label does not fit and to refute the charge of confessionalism, two points need to be addressed. First, do postliberals and liberationists use background theories and, if so, do they use them in such a way that promotes a wide coherence and wide consensus? Recall that one element that widens the reflective equilibrium process is the use of various background theories for the purpose of evaluating alternate sets of considered judgments and principles or helping adjudicate conflicts between reflective equilibria in the pluralistic public realm. In what follows, I will show several examples of how Boff and various postliberals use (or endorse using) background theories which widen the simple coherence and restricted consensus of

---

[22] Nielsen, *After the Demise*, p. 199.
[23] See Lindbeck, *Nature of Doctrine*, pp. 33, 35.
[24] Boff, *Theology and Praxis*, pp. 111, 119, 125. See Lindbeck, *Nature of Doctrine*, pp. 35, 65.

narrow reflective equilibrium. One can detect a use of background theories in what I construe to be two general apologetic approaches postliberals and liberationists could or do endorse. I will designate them as non-Christian-specific apologetics and Christian-specific apologetics.

Non-Christian-specific apologetic arguments bring to the foreground philosophical arguments supportive of the assumptions entailed in the Christian beliefs being defended. Lindbeck injects a historical theological perspective relevant to this form of apologetics when he points out that Thomas Aquinas used philosophical proofs for the existence of God as "'probable arguments' in support of faith." Lindbeck reads Aquinas as advocating a "subsidiary use of philosophical and experiential considerations in the explication and defense of the faith"[25] because such philosophical reasoning can "represent genuine means by which the human mind comes to know of the existence of a transcendent being." Lindbeck also adds that Aquinas soberly "does not pretend that very much has thereby been achieved" regarding knowledge of the Christian God. Aquinas's discussions of the metaphysical attributes of God "do not tell us who [the Christian God] . . . is, but rather indicate the context within which scriptural and creedal descriptions of who God is . . . can be given a specifiable referent." In other words, philosophical arguments for or about God can at best support broadly theistic claims, but they cannot establish Christian-specific claims about the God of the Bible. Nevertheless, even if the theological content of these sorts of metaphysical arguments is such that nothing "of importance for salvation" is said,[26] Lindbeck seems to concede that the apologetic force of such discussions could be significant, and postliberal theology "need not exclude" them. When Lindbeck asserts that philosophical arguments should not be seen as "standing at the center of theology,"[27] he can be read as affirming how they might nevertheless be apologetically useful as background theories. An

---

[25] Lindbeck, *Nature of Doctrine*, p. 131.

[26] George A. Lindbeck, "Discovering Thomas: The Classic Statement of Christian Theism," *Una Sancta* 24 (1967), pp. 47, 50. The relations between non-Christian-specific notions (e.g., transcendent being) and Christian-specific ones (e.g., the God portrayed in scripture and creed) can only be, as William Placher puts it, "ad hoc conjunctions and analogies." William C. Placher, *Unapologetic Theology: A Christian Voice in a Pluralistic Conversation* (Louisville: Westminster/John Knox, 1989), p. 154.

[27] Lindbeck, *Nature of Doctrine*, pp. 131, 129.

argumentative use of philosophical background theories for or about theism can give justificatory support in some situations and to some audiences for the reasonableness of the theistic presuppositions of Christian-specific God-talk.

Given revisionary apologetic strategies discussed in the previous chapter, the question naturally arises: would a transcendental argument in the spirit of Ogden's "moral proof" for the reality of God (in a revised form, of course) be usable for wide reflective equilibrium apologetics – and would such an argument be acceptable to postliberals? I suggest that it would on both counts. That is, "God" could be proposed as an eminently fitting, highly insightful and/or useful condition for moral activity construed in a certain way. Indeed, it is much more difficult for nontheistic or atheistic moral theorists to rule out claims about God as an eminently fitting condition for some construals of moral activity than to rule out an unqualified metaphysical claim about God as the logically necessary and unique condition of all moral activity.

Kathryn Tanner gives a general endorsement of this type of argument, proposing the use of transcendental arguments that have been "[q]ualified so that proposed conditions are not considered necessarily unique."[28] Hence, I see no reason why postliberals could not include arguments of this sort (utilizing, in the process, whatever theories of morality, the human person, religion, etc. that they deem fitting) in apologetic dialogue with those still interested in philosophically oriented theistic grounding for morality. In other words, such theistic arguments are not always apologetically effective, but they could be persuasive for some cultured despisers of religion.[29] Moreover, using transcendental arguments in this qualified form would help revisionists to avoid overstating what such arguments can achieve (a problem for the early Tracy and an ongoing problem for Ogden). It would also help postliberals to avoid understating (as they tend to

---

[28] Kathryn E. Tanner, *God and Creation in Christian Theology: Tyranny or Empowerment* (New York and Oxford: Blackwell, 1988), p. 23.

[29] Any mode of argumentation, be it a revised deductive or some other mode, which suggests God as a grounding for morality will have to address the ontological and epistemological issues which ensue in a way that is intelligible in a postmodern milieu. Hence it follows that part of the store of background theories one might need to use in non-Christian-specific wide reflective equilibrium apologetic arguments (such as the revised transcendental deductive one mentioned above) would be theories addressing issues such as what it means to say something is moral, true, or real and how language can refer to it, and so on.

do) whatever virtues, so to speak, there might be in engaging in philosophical reflection about transcendent being for apologetic purposes.

Boff also endorses the use of non-Christian-specific apologetics – even to the point of embracing "transcendental reflection," much along the lines of Ogden and the early Tracy.[30] Boff makes only a few explicit methodological remarks about theoretical credibility, but he clearly asserts that fundamental (or as Boff calls it, "first" or "natural") theology is indispensable for Christianity to help secure its "rational warranty" and "to justify its theoretical status." Boff argues that there is a full "breach," or epistemological "discontinuity," between Christian theology proper and natural theology.[31] By stipulating this breach, he indicates that natural theology is situated "at zero degrees on the theological scale"; it remains "pretheological," having to do with defending the presuppositions of Christian belief (hence a non-Christian-specific form of argument).[32] Pretheological though it may be, Boff nonetheless asserts that "were the 'question of God' as discussed in 'natural theology' to be decided in the negative . . . theology would fall to pieces."[33] He is aware that this kind of philosophical reflection is not affirmed in all intellectual sectors today, potentially weakening its apologetic force. He acknowledges that "the possibility of knowledge of the supernatural, the metaphysical, the divine . . . [is] determinedly and typically disputed in our contemporary culture, especially in current philosophy."[34] Furthermore, he questions the usefulness of an "out-dated . . . philosophico-anthropological discourse . . . [which] remains mute vis-à-vis the social relationships of human beings . . . reducing itself to the detection of the common traits of all human beings in their transcendentality."[35] Nevertheless, Boff himself is not averse to speaking of human nature rather philosophically as

[30] Boff, *Theology and Praxis*, p. 80.

[31] Ibid., pp. 81, 82, 109; see p. 281 n. 2.

[32] Ibid., pp. 80, 74.

[33] Ibid., p. 82. Ogden would probably peg Boff as exemplifying the apologetic stance "mainstream Christian theologies have typically" taken (of which Ogden is highly critical) – that is, allowing for a defense of "the credibility of the necessary presuppositions of witness . . . as a pretheological task [while] . . . the credibility of witness itself, as distinct from its presuppositions, has been excluded from the scope of [critical] theological reflection." Schubert M. Ogden, "Toward Doing Theology," *Journal of Religion* 75 (1995), pp. 8–9.

[34] Boff, *Theology and Praxis*, p. 272 n. 64.

[35] Ibid., p. 11.

having an existential "'something' constitutive of being itself, as an
ontic dimension, such as will render the human being a being-open, a
being-called" in relation to God.[36] He insists that liberation theology's
preferential option for the poor does not preclude "metaphysical or
transcendental questions . . . precisely because the poor are not only
poor, but men and women called to eternal communion with God."[37]
Beyond this rather general and only slightly qualified endorsement of
the apologetic use of transcendental arguments (with experiential-
expressive shadings), Boff does not elaborate. Instead, he explains the
brevity of his comments about fundamental theology by saying that
the "pressure of historical urgency" causes him to focus instead on
other issues more pertinent to the needs of the Latin American
Christian communities.[38] The same criticism I directed toward Ogden
and Tracy in the previous chapter would apply to Boff's experiential-
expressive claims about human nature and his endorsement of metaphysical arguments. Boff will need to make a linguistic-historical
turn on these issues and, by all indications, is poised to do so since
he has already voiced some reservations about making speculative
claims about the transcendentality of human beings. He would not
have to abandon natural theology but could use revised transcendental arguments as part of what I am calling non-Christian-specific
apologetics.

Another strategy for defending the validity of Christian discourse
takes the form of what I am calling Christian-specific apologetic arguments. These can be indirectly or directly apologetic. Indirect Christian-
specific apologetics would depend on the "persuasive power" of constructive theological formulations standing at the center of Christian

[36] Ibid., p. 96. At first glance, Boff's theological anthropology seems to posit something analogous
to Ogden's notion of basic faith which all humans inescapably have at the nonsensuous level of
existence. However, closer examination suggests that Boff's notion of humanity's constitutive
openness to God is derived theologically ("from a point of departure in revelation") not
phenomenologically (p. 96). Thus, Boff's experiential-expressive sounding statements might be
characterized as belonging to the type of liberal theology about which Lindbeck (with Lonergan
in mind) says the following: this type focuses on "the special religious experience of the gift of
God's love (and this is postulated on the basis of theological rather than philosophical considerations)" (*Nature of Doctrine*, p. 44 n. 18).
[37] Clodovis Boff, "Epistemology and Method of the Theology of Liberation," tr. Robert R. Barr,
in *Mysterium Liberationis: Fundamental Concepts of Liberation Theology*, ed. Ignacio Ellacuría, S.J., and
Jon Sobrino, S.J. (Maryknoll: Orbis, 1993), p. 61.
[38] Boff, *Theology and Praxis*, p. 7.

theology, in the spirit of Barth's aphorism: "a good dogmatics is the best apologetics."[39] Or, to use the language of wide reflective equilibrium, I have in mind an argument whose persuasive force is primarily a factor of how profoundly and widely the theologian displays the coherence among Christian beliefs and doctrinal principles – buttressed and tested for feasibility by the critical force of a variety of background theories (e.g., philosophical, literary, anthropological, sociological, etc.). It will help to give at least one brief example of dogmatics with an indirect apologetic effect which can be found in Frei's descriptive theological exposition on Jesus' death and resurrection. This theological exposition not only contains the three elements of wide reflective equilibrium as mentioned above but also brings those elements into relation with each other in a way that reflects the purposes of wide reflective equilibrium. What is of particular interest to me here is Frei's use of background theories which is, after all, what makes reflective equilibrium wide and not narrow.

The church's proclamation of Jesus' crucifixion and resurrection as told in the biblical narrative, which Frei calls "the cornerstone of the Christian tradition,"[40] is recognizably a stable belief – that is, category (a) of a Christian wide reflective equilibrium. This stable belief has received various creedal and doctrinal formalizations from the time of the early church ecumenical councils and onward. Frei comments on one sixteenth-century doctrinal statement in Article IV of the Church of England's Thirty-nine Articles: "Christ did truly rise again from death, and took again his body, with flesh, bones, and all things appertaining to the perfection of man's nature . . . "[41] This Article, when construed in terms of postliberal rule theory, specifies that the resurrected Christ should be spoken of as identical in human nature to the Christ who died on the cross. When read as a regulative doctrinal principle, it resembles category (b) in wide reflective equilibrium because it "economically systematizes" (as Daniels would say) the corresponding Christian communal beliefs about Jesus in category

[39] William C. Placher, "Revisionist and Postliberal Theologies and the Public Character of Theology," *Thomist* 49 (1985), p. 405.

[40] Hans W. Frei, "Theological Reflections on the Accounts of Jesus' Death and Resurrection," *Christian Scholar* 49 (1966), p. 263.

[41] Hans W. Frei, "How It All Began: On the Resurrection of Christ," *Anglican and Episcopal History* 58 (1989), p. 139.

(a). So far we have a narrow doctrinal reflective equilibrium. However, Frei employs a number of background theories so that his dogmatic proposal is not simply a narrow coherentist match of belief and regulative doctrine but is an attempt to achieve a wider (and hence more publicly intelligible) reflective understanding of what it means to say that the unsubstitutable "identity of the crucified Jesus and that of the risen Lord are one and the same."[42]

One background theory Frei draws from is a literary theory of realistic narrative which he uses to read the gospels as "history-like" accounts of Jesus – that is, "unlike myths and allegories, they literally mean what they say."[43] To take these biblical texts as history-like realistic narratives means to take them primarily as accounts "adequate to" the reality of the events of Jesus' life, death and resurrection. The gospels, while not "an absolutely accurate record," are nevertheless an "indispensable means for grasping, even though not explaining, the mystery of Christ's resurrection as a real event."[44] The fact that Frei later distanced himself from any systematic use of this hermeneutical theory for interpreting the Bible does not weaken the importance of my identification of realistic narrative as a background theory in this dogmatic wide reflective equilibrium exposition. Frei's change of opinion regarding how much to depend theologically on this theory evinces the kind of self-critical dynamism which marks a wide reflective equilibrium approach – namely background theories must also be open to revision.

In order to argue that Jesus' "singular human identity is . . . most fully accessible to the reader in the passion–resurrection sequence," Frei employs several philosophical background theories on personal identity, principally, theories of "intention action" and "self-manifestation" description. The former answers the question "What is the person like?" by focusing on the intentions a person carries into action and the latter answers the question "Who is that person?" by describing the

[42] Frei, "Theological Reflections," p. 274; original in italics.
[43] Hans W. Frei, *The Identity of Jesus Christ: The Hermeneutical Bases of Dogmatic Theology* (Philadelphia: Fortress, 1975), p. xiv. The literary theorists Frei draws from include Cleanth Brooks, René Wellek and Erich Auerbach. See Hans W. Frei, "Remarks in Connection with a Theological Proposal" in his *Theology and Narrative: Selected Essays*, ed. George Hunsinger and William C. Placher (New York and Oxford: Oxford University Press, 1993), p. 33.
[44] Frei, "On the Resurrection," pp. 141, 140, 142.

persistence of the subject's identity through life's transitions.[45] When the intention-action and self-manifestation descriptions are combined with a history-like reading of the narrative (Frei focuses primarily on Luke), the questions "What is Jesus like?" and "Who is Jesus?" are depicted as being most explicitly answered in a realistic narrative reading of the passion–resurrection sequence. Frei's concluding point is Anselmic: reading the narratives realistically, with the aid of these clarifying categories from philosophical anthropology, renders Jesus' being and identity in such a way that for the believer, "his nonresurrection becomes inconceivable." Even the agnostic who finds the story "implausible" can no longer write it off as "myth."[46] I will not digress to elaborate upon or assess (doctrinally, philosophically or literarily) Frei's subtle argument. The point I wish to highlight is the method being employed. It is via the conjunction of two different sets of background theories (literary theory and philosophical anthropology) that Frei attempts to account for what the communal plain sense claims and church doctrine regulatively systematizes – that is, the passion narratives should be read more nearly as a story of the bodily resurrection of Jesus than as, say, a myth about the renewal of the disciples' faith. If Frei's dogmatic treatment of Jesus' death and resurrection can plausibly be viewed as an attempt to give a coherent and intelligible construal of Christian beliefs and doctrinal principles in light of various publicly accessible background theories, then it is reasonable to say that postliberal dogmatics can function as (among other things) wide reflective equilibrium arguments having indirect apologetic force.[47]

---

[45] Frei, "Theological Reflections," p. 276. See Frei, *Identity*, ch. 9 and pp. 126ff. and "Theological Reflections," pp. 278ff. These theories were developed in conjunction with Frei's reading of, among others, Gilbert Ryle and P. F. Strawson. Tracy finds Frei's anthropological background theory persuasive and agrees that it "should continue to be *the* principal Christian model for the Christian agent as a responsible self before God and the neighbor." David Tracy, "On Reading the Scriptures Theologically" in *Theology and Dialogue: Essays in Conversation with George Lindbeck*, ed. Bruce D. Marshall (University of Notre Dame Press, 1990), p. 54. That Tracy advocates using other anthropological theories as well simply demonstrates the above-mentioned point made by Daniels. That is, dialogue between opposing positions often begins at the level of background theories. In the case of dialogue with Ogden, these background theories function polemically. Note Frei's critique of Ogden's existentialist hermeneutics which emphasize a "remote 'existentiell' selfhood" at odds with the literal sense ("Theological Reflections," p. 305).

[46] Frei, *Identity*, pp. 145, 143.

[47] Some postliberals have noted the apologetic force of Frei's writings. George Hunsinger suggests that Frei's dogmatic exposition may be taken "as a kind of ad hoc apologetics . . . falling within the scope of dogmatic theology" ("Hans Frei as Theologian: The Quest for a Generous Orthodoxy," *Modern Theology* 8 [1992], p. 117).

Could Boff envision dogmatics as having an indirect apologetic function – once the theologian has moved across the epistemological "breach" from fundamental theology to Christian theology proper? Specifically, could he endorse indirect Christian-specific apologetic arguments within a wide reflective equilibrium conceptuality which addresses the validity not of the presuppositions of Christian beliefs but of the beliefs themselves? To my knowledge, Boff has not engaged in a dogmatic exposition (similar to Frei's discussed above); nevertheless, he does give some methodological clues for how he might widen the reflective equilibrium of Christian beliefs and theology's regulative code of faith by means of background theories. A conceptuality analogous to background theories is found in his system under the designation of theoretical "mediations."[48] These mediations function within what Boff calls the process of the production of theological cognitions (a concept he develops with notions borrowed from Louis Althusser and Thomas Aquinas), within which dogmatics takes place. A central Althusserian notion which Boff adapts for theology is that of the three "generalities" or stages in theoretical practice. Generalities are what are treated, known and produced in theoretical practice. The goal is the production of knowledge which is the last or third generality. The second generality is the conceptual framework used to rework some datum or subject matter which is the first generality. Boff synthesizes Althusser's three categories of theoretical practice with Aquinas's theological notions in order to develop a methodological schema in which "the *principia* of theology" are seen "as occupying the position of a second generality." The principles of faith are the formal object which "gives shape to" theology's material object or "first generality, rendering it a finished product in the form of [a] third generality."[49] This finished product is properly theological in that it is ruled by theology's code of faith which (as a second generality) reworks the material object.

Different kinds of mediations are at work at several points in this Christian-specific cognitive process. At the level of the first generality, Boff explains that "[t]here is no question of practicing upon an absolutely 'raw' material, a brute 'pure' fact, an object 'in itself.' "[50]

---

[48] See Boff, *Theology and Praxis*, pp. xxiv, 234 n. 7.
[49] Ibid., p. 74.
[50] Ibid., p. 71.

Much of Boff's text focuses on social-scientific mediations (e.g., political science, economics, history, sociology, etc.) which liberation theologies use to grasp socio-political material objects. Political reality must be mediated by the social sciences before the theologian can rework it with a theological second generality. In more metaphorical language, in order to read the political, theology "receives its text from [the] social sciences and practices upon it a reading in conformity with its own proper code." One can extrapolate from this that any number of other mediations could be used as well: philosophy, psychology, literary theory, the natural sciences, and so on. Mediations are also at work in the construction of theology's formal object, which should not be conceived as revelation springing pristinely from scripture or "like meteors" fallen from heaven.[51] What it means to say that theology's grammatical code of faith is produced via hermeneutical mediation in relation to scripture will be discussed in the next chapter. Suffice it to say here that at all phases of theological practice, "mediations of reason are ever present, however veiled or disguised." Good theological method will bring "acritically mediated theology" into the light of "critically mediated theology."[52] Using the language of reflective equilibrium, we can say that wide reflective equilibrium strives to be explicit in its use of critical background theories, while narrow reflective equilibrium disguises its acritical and implicit use of background theories. By maneuvering through Boff's technical language, one can describe mediations as functioning within his methodological system in relation to religious discourse and the principles of faith in a way that is analogous to how background theories interact with beliefs and principles in Christian-specific wide reflective equilibrium arguments. That is, mediations widen the coherence of what goes into a theological product. The theological product of this process would then be poised to function apologetically in an indirect way.

A direct Christian-specific apologetic approach entails theological arguments tailored to a specific non-Christian interlocutor (or community of interlocutors) with the intent to persuade that person (or community) of the validity of the Christian web of beliefs. William Werpehowski's "Ad Hoc Apologetics" provides a postliberal illustration

---

[51] Ibid., pp. 31, 74.
[52] Ibid., p. 25.

of this approach. Werpehowski's article, whose title is identified with a phrase from *The Nature of Doctrine*, helpfully attempts to fill in Lindbeck's apologetic strategy by giving, among other things, a "specific and plausible account of how an apologetic exchange might take place between believer and unbeliever." Werpehowski does not introduce his proposal, as I have done, in terms of its relation to Christian- or non-Christian-specific apologetic approaches; nor does the conceptuality of wide reflective equilibrium overtly factor into his discussion (although he does mention "the idea of reflective equilibrium" in Rawls).[53] Nevertheless, I believe Werpehowski's comments can be used fairly as a point of departure for what I am calling direct Christian-specific wide reflective equilibrium apologetic argumentation. For a liberationist perspective on direct Christian-specific apologetics, I will refer to José Míguez Bonino's views along with those of Gutiérrez and Boff.

Werpehowski's article is directly relevant for liberationist apologetics because one specific example he explores is a hypothetical interaction with the atheistic views of a Marxist. We need to be careful, however, not to conflate North American postliberal conversation with Marxists and Latin American liberationist conversation with Marxists. The contexts of these two types of apologetic exchange are different and, hence, what is perceived as the pressing issues for consideration often may be different. Werpehowski's apologetic approach is oriented to the question of "how certain contributions from one side can correct and criticize the other's position," having in mind "the purposes of common interest and activity" (which remain unspecified).[54] By contrast, Míguez Bonino notes that central to the Marxist–Christian interaction in the Latin American liberationist context is the sustained reference to a concrete "common revolutionary project." For this reason, in encounters between liberation theologians and Marxists, "it is not an intellectual dialogue that leads to co-operation; rather the objective conditions prompt a common action, and it is within this co-operation

[53] William Werpehowski, "Ad Hoc Apologetics," *Journal of Religion* 66 (1986), pp. 284, 296 n. 30. Mention of *ad hoc* apologetics is made by Lindbeck in *Nature of Doctrine*, p. 129. The notion is also found earlier in Frei, *Identity*, p. xii and Hans W. Frei, "An Afterword: Eberhard Busch's Biography of Karl Barth" in *Karl Barth in Re-View*, ed. H. Martin Rumscheidt (Pittsburg: Pickwick, 1981), p. 114.
[54] Werpehowski, "Ad Hoc Apologetics," p. 296.

that dialogue takes place."[55] Gutiérrez makes a similar point when
he states that in Latin America "the oppressed and those who seek to
identify with them face ever more resolutely a common adversary, and
therefore, the relationship between Marxists and Christians takes
on characteristics different from those in other places." Given these
differences, we can better appreciate Gutiérrez's remark that a North
Atlantic "theoretical dialogue with Marxism . . . holds little interest for
Latin America."[56] He knows that the most credible justification of the
Christian faith to Latin American Marxists is one that shows how the
church does, or at least could, outdo Marxism in its commitment to the
struggle against oppressive economic and political structures. His
point, however, should not be taken outside of its polemical context.
He and other liberation theologians are not uninterested in bringing
theoretical dimensions of Christian and Marxist reflective equilibria
into dialogue – when appropriate.

Whether in the postliberal context of a project of cooperative intellectual dialogue or the liberationist context of a project of cooperative
action preceding dialogue, there are common elements of apologetic
exchange which can be identified in Werpehowski and liberationists.
One finds a variety of strategies for direct apologetic exchange. One
strategy includes critical analyses meant to demonstrate the inadequacy
of the views of the theologian's interlocutor. We see an example of this
in Míguez Bonino's argument that the Marxist view of the human condition is "insufficient . . . because it does not take seriously enough the
depth of man's alienation and consequently of the problems of power,
of man's self-interest, of the intractability of human relationships."[57]
Werpehowski also suggests criticizing Marxist views on the potential
of humanity to be "utterly its own master and creator" once a socialist
society is achieved.[58]

---

[55] José Míguez Bonino, *Christians and Marxists: The Mutual Challenge to Revolution* (Grand Rapids, Mich.: William B. Eerdmans, 1976), p. 16.

[56] Gustavo Gutiérrez, *A Theology of Liberation: History, Politics, and Salvation*, tr. and ed. Sister Caridad Inda and John Eagleson; author's new introduction and revisions, tr. Matthew J. O'Connell (Maryknoll: Orbis, 1988), p. 60.

[57] Míguez Bonino, *Christians and Marxists*, p. 98. Boff and Gutiérrez would affirm the importance of a theological "apologia" which counters the insufficiencies of Marxist atheistic dialectical materialism by insisting on a spiritual dimension to human existence (Boff, *Theology and Praxis*, pp. 13, 55; see Gustavo Gutiérrez, *The Truth Shall Make You Free: Confrontations*, tr. Matthew J. O'Connell [Maryknoll: Orbis, 1990], pp. 6off.).

[58] Werpehowski, "Ad Hoc Apologetics," p. 295.

A second strategy for apologetic exchange includes defensive arguments meant to respond to Marxist critiques of Christian beliefs. Werpehowski suggests that a likely defensive "conversational scenario" would take on Marxist attacks on religion in general as "an illusory projection of human needs" reflecting the alienation of persons within a capitalist economic system.[59] Míguez Bonino also recognizes the need to refute the basic Marxist charge that the "religious element is seen always as an ideological screen, as a false consciousness of a real human need."[60] I suggest that using the conceptuality of wide reflective equilibrium clarifies how such an attack could be addressed within an apologetic exchange. This aspect of Marxist–Christian debate might focus on conflicting background theories about the nature of religion and the relation of religion to socio-economic structures. I would suspect that, in actuality, most Christian–Marxist apologetic discussions would probably need to begin with these (and other) background theory issues. That is, before further constructive dialogue could proceed, the Marxist would need to be disabused of, or at least would have to suspend temporarily, his or her view that Christianity is reducible to an ideological projection of the needs of the alienated masses.

A defensive apologetic would also need to respond to those legitimate criticisms made by Marxists which are acknowledged as unmasking problems and weaknesses in Christianity. Werpehowski concludes that certain Marxist charges about Christianity's "anti-humanity . . . may strike home."[61] Boff argues that "we must give Marx credit for enabling us to see that a theology . . . that fails objectively to recognize a given real historical situation and do it justice, necessarily spins out a vacuous discourse bereft of any credibility – a 'mystifying' discourse."[62] His *Theology and Praxis* is in part an apologetic engagement with Marxism which focuses on a methodological response to this challenge – hence, his argument for how theology should make methodical use of social scientific mediation in order to address political issues in a rigorous and ideologically vigilant way.

Also integral to a defensive apologetics is the clarificatory task of

---

[59] Ibid., p. 297.
[60] Míguez Bonino, *Christians and Marxists*, p. 49. Boff refers to this as the "antidogmatist critique" (*Theology and Praxis*, p. 295).
[61] Werpehowski, "Ad Hoc Apologetics," p. 298.
[62] Boff, *Theology and Praxis*, p. 13.

presenting the Christian web of beliefs as a coherent whole in a way
that can counter how one's interlocutor may be misconstruing or
misidentifying the "internal logic of the Christian faith itself."[63] Giving
a presentation of the web of Christian beliefs would move the theologian to a descriptive or, more traditionally, dogmatic mode of discourse
(as illustrated above in reference to Frei's christological exposition).
Even if dogmatic wide reflective equilibrium theological formulations
do not have a primarily apologetic intent and thrust, they may have an
important place as a component within a direct Christian-specific
apologetic interchange.

A third apologetic strategy which Werpehowski discusses attempts
to identify points of commonality between the "'reflective equilibrium'
internal to [each] . . . position" in an effort to convince the Marxist
that the Christian reflective equilibrium is a more plausible way of
accounting for the views of reality which they find they share in common. Werpehowski observes that there are some "limited alliances" of
Christian and Marxist considered judgments about social justice and
about human tendencies toward the "practice of domination and
tyranny."[64] Finding this commonality of views allows the theologian
then to argue, for example, that Christian beliefs and principles about
"human need and human failure" may better account for the human
realities which Marxists and Christians both acknowledge in different
ways. For Werpehowski, if the Marxist could adopt "an approximation"
of the Christian view of human failure (doctrine of sin), it may be
possible for the theologian to speak further to the Marxist of other
Christian beliefs and principles, such as the "thoroughgoing human
need for a source of reconciliation and trust" which transcends human
limitations.[65] In this way, the theologian attempts to move the conversation toward a more substantive consensus which could allow the
Marxist to see the coherence between (1) the Marxist–Christian point
of commonality that has been identified and (2) the larger web of
Christian beliefs to which that point is connected.[66] This strategy

---

[63] Werpehowski, "Ad Hoc Apologetics," p. 297.

[64] Ibid., pp. 295, 296.

[65] Ibid., pp. 297, 296. I will comment below on one possible way of understanding this notion of
"approximation."

[66] This kind of argumentation is not dissimilar in method to what Ronald Thiemann calls "holist justification." See Ronald F. Theimann, *Revelation and Theology: The Gospels as Narrated Promise* (University
of Notre Dame Press, 1985), pp. 75ff.; see p. 173 n. 11 for a reference to reflective equilibrium.

exemplifies Rawls's notion of overlapping consensus because it tries to secure a certain number of shared theoretical and practical commitments which each interlocutor can agree on for reasons internal to their own reflective equilibrium.[67] Similarly, the liberationist Christian–Marxist encounter also forms an overlapping consensus where a collaborative political project is shared for reasons internal to each one's reflective equilibrium.

In part, the plausibility of the direct Christian-specific apologetic strategy I have just outlined hinges on whether it makes sense at all to speak of Marxist–Christian "approximations" or partial translations of considered judgments which can form the basis for an overlapping consensus in an apologetic exchange. Readers of Lindbeck are familiar with his polemic against liberal theology's apologetic attempt to translate the Christian faith into a contemporary idiom.[68] If Lindbeck were interpreted as promoting the notion that most aspects of the Christian paradigm are completely incommensurable with, and hence untranslatable into, other religious and nonreligious discourses, then it would be understandable for revisionary theologians such as Tracy to conclude that Lindbeck is rejecting any significant notion of a public shared rational space.[69] However, Lindbeck need not be read as rejecting the notion of translatability *per se*, since what he criticizes are translations which are done "systematically" so that the "contemporary framework is controlling" and the Christian semiotic system is distorted.[70] Moreover, Lindbeck's use of the term "incommensurable" regarding comparative religion approaches is meant to make the very specific point that "no common framework" exists "within which to compare different religions."[71] Incommensurable does not mean incomparable or completely untranslatable; rather, it means that there "cannot be any neat and simple way of settling the issues between" two very different conceptual paradigms (in Thomas Kuhn's sense of the word) on a "point

---

[67] For a discussion of overlapping consensus among Christians and non-Christians in public debate, see Kathryn Tanner, "Public Theology and the Character of Public Debate," *The Annual of the Society of Christian Ethics* (1996), pp. 79–101.

[68] See Lindbeck, *Nature of Doctrine*, p. 129.

[69] For a discussion of the notions of incommensurability and untranslatability, see Placher, *Unapologetic Theology*, pp. 48ff.

[70] George Lindbeck, "Scripture, Consensus and Community," *This World: A Journal of Religion and Public Life* 23 (1988), pp. 14, 15.

[71] Lindbeck, *Nature of Doctrine*, p. 49.

after point" or systematic basis.[72] Richard Bernstein adds a philosophical clarification when he interprets Kuhn's thesis about incommensurable paradigms as raising not an issue of translation but an issue
"of *problems* and *standards*."[73] In other words, I may be able partially to
translate a rival paradigm into language I can understand so as to grasp
the meaning of what that paradigm is about, but I may still judge it
to be incommensurable with my paradigm because it deals with
problems and entails standards for which I have no use.

Lindbeck assumes that extrabiblical concepts taken from various
sources will be absorbed (to use his now famous metaphor) into the
biblical world.[74] This is what I take Lindbeck to mean when he says
that a theologian "may inscribe neo-Platonism within the biblical text,
as did Augustine, or Aristotelianism, as did Aquinas, or late medieval
nominalism, as did Luther . . . and there is nothing . . . to prevent
others from trying to do the same with Whiteheadianism or Marxism.
It may, in fact, be an obligation."[75] Surely this absorption process
entails some translation in the sense of charitably optimizing agreement with an alternative viewpoint, as Donald Davidson would say.[76]
Some revisionary theologians may promote the kind of systematic
translation or interpretation "without remainder"[77] of which Lindbeck
is so critical, but the Davidsonian point I am injecting into this con-

[72] George A. Lindbeck, "Theological Revolutions and the Present Crisis," *Theology Digest* 23 (1975), p. 315. Lindbeck makes this argument in relation to paradigm shifts in Christian theology. Terrence Tilley applies this point for interreligious dialogue. For example, in Theravada Buddhism and Roman Catholicism, "what counts as a problem differs: a Catholic doesn't have to solve the problem of how dharma can work when no 'soul' transmigrates, and a Buddhist doesn't have to explain how the bread and wine . . . can be the body and blood of Jesus Christ." Terrence W. Tilley, "Incommensurability, Intratextuality, and Fideism," *Modern Theology* 5 (1989), p. 90.
[73] Richard J. Bernstein, *Beyond Objectivism and Relativism: Science, Hermeneutics, and Praxis* (Philadelphia: University of Pennsylvania Press, 1985), p. 85. Placher notes that Kuhn "never really meant to deny" the (at least partial) translatability of incommensurable paradigms; rather, he only meant to indicate that when choosing between paradigms, one looks at each one's success and decides for reasons often more like art than science which "success was more important" (*Unapologetic Theology*, pp. 49, 50).
[74] See Lindbeck, *Nature of Doctrine*, p. 118.
[75] George Lindbeck, "Barth and Textuality," *Theology Today* 43 (1986), pp. 368–69.
[76] See Donald Davidson, "On the Very Idea of a Conceptual Scheme" in *Post-Analytic Philosophy*, ed. John Rajchman and Cornel West (New York: Columbia University Press, 1985), p. 142. See also Bruce D. Marshall, "Absorbing the World: Christianity and the Universe of Truths" in Marshall, ed., *Theology and Dialogue*, pp. 74–75.
[77] Schubert M. Ogden, *Christ Without Myth: A Study Based on the Theology of Rudolf Bultmann* (Dallas: Southern Methodist University Press, 1961), p. 146; original in italics.

strual of wide reflective equilibrium apologetics in no way suggests or logically entails that kind of translation.

In light of this, one way to interpret Werpehowski's notion of Marxist approximations of Christian beliefs is to say that the Marxist absorbs, or partially translates, some Christian beliefs into his or her semiotic system. There can never be translation "without remainder," as Werpehowski says, from one semiotic system to another,[78] but there is no reason to reject that significant translation can take place back and forth in the process of conversation. If this can occur, then a minimal common ground (albeit contextual and perhaps tenuous) can be established and interchanges (apologetic, mutually critical, etc.) can proceed – even if the shared rational space is simply posited as a "heuristic fiction" (as Tracy describes Richard Rorty's position).[79] There is no reason to rule out in advance the possibility of participants from different traditions of inquiry engaging each other in good faith, mutually critical dialogue and working toward at least moments of overlapping consensus. It happens already.

The problem of fallibilism

Examining some postliberal and liberationist apologetic strategies in terms of a wide reflective equilibrium conceptuality has hopefully clarified how postliberal or liberation theologians could, do, and I believe, should engage in apologetic arguments of coherence and consensus. However, no matter how clarifying a wide reflective equilibrium conceptuality may be for postliberal or liberation apologetics, it cannot be a useful resource if it is incompatible with basic postliberal or liberation methodological and theological commitments. Recall that one element of wide reflective equilibrium as a coherence argument is a certain fallibilism – that is, because one's position (though currently justified) may not be true, one has to leave open the option of revision. With the influx of new data, revision to one's reflective equilibrium is permitted or may even be compelled. Another

[78] Werpehowski, "Ad Hoc Apologetics," p. 295. Although Werpehowski does not mention Ogden explicitly here, it is reasonable to think he has Ogden and other revisionary theologians in mind (see p. 282 n. 1).
[79] David Tracy, "Theology, Critical Social Theory, and the Public Realm" in *Habermas, Modernity and Public Theology*, ed. Don S. Browning and Francis Schüssler Fiorenza (New York: Crossroad, 1992), p. 19.

way to put this is to say that fully critical reflection entails the risk of revisability.

I believe Boff would concur with this fallibilism principle and its revisability entailment since the notion of the production of theological cognitions entails some "recasting" of theology's formal object (second generality). While he recognizes that "normal" theological science takes place under a central, stable, ruling grammatical paradigm, "the logic of scientific progress is dialectical, in the sense that it is necessarily achieved under the sign of resistance to knowledge already constituted." Some dialectical recasting of theology's formal object takes place within normal theological science itself and not merely in times of "crisis."[80] Boff observes that "it is doubtless painful for Christian awareness to have to do its symbolic universe all over again – recast it – with the help of new comprehensive syntheses," or as I would call them, new wide reflective equilibria. (In giving examples of the type of recasting that occurs during theological crises, he cites many of the same examples as Lindbeck did above: "the encounter with Hellenism in the apostolic and patristic age, . . . the encounter with Aristotelianism in the Middle Ages, and . . . with the 'human sciences' today.")[81] Doctrinal recasting always occurs against the backdrop of the communally authoritative grammatical framework. There is no question of an abandonment of the religion's code of faith in the recasting process, but doctrinal revisions are possible and even inevitable during hermeneutical mediation. This is consistent with what occurs in wide reflective equilibrium in moral theory.

This question is more thorny for postliberals, given their characteristic emphasis on theology as an intratextual descriptive undertaking. Can a wide reflective equilibrium view of the normativity of beliefs and principles do justice to how postliberal theologians would wish to ascribe "epistemic primacy" to the patterns encoded in the Bible, especially since the beliefs and principles based on those paradigmatic biblical patterns are what Christian communities resist revising or abandoning?[82] I believe that concerns about wide reflective equilibrium under-

[80] Boff, *Theology and Praxis*, pp. 80, 74. The terms "normal" science and "crisis" are allusions to Thomas Kuhn's *Structures of Scientific Revolutions* (see pp. xxix, 236 n. 21).

[81] Ibid., p. 266 n. 7.

[82] Bruce D. Marshall, "Truth Claims and the Possibility of Jewish–Christian Dialogue," *Modern Theology* 8 (1992), p. 223.

mining postliberal descriptive theological methods could be allayed by showing that the notion of revisability can coexist with the notion of commitment to a normative core of beliefs and principles.

It is necessary to understand why wide reflective equilibrium entails the principle that all considered judgments and principles must be held open to revision. For Daniels and Nielsen, the principle of revisability is a factor of a nonfoundationalist stance – that is, no belief or principle may be taken to be indubitable, and hence none may be granted "special epistemological priority." At most there is the "*effect*" of basicality in that one's beliefs and principles provide a "provisional fixed point," but no foundations are intended or established because revision of any belief or principle is always in theory permitted.[83] If the temptation to foundationalism is not a factor (and it is not for postliberals), then the notion of revisability *per se* is put into its proper perspective and is compatible with a postliberal approach which privileges the stability (not the indubitability) of the core beliefs and principles Christian communities hold.

Proponents of wide reflective equilibrium are not suggesting that it is necessary or even possible to revise all one's beliefs and principles at the same time. We are, as Nielsen says, sailors "rebuilding the ship at sea, modifying and adjusting here and there until we get a coherent and consistent set of beliefs."[84] If revisions are undertaken, they are undertaken slowly enough so that the ship remains seaworthy. There is no incentive to be destructively revisionary. Furthermore, proponents of wide reflective equilibrium emphasize that to say that all beliefs must be held open to revision is not to say that one does not have a firmly held set of considered judgments and principles. As noted above, Daniels calls this a "provisional fixed point"; Nielsen speaks of the moral "norms . . . that we would most resist abandoning – the ones that humanly speaking are bedrock for us."[85] Nielsen argues that there is no avoiding these culturally (and postliberals would add religiously) embedded norms which "cannot but have an *initial* authority" and are essential in any wide reflective equilibrium process.[86] Specifying openness to revision is meant to indicate that a wide equilibrium is not

[83] Daniels, "Wide Reflective Equilibrium," pp. 265, 267.
[84] Nielsen, *After the Demise*, p. 203.
[85] Daniels, "Wide Reflective Equilibrium," p. 267; Nielsen, *After the Demise*, p. 199.
[86] Nielsen, *After the Demise*, p. 228.

something one automatically has but is something one works towards reflectively. In the process, if a belief one initially held is found to be incompatible with some new considerations one finds compelling (e.g., background theories or aspects of a competing worldview), one may have to revise or even reject that initial belief.

Postliberals have made analogous comments about revising the Christian web of beliefs on the basis of considerations external to that web. Werpehowski suggests that apologetics involves "[c]ommitment to common exchange" which is open to giving and receiving criticism and "engaging the ... option of correction" to Christian beliefs.[87] Bruce Marshall states that "[e]ncounters with external truth claims can lead Christians ... to change their established beliefs." His suggestion that revisions are "logically bound to take place in a partial and piecemeal fashion, against a background of stable belief"[88] echoes Nielsen's metaphor cited above about modifying one's "ship" at sea. Given these comments, there is arguably no formal inconsistency between the revising process in wide reflective equilibrium and the revising process postliberals already recognize – as long as postliberals are open to the critical assessment of any Christian belief and principle as needed (since fully critical reflection entails the risk of revisability).

Daniels's and Nielsen's point above about some of our currently held beliefs being a provisional fixed point having initial authority is largely a functional approach to normativity. That is, one unavoidably comes to the reflective process with normative beliefs and principles. (Indeed those beliefs and principles are historically what identify a worldview as being Christian or Jewish or secular humanist, etc.) There is no tenable reason I can see why viewing core Christian beliefs and principles as functionally basic in this way cannot provide an adequate formal account of how postliberal theologians wish to describe the normative role of, for example, the beliefs drawn in part from the plain sense of scripture for Christian communities. Moreover, calling core Christian beliefs and principles functionally normative is all the epistemic primacy a nonfoundationalist stance permits. The benefit for apologetics is that this functional view of the normativity of core beliefs and principles allows postliberals to engage in genuine public debate, which entails not only defending one's theological

---

[87] Werpehowski, "Ad Hoc Apologetics," pp. 299, 298.
[88] Marshall, "Absorbing the World," p. 93.

claims but also openness to revising one's position in the process of mutually critical dialogue.

Undeniably, postliberal attention has been focused on issues other than the conditions for revising the Christian web of beliefs as a result of public dialogue. One important postliberal theological concern is on how, in a postmodern "age where old foundations and legitimating structures have crumbled," the church may foster the resources to build Christian community, given its adherence to a normative scriptural tradition.[89] Emphasizing the communal resources provided by this tradition may be different from, but can also be practically compatible with, what I have been discussing about revisions to one's web of beliefs in a wide reflective equilibrium approach. In postmodernity's foundationless world, a wide reflective equilibrium method would seem to offer an effective way of promoting the postliberal focal value of normative redescription of the church's attempts to render a "habitable" or "'followable' world."[90] Liberationists, on the other hand, have been deeply engaged in a certain kind of public apologetic argumentation – mostly related to countering Marxist polemics against religion. To the extent that demonstrating the credibility of Christian beliefs and practices can assist effective cooperation among Christians and non-Christians participating in the struggle for social justice in Latin America, a wide reflective equilibrium approach to pursuing the credibility of theological claims can aid liberation theologians in promoting the focal value of solidarity with the oppressed.

THEORETICAL AND PRACTICAL ASSIMILATIVE POWER

When Werpehowski states that apologetics includes demonstrating that the Christian web of beliefs can give a more plausible account than Marxism of what Christians and Marxists believe in common, I suggest that he is making a point about what Lindbeck calls "assimilative power." The way in which a religion displays its "ability to provide an intelligible interpretation in its own terms of the varied situations

---

[89] Lindbeck, "Scripture, Consensus and Community," p. 22; cf. p. 24. For Lindbeck, the point about the use of an authoritative text applies equally well to text-based religious communities as it does for constitutionally based communities of citizens (see p. 18).

[90] Ibid., pp. 19, 21. The term "followable world" is borrowed from Ronald F. Thiemann, "Radiance and Obscurity in Biblical Narrative" in *Scriptural Authority and Narrative Interpretation*, ed. Garrett Green (Philadelphia: Fortress, 1987).

and realities adherents encounter" is a demonstration of assimilative power. When a belief system is submitted to the test of assimilative power, its validity is argued for in light of "an accumulation of successes or failures in making practically and cognitively coherent sense of relevant data."[91] Lindbeck makes a similar point when discussing competing theological paradigms. He explains that the conflicts between them are settled as "one of the alternatives gradually establishes itself as the more comprehensive and fruitful" paradigm.[92] Lindbeck seems to be describing here something analogous to what philosophers of science call theory "fertility" – that is, the way a scientific hypothesis or theory continues to enable scientific researchers both to assimilate accumulated data and anticipate unexpected data in ongoing scientific practice.[93] Wide reflective equilibriumists seem to have something like this in mind when they speak of testing the feasibility of competing sets of principles and beliefs. Nielsen, who has a knack for making wide reflective equilibrium method sound commonsensical, summarizes what this kind of cognitive and practical adequacy testing means for wide reflective equilibrium. An adequate moral position "perspicuously displays" how its account "(a) fits together into a coherent whole . . . better than alternative accounts, (b) squares best with our best knowledge . . . about the world . . . and (c) most adequately (of the alternative accounts of morality) provides guidance . . . in knowing what to do . . . [and] making extrapolations from the judgments at hand."[94] All these notions (assimilative power, theory fertility and feasibility) point to an evaluation of the theoretical and practical comprehensiveness and fruitfulness of a paradigm – be it a theological model, a scientific hypothesis, a moral position, or a religious worldview.[95]

Making use of testing procedures for theoretical and practical assimilative power seems well suited to postliberal and liberation theology. Because of the nature of its emphasis on fostering Christian

[91] Lindbeck, *Nature of Doctrine*, p. 131.
[92] Lindbeck, "Theological Revolutions," p. 315.
[93] See Ernan McMullin, "The Fertility of Theory and the Unit for Appraisal in Science" in *Essays in Memory of Imre Lakatos*, ed. R. S. Cohen, et al. (Dordrecht: D. Reidel, 1976), p. 401.
[94] Nielsen, *After the Demise*, pp. 203, 204.
[95] Francis Schüssler Fiorenza proposes something similar in his reflective equilibrium model. He uses the notion of "retroductive warrants," comprising theory fertility, the use of practical judgment and appeals to experience ("Systematic Theology," pp. 77ff.).

forms of life, postliberal theology is concerned with "practical as well as . . . theoretical" questions.[96] Postliberal theology does not wish to close itself off from social realities but tries to absorb them into the scriptural world of the believer. Lindbeck acknowledges that addressing theologically the issue of how to respond grammatically and relevantly to contextual challenges requires skills in addition to intratextual ones – especially when those realities are socio-political ones. The theologian must cultivate skills for reading "the signs of the times" as well as scripture. Part of the theological task is to discern which situations "should be cultivated as anticipations or preparations for the hoped-for future, the coming kingdom" according to "eschatologically and empirically defensible" criteria.[97] Evaluation of what is eschatologically defensible is theological; evaluation of what is empirically or practically defensible requires nontheological skills. Unlike liberationists, postliberals have not focused much on what would be needed methodologically to test for the practical adequacy of the Christian reflective equilibrium in particular socio-political contexts. More elaboration from Lindbeck is needed regarding how the intratextual skills one uses in the theological redescriptive task should be related to the nontheological skills one uses to discern the empirically defensible possibilities in the current situation. What is the connection between the competency for reading the Bible and the competency for reading the world? Since Lindbeck has invoked Barth's adage about the theologian needing to work with the Bible in one hand and the newspaper in the other, it seems that his intratextual theological method would be enhanced if it were accompanied by a fuller methodological discussion of the use of background theories for interpreting socio-political realities and evaluating the fruitfulness of one's theological paradigm in light of those contextual realities.[98]

Boff, as noted above, finds it apologetically necessary (partly in light of the challenge of the Marxist critique of theology) to develop a clear methodological position on theology's use of the social sciences. He might respond to Lindbeck by stating that it is "impossible to remain content with . . . generic statements like: 'You have to have the Bible in

---

[96] Lindbeck, *Nature of Doctrine*, p. 128.

[97] Ibid., p. 125.

[98] See Lindbeck, "Barth and Textuality," p. 376. This claim is under some contention, especially by John Milbank, whose views I will address in ch. 6.

one hand and the daily newspaper in the other,' as Karl Barth . . . would have it."[99] Boff insists on the necessity of using the social sciences to mediate socio-political reality to the theologian who reads that reality according to the code of faith. The "integration of . . . the sciences of the human being – socio-analytic mediation – is the indispensable *theoretical* condition today for rigorous theological discourse, and the essential *practical* condition for the insertion of such [theological] discourse into (political) praxis."[100] This would seem to echo Nielsen's point that an adequate wide reflective equilibrium is one that squares with what we know about our world and guides us in our actions. Hence, for Nielsen and liberationists, testing the theoretical and practical adequacy of one's position requires the use of the social sciences as background theories or mediations.

This appeal by liberationists to the use of social scientific theory for theology's critical engagement with the political is not, however, an attempt to give praxis priority over theory, as many North Atlantic theologians worry. I already noted Gutiérrez's firm rejection of praxis as a criterion of theology in chapter one. Boff is as, if not more, emphatic. He begins *Theology and Praxis* with the explicit rejection of a theology which is either "directly oriented to praxis" or which claims to "transcend history and praxis." To orient theology correctly vis-à-vis praxis, one must navigate between the shoals of both extremes – the extreme of theology so closely linked to praxis that its criterion of validity is praxis and the extreme of theology which pretends to transcend political praxis. The first point is directed especially to political theologies which might be inclined reductively to act as "the *voice of praxis*" in the struggle for justice.[101] Boff is adamant about this point, since the oversimplified invocation of the criterion of praxis can both mask unreflective action and armchair speculation: when some "group is *satisfied* with crying 'Praxis, praxis' . . . thinking that thereby something has been done, we must recognize that this . . . group has scarely gone very far, in terms of either theory or praxis."[102]

However, if the Christian community is called to be accountable to the praxis of transforming history in light of God's kingdom, does

[99] Boff, *Theology and Praxis*, p. 184.
[100] Ibid., p. 11.
[101] Ibid., pp. 14, 15.
[102] Ibid., p. 202.

not theology fall under the same praxiological accountability? Boff's negative answer to this question must be understood in the context of how he understands the relationship between theology and faith and their respective criteriologies. He insists that "praxis neither is nor can be the criterion of (theological) truth," since theology *qua* theoretical practice is completely independent of all praxiological criteria.[103] The distinction he wishes to maintain is between this "*pistic criteriology,*" which has to do with testing the faithfulness of the believer, and "*theological criteriology,*" which has to do with validating Christian claims theoretically – that is, according to the rules proper to theology as a ruled, theoretical discipline. Boff defines theology strictly as "theory *upon* faith, not theory *of* faith."[104] The religious discourse of faith is performative, existentially self-involving, doxological; theological discourse is critical, scientific and argumentative.[105] His point is not that doing theology can never be a personal faith activity. Rather, he wishes to stress that the "*self-implicating*" nature of faith "engages the living subject" in praxis; whereas, the demands placed on theology are for grammatical and "ideo-political vigilance" in matters of religious and theological discourse.[106] There is a sense in which one may correctly speak of a verification of praxis in relation to the believer's performative faith – that is, in a very qualified sense, one's faith is judged by one's works[107] – but theology is not verified by praxis.

Just as Boff insists that praxis cannot be the criterion for theological validity, he also insists that theology depends on praxis. While political engagement does not provide the criteria of validity for theology, it is "*a necessary condition*" for theologically grasping Christian realities in their socio-political context adequately.[108] In short, liberation

---

[103] Ibid., p. 198. A helpful summary of Boff on this point is Aidan Nichols, O.P., "The Story of *Praxis*: Liberation Theology's Philosophical Handmaid," *Religion in Communist Lands* 17 (1989), esp. pp. 56ff.

[104] Boff, *Theology and Praxis*, pp. 199, 113.

[105] Ibid., pp. 111ff., 124ff.

[106] Ibid., pp. 37, 43. I will say more about Boff's strict view of theology in ch. 6 but to preview briefly that discussion, let me add that although he insists that theology as a theoretical discourse is distinct from performative religious discourse, Boff structurally links theological and religious discourse by the grammar they share, making the "line of demarcation" between them, in other words, only a "quasi breach" (p. 116).

[107] See ibid., p. 203. The biblical warrant for this would be the admonition that "[f]aith without *agape* is dead (James 2:14–16; 1 Cor. 13:2)" (p. 101). However, ultimate verification of Christian faithfulness pertains to the eschaton (see p. 203).

[108] Ibid., p. 167.

theology is "impossible without a *minimal contact* with the world of the oppressed."[109] However, a self-conscious connection to Christian praxis is not just a requirement for theologies of the political but for any theology. No theology exists in a vacuum; each theology has its own social location, interests, and so on. Thus, the question is not should the theologian be politically engaged, since theologians are always engaged, indirectly or directly, in some socio-political reality and the issues and ideological interests entailed in that reality. Rather, the question is: "Engagement for whom? Option for what cause? Taking sides with whom?"[110] Answering these questions requires "ideological vigilance" since any theoretical discipline "can have an ideological function . . . however rigorous and disciplined it may be." One has to be vigilant not to reduce theology to being the voice of Christian praxis, and one has to be vigilant against the view that a purportedly nonpolitical academic theology has thereby guaranteed its "nonideologicity."[111]

A primary thrust of *Theology and Praxis* is the argument that what greatly debilitates liberation theology today (and by extension, theologies in general) is its faulty grasp of socio-political realities because of its improper or inadequate use of the social sciences. For liberation theology to grasp the political realities with which the Latin American church is embroiled, those realities must not merely be experienced by the politically engaged liberation theologian but must also be subjected to the proper social scientific analysis. While the liberation theologian's own political commitment to the poor fosters a certain "sensibility," nevertheless, "without analysis, sensibility can remain blind."[112] This warning applies to first-world academic theologians as well. Any claim that a theologian, by dint of sheer proximity or exposure to some political reality, thereby could grasp and expound upon it in a way that will be critically helpful to the Christian community, Boff would consider naive. When we look at Boff's method in light of the notion of

---

[109] Boff, "Epistemology and Method," p. 74.

[110] Boff, *Theology and Praxis*, p. 162.

[111] Ibid., pp. 43, 44.

[112] Ibid., p. 183. This requirement is incumbent as well on those in base Christian communities. Boff concretely recommends that community pastoral animators avail themselves of the resources of trained social scientists for this task. See Clodovis Boff, "The Nature of Basic Christian Communities," tr. Paul Burns, in *Tensions Between the Churches of the First World and the Third World*, Concilium 144, ed. Virgil Elizondo and Norbert Greinacher (Edinburgh: T. & T. Clark; New York: Seabury, 1981), p. 58.

adequacy testing discussed above, we might say that anything less than the theologian's contextual sensibility, aided indispensably by background theories designed to interpret socio-political realities, would constitute an inadequate testing of the assimilative power of any Christian wide reflective equilibrium position. Furthermore, it would constitute an inadequate methodological implementation of the focal value of solidarity.

The two forms of wide reflective equilibrium apologetics outlined above can be distinguished in terms of where their apologetic force lies. In non-Christian-specific apologetics, the force lies solely in the argumentative use of background theories employed in defense of the presuppositions of Christian belief. These arguments might include some kind of theistic "proof," such as a qualified transcendental argument for the reality of God. The second form of apologetics, Christian-specific apologetics, comprises two approaches: indirect and direct. Good dogmatics can have indirect apologetic force and can play a strategic role as one element of a direct Christian-specific apologetic exchange with a non-Christian interlocutor. The force of direct Christian-specific apologetics depends on the extent of the consensus the theologian can establish by means of a multifaceted argumentative strategy displaying the overall coherence and assimilative power of the Christian wide reflective equilibrium. Liberation theologians would insist that the demonstration of practical feasibility cannot proceed acritically. The theologian must make explicit, methodical use of social scientific background theories and develop the appropriate sensibility to contextual realities.

If the above construal of postliberal and liberation apologetics in terms of a wide reflective equilibrium approach is persuasive, most concerns about postliberal and liberation theology as confessionalist and antagonistic toward (or limited in their engagement with) the notion of a shared rational space should be dispelled. Wide reflective equilibrium turns out to be a valuable methodological resource for postliberals to implement their focal value of normative redescription by working reflectively toward a theoretically and practically coherent dogmatic position. Liberation theologians can use a wide reflective equilibrium approach to build political coalitions with non-Christian groups and foster an ideologically vigilant and grammatically pertinent theology which enhances the implementation of their focal value of solidarity with the oppressed. Furthermore, wide reflective equilibrium shows ample promise in being able to sustain the revisionary focal value of fully critical reflection via its use of critical, independent background theories (along with the other apologetic strategies outlined above).

It would appear therefore that wide reflective equilibrium can have broad usefulness for theology – fostering dogmatic coherence at the center of Christian thought and facilitating consensus building on beliefs and practices (religious and political) in the public realm. The apologetic force of arguments for the coherence and feasibility of a belief system can only be provisional because what would constitute success is, to a significant extent, paradigm dependent and could be a matter of strenuous debate in the pluralistic public realm. But then paradigm dependency and overlapping consensus are unavoidable factors of publicly defending any claim to validity after the linguistic-historical turn.

CHAPTER FOUR

Reading the Bible theologically as the church's book

The theologians from the movements I am examining all view Christian theology as involving a complex process of reading and using the Bible as the church's book – that is, as scripture – in theological practice.[1] Entailed in any theological use of scripture is the theologian's decision about how to relate scripture to the church's ongoing ecumenical tradition. Coming to terms with the scripture–tradition relationship is a daunting task in light of the diversity of Christian intracommunal and intercommunal reading practices and the challenges to text-based religion by contemporary modes of thought. New scripture readings from communities on Christianity's margins are seriously competing with traditional ways of reading the Bible, and this presents a dilemma for how theologically to adjudicate among this plurality of readings new and old. In academia, poststructuralism joins the list of other scholarly theories which challenge all of these ecclesial readings. Deconstructive criticism especially has serious implications if it erodes the church's ability to use scripture as a privileged source and norm for community-building and Christian praxis.

The very notion of the church's "book" has come under "a/theological" fire, for example, from deconstructive theologian Mark C. Taylor. According to Taylor, the time has passed for privileging any book viewed as a logocentric, self-enclosed unity, such as the canonically closed book of Christianity. We live in a "liminal" moment, not only in the shadow of the death of God but the death of selves. A/theology does not try to avoid but to enter (or more precisely, "wander") into this

---

[1] David Kelsey clarifies this point: "To take biblical writings simply as 'texts' is, notoriously, not necessarily to take them as 'Christian scripture.' They may be studied as literature or as historical sources ... But it is precisely as 'Christian scripture' that they are used ... to authorize theological proposals." David H. Kelsey, *The Uses of Scripture in Recent Theology* (Philadelphia: Fortress, 1975), p. 90.

deconstructive place in order to find "a new opening for the religious imagination."[2] The unending play of a/theological wandering is hampered when Christianity's book is linked to an authoritative tradition which "regulates and regularizes by establishing a normative canon" and becomes "the rule by which to distinguish proper from improper." This "*regula*" both closes Christianity's book and extends its authority, as tradition, over all other books.[3] The a/theologian attempts to break out of this "unproductive confinement" by identifying gaps and ruptures in the canonical tradition. This deconstructive reading disseminates what has been confined and opens the book into the "text." Ironically, this reading reveals that the book "always includes the other that it struggles to exclude" because "[i]n attempting to secure closure by controlling disruptive otherness, the book opens itself to difference."[4] The text is the book that has been opened by the (erring) reader who has no self (or at least only a "trace") to assert over against the other.[5]

One need not endorse a completely intertextual view of meaning or a poststructuralist view of subjecthood to see that Taylor raises a number of important concerns. Some of his concerns arise from a nexus of intellectual, political, and cultural developments unique to the contemporary scene. Whether one welcomes deconstructive criticism or not, its cultural impact is increasingly widespread. Not all it brings will be theologically useful but, at times, the agendas of Christian theology and poststructuralism may even intersect. For example, some of Taylor's concerns rephrase from a postmodern perspective age-old theological quandaries. His point about a normative canon confining one's reading of books restates the issue of the sometimes tensive relationship between new communal uses of scripture and the church's ongoing tradition. From a pastoral perspective, it is imperative that the scripture–tradition relationship remain stable enough to form Christian communal character capable of resisting the corrosive effects

---

[2] Mark C. Taylor, *Erring: A Postmodern A/theology* (University of Chicago Press, 1984), pp. 6, 11. The wandering metaphor indicates that a/theological thought is not linear and systematic but "transitory" and "nomadic" (p. 11).

[3] Ibid., p. 88.

[4] Ibid., pp. 92, 93. The term "text" is linked at its root to the Latin word for "tissue"; hence for Taylor, a text is a complex, textured fabric. One text comes into being only as it is woven relationally with other texts (pp. 177–78).

[5] Taylor deconstructs subjectivity by positing the notion of the self as "trace" – that is, an "unending play of presence and absence" where boundaries of interiority and exteriority are blurred (ibid., pp. 138ff.).

of secularity and combatting social injustice. For reasons also proper to Christianity (the Spirit "blows where it wills") as well as for reasons echoed by postmodernity, that relationship must also be open to difference and change. To read scripture theologically as the book of diverse, historically extended communities is to read it in continually changing world contexts in which mainstream Christianity meets the margins where new forms of belief and practice are emerging. Hence, for reasons internal to Christianity (recall Paul's claim to have "become all things to all people"), it is imperative that the theologian recognize the dialectical interplay between text and each new context. This finds an echo in the deconstructive call for allowing otherness to disrupt all books.

My contention that a postmodern approach can shed new light on theological issues, nevertheless, is not an endorsement of the a/theological path of incessant wandering as the primary theoretical framework for construing the scripture–tradition relationship in contemporary culture. A number of theologians have called into question for intellectual, ethical and ecclesial reasons the ability of a/theology to find workable solutions for the theoretical and practical problems the church faces today.[6] If one is serious about theology promoting the values of solidarity with the oppressed, thickly describing an identity-forming Christian worldview, and engaging in fully critical dialogue in the public realm, one's hermeneutic must do more than disrupt books and open erring texts. What is needed in order to read the Bible theologically as the church's book in light of Christian communal needs in a textually deconstructive, socio-economically impoverished and pluralistic world? The reading product must be cohesive enough to render a communally habitable world; readings must be open to change and difference within

---

6 Peter Hodgson argues that Taylor's deconstructive approach "is utterly without ethical seriousness" because its call to aimless wandering is a "Nietzschean romantic affirmation of the unyielding law of change and necessity" which "leaves utterly unchallenged . . . structures of domination and oppression." Peter C. Hodgson, review of *Erring*, by Mark C. Taylor, *Religious Studies Review* 12 (1986), p. 258. Delwin Brown finds Taylor's a/theology to be "one-sided," because it fails to address the Christian tradition's "resourcefulness" in supplying "judgments and alternatives . . . worthy of consideration, capable of transformation" (*Boundaries of Our Habitations: Tradition and Theological Construction* [Albany: State University of New York Press, 1994], pp. 130, 132). Yet, see William Beardslee's insightful article for a discussion of how deconstructive biblical criticism can be both ethically serious and constructively critical of the tradition. William A. Beardslee, "Poststructuralist Criticism" in *To Each Its Own Meaning: An Introduction to Biblical Criticisms and Their Application*, ed. Steven McKenzie and Stephen Haynes (Louisville: Westminster/John Knox, 1993), pp. 221–35.

the ecumenical Christian community, and they must be critical of distortions in the text and the tradition. In other words, I am suggesting
that we need to make good on the proper hermeneutical impulses –
the impulse of continuity with the tradition to offset textual and communal fragmentation; the impulse of plurality to combat interpretive
narrowness, especially in relation to marginalized voices of the
oppressed; and the impulse of critique to identify problems such as ideological bias. These impulses were developed in the course of evaluating the hermeneutical approaches of the three theological movements
in this book and are meant to complement their focal values. This
chapter directs attention to where I believe these three impulses are
being helpfully or unhelpfully instantiated methodologically. The goal
is to envision a scripture–tradition relationship such that the tradition
can be both a stable yet flexible *regula*, the book remains open for new
readings, and theology remains attentive to what is other.

   The first section of this chapter addresses the issue of retaining
scriptural meaning in light of the poststructuralist challenge, beginning
with a critical analysis of potential weaknesses in Tracy's attempt to
deflect deconstruction of the church's book. I will argue that a functionalist approach to scripture offers a more theologically appropriate
way of addressing the deconstructive challenge while accommodating
a diversity of Christian intracommunal and intercommunal readings
as well. In the second section of this chapter, I turn to the challenge of
upholding continuity and a plurality of readings of the scriptures (functionally understood). My proposal for a regulative-dialectial hermeneutic draws from postliberal rule theory of doctrine, Boff's dialectical
mode of doctrinal recasting, and revisionists' use of critical exegetical
and hermeneutical tools in order to construct an approach to scripture
and tradition that is stable yet flexibly open to change and critique.

POSTSTRUCTURALISM, THE CLASSIC AND THE PLAIN SENSE

Poststructuralism, especially deconstructive criticism, emphasizes the
essential incompleteness of texts and challenges any theory of interpretation which is governed by an appeal to the "privilege of the logos"
as a self-presence preceding and authorizing thought and writing.[7]

---

[7] Jacques Derrida, *Of Grammatology*, tr. Gayatri Chakravorty Spivak (Baltimore and London: Johns
   Hopkins University Press, 1976), p. 15.

Deconstructive criticism dislodges determinate meaning in all books (whether grounded in authorial intention, textual reference, structural elements, etc.), suggesting that there are only fractured texts and the play of intertextuality. This viewpoint challenges all text-based endeavors, including those of so-called religions of the book. Among the latter, this theory could have a deleterious impact, for example, on those underclasses of believers who are just beginning to reclaim the liberating message of scripture in their communities after having been excluded from ownership of the "book" by ecclesial and academic elites.

One of the strongest polemics for using the Bible as the book of the church of the poor is Gutiérrez's impassioned defense of the right of the oppressed to "repossess" and reclaim a "militant reading of the Bible." He sees the exercise of this right as constituting "an ideological exposé" of how the first world has dominated biblical interpretation, squelching readings by the oppressed – in effect, appropriating their book.[8] True to his focus on the empowerment of those who are oppressed, Gutiérrez argues that "the Bible is to a great extent the expression of the faith and hope of the poor." The privileged reader might gain knowledge of this biblical truth, but it is the suffering of the poor in dialogue with the Bible which unlocks "the complexity of the mystery" that God "has a preferential love for those whom the world passes over."[9] The Bible belongs to the poor not necessarily because they have more spiritual insight but because God has chosen to be preferentially revealed in a "proclamation to the poor," and they live by this normative word about God's presence to them.[10] Poststructuralist theories indirectly issue a challenge to liberation theologians like Gutiérrez by virtue of the way they deconstruct the notion of texts as containing stable, essential (e.g., liberationist) meaning. Are elite academics again taking the Bible away from the poor? Are there other options for construing scripture which safeguard a sense of the Bible as the church's book (hence leaving room for interpretations such as Gutiérrez's) without ignoring the antiessentialist critique of poststructuralism?

[8] Gustavo Gutiérrez, *The Power of the Poor in History*, tr. Robert R. Barr (Maryknoll: Orbis, 1988), p. 101.
[9] Gustavo Gutiérrez, *The God of Life*, tr. Matthew J. O'Connell (Maryknoll: Orbis, 1991), p. xv.
[10] Gutiérrez, *Power of the Poor*, p. 208.

Tracy not only takes on the task of addressing deconstructive criticism but also would not want to save the church's book from poststructuralists only to make it the exclusive property of another set of
elite readers with "the proper credentials."[11] I share his point of
departure but have reservations about his theoretical means for doing
so, namely, his theory of the religious classic. In his appeal to the disclosive power of the biblical classic, Tracy turns the challenge of
deconstruction into an implicit affirmation of the Bible's claim to
attention. He suggests that even in deconstructing Christianity's book,
postmoderns have a textual encounter with its mystery. What is wrong
with neutralizing deconstructive readings by absorbing them into the
fold, so to speak, of the religious classic? The answer, I believe, is
twofold. First, this hermeneutic is often accompanied by problematic
experiential-expressive tendencies. As discussed in chapter two, an
appeal to the notion of a primordial common human experience
underlying the recognition of the truth of the classic belies a genuine
linguistic-historical turn. Correlatively, and this is relevant to the
hermeneutical impulses I am promoting here, Tracy's appeal to the
religious classic risks subverting genuine interpretive plurality. Second,
Tracy's attempt to use the theory of the classic (whether understood
experiential-expressively or not) to counter the poststructuralist
challenge turns out to be a literary theory battle about textual meaning. This is an important subject to debate but one that should be
properly situated within the overarching theological task of reading
the Bible theologically as scripture. I believe that to move forward in
constructing an approach to scripture and tradition – especially one
mindful of the readings of marginalized communities – we need to
situate the debate over textual meaning in terms of what I would call
background theories and refocus primary attention on the way the
Bible is used in Christian communal contexts.

Plurality, deconstruction and the biblical classic

To expand on the discussion of the classic in chapter two, a religious
classic involves a claim to meaning and truth as an "event of disclosure-
concealment of the whole of reality *by the power of the whole* – as, in some

---

[11] David Tracy, *Plurality and Ambiguity: Hermeneutics, Religion, Hope* (San Francisco: Harper & Row,
1987), p. 104.

sense, a radical and finally gracious mystery." Tracy tells us that we
recognize the truth of this event insofar as it resonates with our most
basic common human experience of fundamental trust or (to borrow
from Schleiermacher) absolute dependence on that whole.[12] The
power of the biblical classic is rooted in a particular "journey of intensi-
fication" into this radical and gracious mystery which for each biblical
writer was a specific experience of the event of Jesus Christ. Tracy uses
Paul Ricoeur's discourse theory to explicate how the biblical writers
gave literary form to their religious experiences of this event, suggesting that the Bible may be seen as discourse, a written work of "productive imagination."[13] Meaning is projected "in front of the text as
a possible way-of-being-in-the-world" via the writers' techniques of
composition, genre, syntax, style, and so on.[14] As discourse, the struc-
tured imaginative scriptural text produces a "surplus of meaning"
beyond its authors' intentions, creating a "never-exhausted need for
new interpretation." For Tracy, the event of Jesus Christ is the concrete
re-presentation of an experience of trust which is posited as "always
already present to us as human beings." Among the diversity of scriptural expressions of this re-presentative Jesus Christ event, he identifies three classic forms: "manifestation," "proclamation" and "action."
Manifestation expresses an often mystical participation in the sacred.
Proclamation denotes an awareness of the radical otherness of the
divine whose word comes as an inbreaking which is dialectically
related to manifestation.[15] Theological interpretations of the Bible
traditionally have reflected these two prominent modes of biblical
writings. Schleiermacher, Rahner and Eliade may be seen as focusing
on the "manifestory" mode; Barth, Bultmann and Moltmann may be
seen as typically focusing on the proclamatory claim to attention of
scripture.[16] In addition, there is an experience of the event of Jesus

[12] David Tracy, *The Analogical Imagination: Christian Theology and the Culture of Pluralism* (New York: Crossroad, 1986), p. 163; see pp. 185 n. 35, 201.
[13] Ibid., pp. 199, 128.
[14] David Tracy, "Hermeneutical Reflections in the New Paradigm" in *Paradigm Change in Theology*, ed. Hans Küng and David Tracy (New York: Crossroad, 1989), p. 51; original in italics.
[15] Tracy, *Analogical Imagination*, pp. 129, 234, 235. An example of manifestation in the Bible is the meditative, mystical writings of John which disclose that author's participation in "a manifesta-tion of the love of Jesus Christ" (p. 285). An example of proclamation in the Bible is the keryg-matic writings of Paul which disclose the dialectic of the cross as "decentering, defamiliarizing scandal" and life-changing "amazing grace" (p. 284).
[16] Ibid., p. 285; see pp. 378ff. and 387ff.

Christ entailing transformative praxis, which Tracy calls the historical action mode of interpretation. Here "we are primarily neither hearers of the word [proclamation] nor seers of a manifestation ... [but] we are freed to become doers of the word" in light of the historical actualities of oppression and suffering in the world. As might be expected, he identifies this mode as pertaining to most political and liberation theologies. He argues that liberation theology's historical action mode of interpreting the biblical classic reveals meanings which first-world theologians may ignore "only at the price of willful self-deception."[17]

There is no doubt that scriptural expressions of the Jesus Christ event are diverse – even within these three classic modes; nor is there any doubt that interpretive responses to these classic scriptural expressions are even more plural. Why then should any concern about loss of interpretive plurality arise? On this point, my concern centers on Tracy's re-presentative experiential-expressive framework for the religious classic in general and the Christian classic in particular. When he discusses the classic event of Jesus Christ in *The Analogical Imagination*, Tracy explicitly refers the reader back to his discussions in *Blessed Rage for Order* on re-presentative limit-language which entails the notion of a prethematic experience of basic faith or fundamental trust (as discussed in chapter two).[18] What unites the three classic modes of expression of the Jesus Christ event (Tracy calls them "family resemblances"[19]) is that they all re-present, intensify and transform dimensions of this underlying fundamental trust. When this underlying experience is appealed to not only as the basis for the Bible's public claim to our attention but also as an explanation of the reader's resonance with or complete recognition of its disclosive truth, are not all readings of scripture ultimately pulled into that phenomenological vortex? The risk in an experiential-expressive phenomenological

[17] Ibid., pp. 390, 398. Nevertheless, according to Tracy (as of 1986), no "classic text" in the historical action mode has been produced with the explosive interpretive power of, say, the young Barth's Romans commentary – a classic of the proclamation mode of interpretation (p. 398). The historical action mode does not emerge with the same hermeneutical status as manifestation and proclamation in his earlier writings. The experience of Jesus Christ from which transformative praxis springs is dependent on a prior "originating experience of the power of word [proclamation] or manifestation" (p. 391).

[18] Ibid., pp. 234, 242 n. 7; see David Tracy, *Blessed Rage for Order: The New Pluralism in Theology* (New York: Seabury, 1978), pp. 215, 103.

[19] Tracy, *Analogical Imagination*, p. 376.

hermeneutic of this kind is that genuine interpretive plurality may be
undermined or delimited. Tracy insists that his use of this "general
hermeneutical theory" (in, for example, *The Analogical Imagination*) was
intended to be modestly "clarificatory," guiding the use of technical
literary and critical analyses of scripture.[20] I am not denying that it
is possible and appropriate to conduct in an *ad hoc* way the kinds of
analyses Tracy describes of the biblical text's genre, style, and so on.
However, to the extent that he moves beyond literary analyses to
making claims about the biblical classic's disclosive truth (which we can
recognize by virtue of its resonance with common human experience),
then one may wonder how modest his use of general hermeneutical
theory really is – hence my concern about the loss of a genuine plurality
of ecclesial readings. Furthermore, I am not suggesting that Tracy is
not able to recognize differences in interpretive responses to the Bible
(indeed, he documents them amply); rather, I am concerned that the
significance of those differences may be underappreciated or eclipsed
if they are viewed as mere surface differences rooted in a more fundamental underlying common experience which religious language re-
presents. I agree with Wesley Kort's point that too many important
aspects of theological discourses are obscured when their oppositional
characteristics are downplayed (in the way I suspect a general phenomenological hermeneutic of the classic might do).[21]

Given what we know of Tracy's increased linguistic-historical and
postmodern sensibilities on epistemological issues as discussed in
chapter two, it should come as no surprise that it may be possible to
read some of his discussions of the classic in a more low-key, non-
philosophically loaded way. Taken commonsensically, there is nothing
that is at odds with the impulse of plurality in his suggestion that "the
meaning of the text lies . . . in the now common question, the now common subject-matter of both text and interpreter" – that is, as long as
"now common" means something like the common ground which can
emerge from the back-and-forth of conversation (with the Bible, other
texts and other interpreters), and not common human experience
which allows readers to resonate with the disclosive truth of the religious

[20] David Tracy, "On Reading the Scriptures Theologically" in *Theology and Dialogue: Essays in Conversation with George Lindbeck*, ed. Bruce D. Marshall (University of Notre Dame Press, 1990), pp. 58–59 n. 16.
[21] See Wesley A. Kort, *Bound to Differ: The Dynamics of Theological Discourses* (University Park, Pa.: Pennsylvania State University Press, 1992).

classic.[22] This commonsensical approach is quite compatible with the functionalist view of scripture I will outline below. Thus, if the notion of the classic is rehabilitated in this way as part of an overall linguistic-historical turn, it could effectively promote pluralistic conversation. This is, however, a lingering *if*, whether Tracy has thoroughly rehabilitated the theory of the classic in his current work, I will leave an open question.[23]

When Tracy uses the classic in relation to the poststructuralist challenge specifically, an additional set of problems emerges. He recognizes the challenge to his approach that deconstructionists bring in their attempt to unravel "determinate meaning."[24] In *The Analogical Imagination*, he turns the poststructuralist challenge into an implicit affirmation of the classic's power to disclose the whole as an "always-already presence of ... nonpresence." Tracy suggests that Derrida's intertextual "uncanny moment wherein order becomes chaos, determinacy becomes indeterminacy, differing becomes deferring, difference becomes differance" – could itself be a kind of mystical, "quasireligious" interpretive encounter. Tracy welcomes such "uncommon experiences of the uncanny."[25] In the spirit of catholicism (in the general sense of inclusiveness), deconstructionists are absorbed into the fold (and pulled into the phenomenological vortex as well).

Frei found this kind of defensive strategy unconvincing and questioned whether Tracy's phenomenological hermeneutics could withstand the current bombardment of deconstructionism's "immanent subversion" of all hermeneutical systems. Frei warned that if one's reading of scripture is dependent on a single interpretive theory, one's interpretation will "stand or fall with the theory's own viability."[26] He

[22] Tracy, "Hermeneutical Reflections," p. 42. One could read "common question" in a Davidsonian light as referring to charitable conversation with the other who is different.

[23] Much rides on how one continues to interpret Ricoeur's discourse theory. Tracy reads Ricoeur as taking phenomenology in a Habermasian "communicative direction." See David Tracy, "Theology, Critical Social Theory, and the Public Realm" in *Habermas, Modernity, and Public Theology*, ed. Don S. Browning and Francis Schüssler Fiorenza (New York: Crossroad, 1992), p. 39. For another defense of Ricoeur's hermeneutics in relation to postliberal criticisms, see Mark I. Wallace, *The Second Naiveté: Barth, Ricoeur, and the New Yale Theology* (Macon: Mercer University Press, 1990).

[24] Tracy, *Analogical Imagination*, p. 360.

[25] Ibid., pp. 361, 355, 363.

[26] Hans W. Frei, "The 'Literal Reading' of Biblical Narrative in the Christian Tradition: Does It Stretch or Will It Break?" in *The Bible and the Narrative Tradition*, ed. Frank McConnell (New York and Oxford: Oxford University Press, 1986), pp. 55, 51.

saw Tracy as being in a precarious position, given that deconstructionists make a "strong case" against a hermeneutics of textual disclosure, calling into question especially the Ricoeurian notion of a
metaphorical reference to a possible world in front of the text.[27] But
given that Frei would not predict "decisive victory" for the deconstructionists, I take him as saying that this debate could likely continue
for the foreseeable future, one step removed from what he considered
to be the more center-stage issue of Christian communal scriptural
reading practices.[28]

In *Plurality and Ambiguity*, Tracy speaks of reading the classic dialogi-
cally, still in the Ricoeurian sense of discourse, but now presented in,
again, a more low-key way: discourse is simply a situation where "'someone says something about something to someone.'"[29] Deconstructive
literary critics are absorbed not into an uncanny encounter with the
biblical classic but into a public dialogue with its imaginative plurality
and ambiguity. His strategy is, apparently, to ratchet down the deconstructive impact of poststructuralism. Deconstruction is described as a
useful "interruptive detour" or a "linguistic therapy" akin to ideology
critique which unmasks our epistemological illusions. In this strategy,
Tracy does not so much resolve the poststructuralist challenge; rather,
he uses deconstruction as a critical interpretive pause and then leaves
it behind (but now without the illusion of full presence and with "a
chastened interpretation of texts").[30] He believes that dialogical discourse with the biblical classic will produce meaning resistant to
deconstruction. Conversation with the biblical classic would then continue, hopefully this time including marginalized voices.

I again leave open the question of whether Tracy's appeal to dialogue
with the classic is as modest as he claims. If a general phenomenological hermeneutic is still lurking, the problems discussed above about
the loss of genuine ecclesial interpretive plurality reemerge. Even if
Tracy has currently moved to a low-key version of discourse theory
which can accommodate deconstruction as a therapeutic interruption,
he still risks turning the task of reading the Bible theologically into a
(currently unresolved) debate about who has the better theory for how

---

[27] Ibid., p. 58. For Derrida, referential meaning "is *deferred* along a loosely connected potentially indefinite metaphorical axis" (p. 56).
[28] Ibid., p. 59.
[29] Tracy, *Plurality and Ambiguity*, pp. 53, 61.
[30] Ibid., pp. 63, 60, 62.

meaning and texts are related. Furthermore, the issue of challenging
the dominance of elite readers with proper credentials seems sidelined
(despite Tracy's intentions). In what follows, I present another way to
address deconstruction without losing plurality and without linking
interpretation of scripture to a general theory about literary meaning:
a functionalist approach to scripture, as promoted recently by some
postliberal theologians. I am attracted to a theory of functional plain
senses of scripture because it locates scriptural meaning in the reading
practices of religious communities. Issues such as literary meaning,
metaphorical reference, logocentrism, or différance remain important
as background theory debates, but the primary focus is on assessing
communal uses of scripture.

From deferred meaning to functional plain senses

The postliberal move to a functional approach to scripture can, in part,
be read as a response to an ambiguity about the role of literary considerations in Lindbeck's discussion of intratextuality in *The Nature of
Doctrine*. The ambiguity has to do with his claim that in an intratextual
approach, meaning is "immanent" in scripture. On the one hand,
Lindbeck characterizes intratextuality as an approach which "depends
heavily on literary considerations" for determining the internal "interpretive framework that designates the theologically controlling sense"
of scripture. For example, when the gospels are read as history-like
realistic narratives recounting "the interaction of purpose and circum-
stance" of Jesus' agency (this was Frei's intention in *The Identity of Jesus
Christ*), what emerges is Jesus' ascriptive, unsubstitutable identity, not
his "metaphysical status, or existential significance." Unsubstitutable
agential identity is the controlling sense of the story, and this conclusion is grounded literarily. However, Lindbeck also speaks of the
immanent meaning not in literary but in functionalist categories as
being "what the text says in terms of the communal language of which
the text is an instantiation." He states that the "normative or literal
meaning must be consistent with the kind of text it is taken to be by
the community for which it is important."[31] Statements such as these
can be attributed to Lindbeck's cultural-linguistic theory of religion

31 George A. Lindbeck, *The Nature of Doctrine: Religion and Theology in a Postliberal Age* (Philadelphia:
Westminster, 1984), p. 120.

according to which religions are seen as "comprehensive interpretive schemes ... which structure human experience and understanding." Becoming Christianly religious has to do with interiorizing "a distinctive logic or grammar," acquiring a "vocabulary of discursive and nondiscursive symbols," and using them correctly in a communal context.[32] Religion as a comprehensive idiomatic form of life is often canonically text-bound. Judaism, Christianity and Islam, "all have relatively fixed canons of writings that they treat as exemplary [of] normative instantiations of their semiotic codes" – that is, they all have a book. When the biblical text is construed cultural-linguistically as the "paradigmatic instance" of the Christian language, then immanent meaning will be linked to its proper "use" within Christianity's semiotic system.[33]

How these two perspectives on scripture (literary and functional) are related is not always clear in Lindbeck's writings. From the first perspective, the immanent meaning of the biblical text is located in certain predominantly literary qualities found, so to speak, in the Bible. From the second perspective, the immanent meaning is a factor of how it is used meaningfully in the community for which the text is normative. In *The Nature of Doctrine,* Lindbeck seems at times to work out of both perspectives simultaneously, as illustrated in the following passage which has been quoted in part above: "The intratextual way ... depends heavily on *literary* considerations. The normative or literal meaning must be consistent with the kind of text it is taken to be *by the community* for which it is important ... An intratextual reading tries to derive the interpretive framework that designates the theologically controlling sense from the *literary structure* of the text itself."[34] Note how, in this passage, a literary point is simply juxtaposed with a functionalist one, followed by a conclusion based on (again) a literary consideration. This mixture leaves one unclear about the nature of the relationship between literary and functional perspectives.

Two clarifying discussions on the necessity of distinguishing between literary and functionalist characterizations of biblical texts are found in Frei's "The 'Literal Reading' of Biblical Narrative in the Christian

[32] Ibid., pp. 32, 33.
[33] Ibid., pp. 116, 118. Lindbeck is alluding to Charles Wood's Wittgensteinian approach which equates understanding a text with having "a way of using the text" (*The Formation of Christian Understanding: An Essay in Theological Hermeneutics* [Philadelphia: Westminster, 1981], p. 42).
[34] Lindbeck, *Nature of Doctrine*, p. 120; emphases added.

Tradition: Does It Stretch or Will It Break?" and Kathryn Tanner's "Theology and the Plain Sense." Frei clarifies that the Christian communal sense of scripture should not be associated methodologically with one particular general theory of reading or literary classification. He gives two important reasons for this. First, even if one sees many theological and pastoral benefits in privileging a particular literary reading (e.g., the traditional realistic, narrative sense), the theologian should resist grounding that reading literarily. He argues, for example, that the less the traditional literal sense is "entangled in theory and the more firmly rooted not in a narrative (literary) tradition but in its primary and original context, a religious community's 'rule' for faithful reading, the more clearly it [the literal sense] is likely to come into view, and the stronger as well as more flexible and supple it is likely to look." Frei suggests that the literal sense of scripture should be understood in terms of the socio-linguistic context in which believers work out a consensus in light of the rule of faith for what kind of reading will assume primacy. The "viability, if any," of the traditional reading, which many today associate with the realistic, history-like sense, "will follow excellently from the actual, fruitful use religious people continue to make of it" as their communal sense of the text.[35] A second reason that the literal sense should not be associated with any one theory of reading is that it will (to repeat the point made above with regard to Tracy) "stand or fall" according to that theory's validity in relation to new hermeneutical theories that appear on the intellectual scene. Given the deconstructionist subversion of literary meaning, all hermeneutical theories which posit a stable textual meaning are called into question. Frei observes that even "the less high-powered general theory that upholds the literal or realistic reading of the Gospels may be just as perilously perched as its more majestic and pretentious hermeneutical cousin [e.g., phenomenological hermeneutics]." For these reasons, Frei argues that all theological accounts of how Christian communities designate a "primary or 'plain' sense" of scripture should be oriented principally to a thick descriptive analysis of communal ruled use and only secondarily and in a low-key way to any literary theory.[36]

[35] Frei, "Literal Reading," pp. 61–62, 37.
[36] Ibid., pp. 51, 64, 72. The fact that realistic narrative readings have predominated historically Frei attributes not to a property in the text but to the guidance of a "(largely but not wholly) informal set of rules" about, among other things, Jesus' ascriptive identity which engendered this realistic narrative interpretive mode (p. 68). For more on these rules, see n. 86 below.

Tanner further clarifies the importance of viewing the ecclesial plain sense functionally in terms of conventions of Christian practice and, in so doing, brings the impulses of plurality and continuity to the fore. Borrowing from David Kelsey's and Charles Wood's functionalist approaches to scripture and canon, Tanner emphasizes that the plain sense is not a "property" of the Christian community's scripture; rather, the plain sense has to do with "the way the text is used" in communal practices.[37] As such, it is a "product of" a community's interpretive practices. Once a particular use of scripture has become "relatively sedimented," it shapes Christian belief and practice and is normative for further readings of scripture.[38] The plain sense may be materially designated to be "a historical account of events, prescriptions for actions ... [or] narrative depictions of divine identity, etc." Formally, however, the plain sense is not any one material depiction but is functionally defined in light of "communal habits" for scriptural use.[39] Tanner echoes Mark Taylor when she raises the concern that the plain sense of the Bible, functionally viewed, might tend to be "captive" within a seemingly "rigid monopoly" of communal interpretive conventions. She specifies two practices (already at work in the Christian tradition) which provide conditions for the plain sense to be used in a "self-critical, pluralistic and flexible way."[40] First, she argues (against Taylor) that "canonizing a body of texts which work as scripture" will "force a certain degree of interpretive license." When a community takes a text to be fixed, limited and unrevisable and gives that text "universal relevance" over its (changeable) communal life, creative exegetical efforts will be imperative in order to draw from the text "more significance ... than is initially apparent

---

[37] Kathryn E. Tanner, "Theology and the Plain Sense" in *Scriptural Authority and Narrative Interpretation*, ed. Garrett Green (Philadelphia: Fortress, 1987), p. 62. Tanner's and Frei's proposals for a functional plain sense are similar to Stanley Hauerwas's attempt to ground the meaning of scripture in (to borrow Stanley Fish's term) an "interpretive community." However, there are some differences. Hauerwas's point is that the community, not the individual, whether the fundamentalist believer or the biblical critic, is the locus for determination of meaning (see Stanley Hauerwas, "Stanley Fish, the Pope, and the Bible" in his *Unleashing the Scripture: Freeing the Bible from Captivity to America* [Nashville: Abingdon, 1993], p. 25). Tanner and Frei are not trying to address the debate over communal vs. individual interpretive authority. Their point is merely to locate meaning in use. Some communities may well read the Bible in individualistic ways.

[38] Tanner, "Plain Sense," p. 63; see p. 69.

[39] Ibid., pp. 65, 66.

[40] Ibid., pp. 67, 75.

there."[41] Second, she suggests that classifying scripture under the rubric of narrative will make the communal use of the text flexibly "open-ended." A narrative plain sense does not specify how to move from the story to practice. Construing the Bible narratively (as opposed to, for example, as "cultic regulations or general teachings about beliefs and behaviors") involves "exegetical ingenuity" in order to position "the particulars of one's own life within a story."[42] Tanner's point (and mine) is not to endorse a particular literary reading (since she does not rule out that a similar effect could be "produced by some other, non-narrative identification of the plain sense"); rather, she is advocating communal uses of the Bible that do not engender "a monolithic Christian practice" but allow the text to promote a communal life which is "inclusive of difference and unperturbed by change."[43]

An orientation which locates scriptural meaning in use directs primary attention away from debating with poststructuralists about literary meaning – a debate which properly belongs in the background – and refocuses it on assessing Christian communal reading practices. Any adequate theological assessment of the flexibility and community-shaping power of a communal plain sense requires thick description. The theological exercise of redescribing the functional plain senses of various communities highlights how differences abound in Christian reading practices. (To borrow a poststructuralist notion, there has always been a sort of ecumenical ecclesial analogue to the endlessly deferred meaning of deconstruction.) Because a functionalist approach posits no underlying common horizon of understanding, the plurality of Christian communal reading practices is a genuine plurality. How then is the theologian to account for continuity? If one is thinking intracommunally, the theologian could appeal to the plain sense within that community which has become conventional or sedimented and, hence, is already functioning normatively in relation to new readings that arise within that community. However, appealing to a community's conventional sense could turn hegemonic in relation to newly

---

[41] Ibid., pp. 72–73. Boff makes a similar point about creative interpretation of canonical texts, stating that the fact of the "closure of scripture," while "prohibitive of certain meanings," at the same time makes "possible a multiplicity of readings." Clodovis Boff, O.S.M., *Theology and Praxis: Epistemological Foundations*, tr. Robert R. Barr (Maryknoll: Orbis, 1987), p. 140; the latter quote is italicized in the original.

[42] Tanner, "Plain Sense," pp. 74, 73, 75.

[43] Ibid., pp. 78 n. 27, 75.

emerging readings whose meanings seem to differ significantly from that plain sense. If one is thinking intercommunally or ecumenically, the situation becomes even more complex because there may not be a consensus reading across diverse congregations and contexts to which to appeal for continuity. Whether addressing how to establish intra-communal continuity in light of newly emerging readings or inter-communal ecumenical continuity, the theologian needs resources beyond a functionalist approach alone.

UPHOLDING CONTINUITY, PLURALITY AND CRITIQUE

Among the theological movements I am examining, there are a number of proposals for how to address the challenge of upholding continuity amid plurality in theological reading practices. Ogden employs a "canon within the canon" approach; Tracy tries variously to construe the Jesus Christ event as a "working canon"; postliberals appeal to grammatical rules for reading; Boff finds dialectical relationships within and between present communal reading patterns and those in the early Christian communities. The two revisionists' approaches coexist some-what contentiously and will serve to situate my alternative proposal for a regulative-dialectical model. Ogden's appeal to a normative canon within the canon has been called into question by Tracy whose colle-gial critique of his fellow revisionist's norm affirms all three hermeneu-tical impulses (plurality, continuity and critique). I agree with Tracy's reservations regarding Ogden's approach and affirm some of his formal criteria of normativity. His specific construal of a working canon, how-ever, is problematic – namely, his recent proposal for normativity developed in conversation with what he calls "the Frei–Lindbeck pro-posal" for a realistic plain sense of the passion narratives which he characterizes as making a positive contribution to his own "Catholic sense of how the Scripture is the church's book."[44] My proposal emerges from an appreciative critique of Lindbeck's rule theory of doctrine and Boff's dialectical method of doctrinal recasting, supple-mented by important resources from revisionary views on the use of critical exegetical and interpretive tools. I will endeavor to show that this regulative-dialectical model could effectively adjudicate

[44] Tracy, "On Reading Scriptures," pp. 36, 37.

among diverse plain senses in a way that incorporates the impulses of plurality, continuity and critique.

Apostolic authority and relative adequacy

For Ogden, envisioning continuity in ecclesial reading practices would mean holding such readings accountable to the same norm of appropriateness. He develops this norm by synthesizing the early church's criterion of canonicity (that is, apostolicity) and conclusions drawn from recent historical-critical studies of the New Testament. Ogden observes that the results of recent historical criticism demonstrate that none of the New Testament writings is properly an apostolic writing and, hence, the "historical judgments" involved in the early church's application of the criterion of apostolicity were "mistaken."[45] If one wishes (as Ogden does) to apply at least the spirit of this criterion as the norm of appropriateness today, then one must concede that the standard for it can only be the "earliest stratum of Christian witness that we today can construct" via historical-critical methods.[46] Hence, "the locus of the *auctoritas canonica* is not the New Testament itself, to say nothing of the Old, but the original witness that is prior to the New Testament," namely, the historically reconstructed apostolic community's "Jesus-kerygma."[47] His norm for continuity, therefore, is the canon within the canon or, more precisely, the "canon *before* the canon" that was "explicitly authorized by Jesus."[48] Christian communal reading practices are deemed appropriately in continuity with the

---

[45] Schubert M. Ogden, *The Point of Christology* (San Francisco: Harper & Row, 1987), p. 103. Ogden depends on Willi Marxsen to show that the early church's procedures for establishing apostolicity were not a question of what we would today call historical authorship. The early church determined apostolicity on the basis of content: "'one reasoned in a circle: only that could and should be canonical which was apostolic; if its apostolicity was uncertain, or disputed, one considered its content. One asked whether its content agreed with what one took to be canonical – for one naturally supposed that one had the right doctrine in that one stood in the right apostolic tradition.'" Schubert M. Ogden, *On Theology* (San Francisco: Harper & Row, 1986), p. 55.

[46] Ogden, *Point of Christology*, p. 103.

[47] Ogden, *On Theology*, pp. 56, 65. Ogden borrows the term Jesus-kerygma from Willi Marxsen (see *Point of Christology*, pp. 53f.).

[48] Schubert M. Ogden, "*Fundamentum Fidei*: Critical Reflection on Willi Marxsen's Contribution to Systematic Theology," *Modern Theology* 6 (1989), p. 6; *Point of Christology*, p. 102. Part of Ogden's proposal is his polemic against any quest for the historical Jesus as a norm of appropriateness. Not only is "the earliest stratum of witness now accessible to us by critical analysis of the gospels ... itself witness to Jesus" but, furthermore, Jesus is "infinitely more than any norm, because he is the primal source of all norms" (*Point of Christology*, pp. 101, 102).

normative tradition if they are judged to be congruent with the Jesus-kerygma.

Tracy's divergence from Ogden falls into roughly three interrelated categories which can be associated with the hermeneutical impulses of plurality, continuity and critique. An impulse for plurality is at work in Tracy's argument against making the Jesus-kerygma the primary criterion for Christianly appropriate readings of the scriptures. Both Tracy's Roman Catholic and Gadamerian "preunderstanding" about the nature of tradition cause him to adopt a very different attitude from that of Ogden regarding how one determines normativity.[49] He argues that a definitive, exclusive norm for appropriateness – whether the historically reconstructed Jesus-kerygma, or any other single element – neglects the "enriching diversity of the whole scriptural (and, in principle, postscriptural) witness." To neglect this diversity is to risk "losing the full reality of 'tradition,'" which must be seen as continuing "*as tradition* by ever-new interpretations, ever-new reformations." Tracy has consistently approached scriptural interpretation with the attitude that the theologian enters into "conversation with the tradition with a fundamental trust" in the whole tradition's range of classic symbols and expressions.[50]

Tracy's attempt to make good on the impulse of continuity is also part of his distancing from Ogden's appeal to the normative Jesus-kerygma. Tracy stresses that the unifying principle of the "remarkably pluralistic" New Testament and later Christian communities "is not any single interpretation of the [Jesus] Christ-event (any particular Christology) but the event itself" to which the biblical writers gave witness. All subsequent Christian communal interpretations of the Jesus Christ event must be shown to be in "appropriate continuity" with the witness expressed in the New Testament as a canonical whole.[51] Theologically speaking, the Jesus Christ event is a formal norm which requires hermeneutical and theological elaboration as to its meaning. The theologian's task is to propose a "'working canon,' some guiding rubric" for material continuity with the New Testament witness to this event. Tracy specifies that his notion of a working canon is an

[49] See Tracy, *Analogical Imagination*, pp. 244 n. 13, 137 n. 16.
[50] Ibid., pp. 290 n. 29, 237, 236.
[51] Robert Grant, with David Tracy, *A Short History of the Interpretation of the Bible*, 2nd edn. (n.p.: Fortress Press, 1984), p. 178.

explicit "abandonment of a search for 'a canon within the canon'" (which characterizes Ogden's approach); the working canon entails the important proviso of "relative adequacy."[52] While I disagree with the experiential-expressive framework Tracy often employs for construing the Jesus Christ event in his early work, I agree with his proposal that continuity with the tradition should not be based on a single canon within the canon and that the norming process should only ever lay claim to relative adequacy. His stress on relative adequacy is especially appropriate since that is all the normativity we can hope to get over-lapping consensus on, given ecclesial plurality.

We also see an impulse of critique at work in Tracy's effort, in effect, to resituate Ogden's method of establishing normativity within an overall approach to reading the Bible critically. Tracy suggests that Ogden's method mistakenly takes an internal textual corrective (the Jesus-kerygma) to be the central Christian norm. Tracy affirms that the historical retrieval of the original apostolic witness is an important corrective of "developments and distortions in the tradition";[53] how-ever, he judges that Christianity's norm for appropriateness does not stand exclusively at its genetic origins. The earliest apostolic witness should be seen not as preeminent but functioning alongside other internal textual correctives (such as the "doctrines of early Catholicism" as found in the pastoral epistles[54]) and other external correctives, such as the interpreter's use of historical- and literary-critical methods, genre analysis, various hermeneutics of suspicion and ideology critique (the latter Tracy draws in part from Ogden's own program of deideologization).[55] Furthermore, while he joins Ogden in deeming historical criticism to be one among many vital exegetical tools, Tracy goes beyond Ogden to take a critical view of some of its effects – particularly the way "traditional Christian readings of the Scriptures as 'history-like' narratives have been interrupted by modern historical critical readings." He engages a critical impulse to question any attempt of historical inquiry "to deny its own hermeneutic character and mask its own historicity."[56]

[52] Tracy, *Analogical Imagination*, pp. 254, 290 n. 29.
[53] Ibid., p. 236.
[54] Ibid., pp. 266–68.
[55] Ibid., pp. 238ff., 246 n. 26 and "Hermeneutical Reflections," pp. 51ff. See also Ogden, *Point of Christology*, p. 94.
[56] Tracy, *Plurality and Ambiguity*, pp. 35, 31.

Tracy's efforts to find genre-sensitive, critical, tradition-inclusive ways to elaborate the meaning of the scriptures have recently converged with his growing interest in two areas: attending to the readings of oppressed Christian communities (as noted above); and highlighting the kind of realistic narrative plain sense he associates with postliberal theology. He calls on academic theologians to listen more closely and preferentially to the claim to attention of new readings of scripture from the underside of history which he calls "prophetic-mystical dialectic" readings – a category that seems to rework the manifestation-proclamation-historical action mode under the influence of especially liberation theologies.[57] With increasing force, he voices agreement with those theologies that "Christian theology must move . . . into the concrete histories of suffering and oppression." Attending to scriptural readings of the oppressed breaks open the Bible, initiating such a profound hermeneutical revolution that we cannot "even guess at the moment where the new Christian theological hermeneutics . . . will eventually lead."[58] In the meantime, we are left with a plurality of readings emerging from diverse, especially marginalized contexts. A ramification of this plurality of church readings is that "[t]he central theological question has become how to understand anew, on theological grounds, the unity amidst so wide and potentially rich a diversity of readings."[59] It is precisely in order to address this question that Tracy has recently found it instructive to focus on the importance of the realistic reading of the passion narratives.

Tracy now specifies that appropriate continuity with the Jesus Christ event expressed in the New Testament means fidelity to the realistic, history-like sense of the passion narratives. This "foundational plain sense" is the "working canon" he currently proposes for unifying diverse Christian readings.[60] Tracy observes that his earlier writings were unable

---

[57] See Tracy, "On Reading Scriptures," pp. 51ff. I read Tracy's category of prophetic-mystical dialectic as a change from his strategy of subordinating the historical action mode to manifestation and proclamation which perpetuates a separation of ethical action and religious encounter with the divine (see n. 17 above). A subordination of ethical action to divine encounter would seem to be especially inappropriate when the religious encounter is a *"via negativa"* of suffering as experienced by the oppressed. See David Tracy, *Dialogue with the Other: The Inter-Religious Dialogue* (Louvain: Peeters; Grand Rapids, Mich.: William B. Eerdmans, 1990), p. 120.

[58] Tracy, *Dialogue*, pp. 119, 120.

[59] David Tracy, "Reading the Bible: The Plurality of Readers and Possibility of a Shared Vision" in his *On Naming the Present: God, Hermeneutics, and Church* (Maryknoll: Orbis; London: SCM, 1994), p. 120.

[60] Tracy, "On Reading Scriptures," pp. 46, 52.

to do what Frei in *The Identity of Jesus Christ* accomplishes – that is, to demonstrate "how and why" the normative Christian confession about Jesus Christ "is rendered in its fullness only in and through the details of the interaction of the unsubstitutable character of Jesus and the specific circumstances of his passion and resurrection."[61] Tracy claims that this realistic narrative sense of Jesus' death and resurrection serves both to unify and "reopen rather than close Christian theological attention to other . . . readings." The Bible's "radical diversity" (such as the "nonclosure of Mark 16:8" or the "meditative, disclosive, iconic power" of the Gospel of John[62]) and interpretations as diverse as African-American, French mystical, German metaphysical, Latin American liberationist, feminist, and so on, are unified because each "has its own way of assuring fidelity to the plain sense of the passion narratives."[63] Tracy does not, however, appropriate the Frei–Lindbeck realistic narrative reading uncritically. He warns against construing "realistic" only in terms of a particular "Anglo-Saxon moral realism," and he urges more comparison between biblical "narrative" and the historical-critically retrieved Jesus-kerygma and other nonnarrative New Testament genres.[64] Attention to genre diversity in the New Testament only confirms for Tracy the presence of the normative force of the common passion narrative.

Tracy's approach is an interesting way of synthesizing what he deems the best of Ogden's, postliberal and liberationist hermeneutics. It is ironic that a qualification to Tracy's proposed narrative norm should come from postliberal theology. Although Tracy says he is agreeing with postliberals on the traditional plain sense (and to a large extent he is), there are subtle differences which are nevertheless significant. Tracy writes that he insists along with Frei that the plain sense of the passion "with or without the aid of literary criticism . . . has

---

[61] Ibid., p. 39.

[62] Tracy, *On Naming*, pp. 125, 127, 128.

[63] Tracy, "On Reading Scriptures," pp. 48–49. Tracy acknowledges important differences in the genres of the gospels but nonetheless asserts that they share a common passion narrative with a "relatively history-like, realistic character" (*Dialogue*, p. 114). He states rather than argues his case, and it is beyond the scope of this book to delve into the exegetical and literary debate on this issue. I would venture to suggest that any sense of a common passion narrative has more to do with the way the mainstream Church tradition has read the passion narratives than with some structural literary similarity among the passion accounts themselves.

[64] Tracy, "On Reading Scriptures," p. 48; cf. pp. 40ff. I would classify Tracy's (important) critiques as belonging to background theories.

traditionally been, is and should be both realistic and history-like." It is true that postliberals have affirmed the historical primacy of this plain sense and have advocated in different ways its ongoing benefits for the church today; however, they stop short of saying (with Tracy) that it "*is* the plain sense of the Christian community."[65] Lindbeck recognizes the widespead "loss of the once-universal classic hermeneutical framework" which is heavily contested today; hence, while arguing for the benefits of this reading, he realizes that it is not the *de facto* normative reading in many Christian communities.[66] Frei, as noted above, suggests that any theological argument for the ongoing validity of the realistic, history-like sense should be based primarily on the fruitfulness of its use in Christian communities. Similarly, Tanner argues that "*to look for* the plain sense as a function of communal practice" is an approach that "does not tell you beforehand *what* you will find when you look."[67]

The conclusion these postliberal comments point to is that theologians should focus on thick description of communal reading practices – description thicker than Tracy gives us when he suggests that various mystical, metaphysical, "and almost all feminist readings" remain congruent with the realistic, history-like sense of the passion.[68] This claim strikes me as too thin, given that privileging the realistic, history-like reading is not the plain sense of the gospel in all Christian communal readings (even influential ones). Tracy may correctly identify its underlying presence in most Latin American liberationist prophetic-mystical readings. However, I doubt that Rita Nakashima Brock, for example, would accept that her feminist communal plain sense (which draws heavily from the Gospel of Mark) must be shown to be in harmony with the realistic, history-like reading of the gospels in order to be Christianly appropriate – especially if that reading is primarily "the realistic hero's quest of Luke."[69] North American feminist theologians

[65] Ibid., pp. 38, 39. See n. 36 above for Frei's historical understanding of why the plain sense has largely been the literal, history-like sense.
[66] George Lindbeck, "Scripture, Consensus, and Community," *This World: A Journal of Religion and Public Life* 23 (1988), p. 6; see *Nature of Doctrine*, p. 124.
[67] Tanner, "Plain Sense," p. 65.
[68] Tracy, "On Reading Scriptures," p. 48.
[69] Tracy, "The Return of God in Contemporary Theology" in his *On Naming*, p. 37. Brock explicitly criticizes the notion of a hero-savior Jesus as undergirding psychologically unhealthy, even potentially abusive, human relations. See Rita Nakashima Brock, *Journeys by Heart: A Christology of Erotic Power* (New York: Crossroad, 1988). I will discuss this at greater length in ch. 6.

interested in scriptural normativity often focus on Jesus' prophetic message in such a way that what Tracy calls the traditional plain sense's "realism of the cross and the realistic vindication of the resurrection" is intentionally eclipsed because these theologians reject the notion of (as Rosemary Radford Ruether would say) the salvific death of a "'once-for-all'" (male) savior.[70]

I do not dispute Tracy's claim that "[i]f there could be agreement on this material christological principle" (i.e., that the Jesus Christ event has its fullest rendering in the history-like sense of the passion), "then there would also be a fuller substantive ecumenical theological criterion than previously available."[71] But given that there is dwindling ecumenical consensus (and if Lindbeck's predictions are on the mark, there probably will be less in the near future), we need to explore other conceptualities which could shed light on addressing the challenge of upholding continuity with the tradition yet with openness to the plurality of Christian readings.

A regulative-dialectical model

In outlining this model, I do not propose a particular material norm for continuity in scriptural reading practices. Such norms are essential for theologians to formulate, but they are appropriately presented within fully developed (preferably wide reflective equilibrium) constructive theological proposals and not in essays on theological practice such as this one. My task here is to explicate what is essentially a heuristic model for thinking about reading the Bible theologically as the church's book. The particular problem I am addressing is how to identify continuity amid diverse reading practices while avoiding rigidity and insularity. A model that I believe is useful in this regard entails a critical retrieval of conceptual resources from Lindbeck's rule theory of doctrine and Boff's dialectical method of doctrinal recasting, in light of revisionary provisoes about using critical exegetical and hermeneutical correctives when interpreting scripture. Rule theory provides the conceptuality for accounting for grammatical continuity (or discontinuity) amid a diversity of reading practices. The dialectical process of

---

[70] Tracy, "On Reading Scriptures," p. 48; Rosemary Radford Ruether, *Sexism and God-Talk: Toward a Feminist Theology*, with new introduction (Boston: Beacon, 1993), pp. 122, 138.
[71] Tracy, "On Reading Scriptures," p. 42.

recasting theology's interpretive framework prevents the Christian *regula* from becoming either too rigid or narrow. Critical exegetical and hermeneutical tools interrogate all readings and even distortions in the church's book itself.

Lindbeck's rule theory proposes that "doctrines qua doctrines" be taken as second-order principles which regulate first-order Christian beliefs and practices, including reading practices. Doctrinal formulations can serve other (nonregulative) functions as well. They can, for example, function as powerful expressive symbols in liturgical settings or as first-order propositional statements.[72] These functions, however, should not technically be associated with doctrines which should be seen as "exemplary instantiations or paradigms" of the grammar encoded in the discourse and practice of Christian communities. The locus for doctrinal continuity in rule theory (used in combination with a cultural-linguistic approach to religion) is, Lindbeck explains, not in "propositionally formulated truths, much less in inner experiences, but in the story [the Christian community] ... tells and in the grammar that informs the way the story is told and used."[73] (For example, Christian doctrine typically specifies that the scriptures should be read within both a monotheistic and trinitarian framework.) Boff expresses a compatible view, as we have seen in the previous chapter. Although he does not speak explicitly of rule theory, he depends on the notion of a regulative Christian grammar to explicate how religious and theological discourses share a code of faith. Christian communal discourse is the locus for this "hermeneutic code," and as believers acquire facility in using it, they are able to read their world Christianly, so to speak. This code provides believers with "eyes for seeing ... a gaze upon the world ... a grammar for reading – for reading all books."[74]

Rule theory is at work in Lindbeck's and (implicitly in) Boff's efforts to distinguish between the grammar and the vocabulary of the Christian religion by specifying that what norms religious or theological discourse "is not its vocabulary but its grammar."[75] Vocabulary differences (often contextually influenced) pervade first- and second-order discourses and reading practices. Different Christian communal plain senses

[72] Lindbeck, *Nature of Doctrine*, p. 80; see pp. 18, 19.
[73] Ibid., pp. 81, 80.
[74] Boff, *Theology and Praxis*, pp. 124, 123; all quotes in italics in the original.
[75] Ibid., p. 125.

of scripture must be analyzed in order to distinguish variances in vocabulary from variances in grammar. So long as the "basic rules" for scriptural use remain the same, differing plain senses can be viewed grammatically "as the fusion of a self-identical story with the new worlds within which it is told and retold."[76] Hence an advantage of this regulative approach to doctrine is that it can envision substantial intra-communal or ecumenical continuity across contextually different or historically changing conditions marked by very different vocabularies. For example, the fidelity Tracy envisions among diverse ecclesial readings of the Bible (ranging from prophetic African American to German metaphysical to feminist) could be conceptualized regulatively rather than in terms of their congruence with a foundational material reading of scripture (the history-like sense of the passion). That is, what accounts for continuity (or degrees of continuity) with the realistic, history-like sense of the passion is the congruence of the grammatical frameworks (the "basic rules") informing each reading. Furthermore, the distinction between vocabulary and grammar provides the necessary conceptual clarification not only for accounting for continuity but also for assessing some of the differences among the plurality of readings. Such clarification is essential especially when new discourses are introduced into Christian reading practices (e.g., the discourse of black consciousness in African American theology or the Korean discourse of *han* in Asian American theology[77]). This regulative assessment will inevitably be a complex, often contentious intracommunal and intercommunal affair. It will require thick descriptions of Christian forms of life and judgments on subtle but often profound grammatical differences.

Some words of clarification on Lindbeck's use of rule theory are in order here. His principal purpose for using rule theory is to explicate "the nature of doctrine" (hence, the title of his book) especially in light of ecumenical dialogue. In this context of ecumenical discussions about what is or is not church-dividing, he uses rule theory to analyze official church doctrines understood as the "communally authoritative teachings regarding beliefs and practices that are considered essen-

---

[76] Lindbeck, *Nature of Doctrine*, p. 83.
[77] See James H. Cone, *Black Theology and Black Power* (New York: Seabury, 1969); Andrew Sung Park, *The Wounded Heart of God: The Asian Concept of Han and the Christian Doctrine of Sin* (Nashville: Abingdon, 1993).

tial."[78] Lindbeck is careful to draw a sharp distinction between doctrinal theology and church doctrine, not only because "[t]hose who agree on officially formulated doctrines may disagree sharply on how to interpret, justify, or defend them" but also because church doctrines do not issue from individual theologians. However, rule theory of doctrine has a broader application (pertaining to his subtitle, "religion and theology in a postliberal age"). Lindbeck applies the insights of rule theory to religions and theologies in general. Religions, when "viewed as a kind of cultural and/or linguistic framework," are seen as ruled by "a distinctive logic" or grammar.[79] Theologians can use rule theory not only to analyze official church doctrines but also as part of their redescriptive and doctrinally constructive task of identifying implicit communal rules or interpretive schemes embedded in Christian speech and action. The theologically identified doctrinal aspects of any Christian communal interpretive framework may or may not be synonymous with any specific church's communally authoritative doctrines. It is this broader application of rule theory in constructive theological work that I have in mind when thinking about the interpretive framework which implicitly or explicitly guides communal uses of scripture and, by extension, theological readings of the Bible as the church's book.[80]

A problematic impression that could be drawn from Lindbeck's application of rule theory is that the theory itself leads to excessive theological conservatism since he uses it to explain how doctrines can be permanent. For example, he uses rule theory to make intelligible the claim that doctrines are "'irreformable'" yet without excluding ostensibly contrary positions.[81] Strictly speaking, however, the theory prescribes neither doctrinal preservation nor innovation but provides a neutral technical perspective for either application. Lindbeck has focused on how rule theory can be used to account for church doctrinal

---

[78] Lindbeck, *Nature of Doctrine*, p. 74. For a helpful analysis of the use of rule theory for doctrinal discussion within ecumenical church dialogue, see Michael Root, "Identity and Difference: The Ecumenical Problem" in Marshall, ed. *Theology and Dialogue*, pp. 165–90.

[79] Lindbeck, *Nature of Doctrine*, pp. 76, 33.

[80] It is beyond the scope of this book to address all the elements which could make up a Christian communal interpretive framework. I am focusing on the implicit and explicit doctrinal rules which guide Christian speech and action (including reading practices). For a philosophical debate related to interpretive frameworks, see Matthew Foster's extended discussion of Hans-Georg Gadamer's concept of the effects of history and Jürgen Habermas's concept of ideology critique (*Gadamer and Practical Philosophy: The Hermeneutics of Moral Confidence* [Atlanta: Scholars, 1991]). See also Tracy, *Analogical Imagination*, pp. 146 n. 80, 137 n. 16.

[81] Lindbeck, *Nature of Doctrine*, p. 9.

continuity; I would like to explore its use in theological practice, specifically on the issue of how grammatical frameworks might be modified in light of a plurality of functional plain senses from contextually diverse communities. This interest in a revisable interpretive framework is not incompatible with Lindbeck's understanding of rule theory, since he affirms that "adjustments also take place in the interpretive scheme" in response to changing worldviews. Nevertheless, we do need to identify limitations in his formulation of the theory for our purposes. I am not disputing that some grammars of the Christian religion may be permanent, but clarification is necessary regarding Lindbeck's appeal to "[t]he deep grammar" or "the indispensable grammar." The problem is the definite pronoun: "*the* deep grammar" or "*the* indispensable grammar."[82] Such formulations make Lindbeck's proposal vulnerable to the kinds of charges he mentions as being typically directed to doctrinal propositionalists: (1) a tendency to legitimate doctrinal "rigidities"; and (2) a tendency to overlook "cultural and individual differences."[83] I find only partial solutions to each in Lindbeck's writings.

One way to avoid the first problem – doctrinal rigidity – when using the concept of "the deep grammar" is to view it as an eschatological concept. Just as linguistics has its "rules of depth grammar, which linguists search for and may at times approximate but never grasp," so Christianity may be seen as having a deep grammar which theologians attempt contextually to articulate in various doctrinal formulations but which remains ungraspable in any definitive manner. Lindbeck makes a similar point regarding growth in the Christian form of life: "For Christians, even mature Christians, this process has just begun" and will continue until the "eschatological fulfillment." By analogy, one might argue that knowledge of *the* Christian grammar is only ever incomplete and remains unconfirmable in any definitive way this side of the eschaton. Lindbeck seems to say as much when he states that "[t]he deep grammar of the language may escape detection."[84]

One way to avoid the second problem (the tendency to overlook cultural and individual differences) is to diversify the base of who determines what comprises "the Christian grammar." Lindbeck envisions a

[82] Ibid., pp. 82, 85; emphases added.
[83] Ibid., pp. 78, 79.
[84] Ibid., pp. 130, 60, 82.

diversity of professional theological and lay perspectives – a view which exemplifies a broad approach to theology (as described in chapter one). He states that when the deep grammar of the Christian faith eludes trained theologians, they must "bow to the superior wisdom of the competent speaker" (presuming they can be identified) from Christianity's "mainstream" – that is, those adherents of the religion who have effectively "interiorized the grammar of their religion." These are the "flexibly devout" who are connaturally well-versed in the Christian idiom and, hence, have acquired an intuitive ability to distinguish cultural (vocabulary) differences from grammatical ones. They may not be theologically trained, but they make up the *"consensus fidelium* against which doctrinal proposals are tested."[85] In dialogue with connaturally knowledgeable, mainstream Christian communities, the theologian can then propose regulative principles as "testable ... hypotheses" instantiating the deep grammar "at work" in Christian speech and action which can then guide reading practices.[86] To the extent that these testable hypotheses reflect the grammar at work among a broad cross section of Christian communities, historically, culturally and geographically, it may be meaningful to employ a working notion of "the Christian grammar." We might say that theological approximations of "the Christian grammar" will entail a complex interplay between the theologian's testable regulative doctrinal hypotheses and the connatural theological sense of Christian communities. A regulative use of doctrines for constructive theological practice is meant to direct the theologian continually back to the interpretive framework embedded in the beliefs and practices of the *consensus fidelium*, creating, in effect, a hermeneutical circle for interpreting scripture in continuity with the tradition, as understood by its broad and diverse base of believers. The circle entails reading the scriptures in terms of the deep grammar interiorized by Christianity's competent speakers who, in

---

[85] Ibid., pp. 82, 100.

[86] Ibid., pp. 109 n. 10, 94. Lindbeck himself proposes three testable hypotheses at work in the language of Nicaea and Chalcedon: (1) "The monotheistic principle: there is only one God, the God of Abraham, Isaac, and Jacob, and Jesus"; (2) "the principle of historical specificity: the stories of Jesus refer to a genuine human being who was born, lived, and died in a particular place and time"; (3) "the principle of ... Christological maximalism: every possible importance is to be ascribed to Jesus that is not inconsistent with the first rules." Lindbeck suggests that these creeds be viewed as products of "the joint logical pressure of these three principles constraining Christians to use available conceptual and symbolic materials to relate Jesus Christ to God in certain ways and not in others" (pp. 94, 95).

turn, connaturally derive that grammar in part from the scriptures themselves.

An eschatological proviso does offset to some extent a tendency toward rigid claims regarding *the* Christian grammar, and a hermeneutical circle as described above is a useful way to open the theologian up to different perspectives among the flexibly devout. However these are only partial solutions. The eschatological proviso is a partial solution because it functions as a check on any particular rendering of the Christian grammar but fails to conceptualize elements necessary to keep the process of doctrinal formulation itself open-ended and flexible. The appeal to the mainstream *consensus fidelium* is only a partial solution because it is not critical enough of the concepts "mainstream" or "consensus." Lindbeck uses these notions in his discussion of how one would identify a wide consensus of competent speakers of the Christian grammar (as distinct from the larger constituency of all churchgoers who have not interiorized the grammar). One of his criteria is that the group be selected from among ecumenically minded Christians, not those from "ingrown sects uninterested in communicating widely."[87] It makes sense for Lindbeck to identify that his cultural-linguistic and regulative doctrinal theories seem most applicable and helpful to mainstream, nonsectarian Christians with some observable competence in using Christian grammar. However, if doctrinal formulations are the product of theologians in dialogue with concrete Christian communities and their reading practices, then it is incumbent upon theologians to attend not only to the harmony of voices in the mainstream consensus but also to those sometimes dissonant voices on the margins striving to be heard and perhaps challenging (explicitly or implicitly) aspects of that consensus. Lindbeck's rule theory allows for doctrinal innovation but does not suggest a method for guiding it in theological practice; he promotes attentiveness to the laity but does not methodologically specify how to offset the tendency toward settling with the status quo of mainstream believers.

Boff does focus methodologically on some of the issues involved in avoiding doctrinal rigidity and avoiding a conservative tendency to overlook differences. He envisions the tradition as a traditioning process in which both elements in the hermeneutical circle (interpre-

[87] Ibid., p. 100.

tive framework and communal readings) shift. As noted in chapter three, for Boff, theology's formal object or code of faith does not fall from the heavens but must be recast from complex, highly dialectical interactions of scripture, tradition, historical experience, and critical mediations. His method of doctrinal recasting works to open the hermeneutical circle, extending it into what I would call a dynamic hermeneutical helix. New reading practices are introduced and the traditioning process remains open to revisions in light of oppositional views.

Boff borrows from Thomas Kuhn to describe theology as a theoretical process marked by a dialectic of resistance to a stable ruling paradigm which is recast overtly in moments of crisis and more subtly in normal theological science.[88] (As I suggested in chapter three, this recasting is consistent with wide reflective equilibrium procedures where revisions and adjustment of beliefs, principles and background theories occur.) Lindbeck also acknowledges the Kuhnian point that when "anomalies accumulate which the old theories cannot integrate," the old theoretical paradigm undergoes revision; yet he tends to think of the Christian religion in terms of its "abiding *regulae fidei* which last as long as the religion itself."[89] For the reasons of ecumenicity discussed above, he emphasizes how theologians continue to struggle "with both the strengths and the weaknesses" of the dominant paradigm within which they work, and that theological revolutions occur, in other words, only under "very exceptional circumstances."[90] While Boff would agree with Lindbeck that the Christian doctrinal tradition historically has been fairly stable overall, his own experience of how liberation theology has precipitated something of a paradigm shift "by opposing 'classic' theology" seems to orient him to a more thoroughgoing dialectical approach.[91] For Boff, dialectic is not just a technique, it is a characteristic of serious reflection, a "*dynamism* of thought," marked by a continual "effort to transcend all fixed points." Dialectical thought

---

[88] See, Boff, *Theology and Praxis*, pp. xxix, 236 n. 21.
[89] George A. Lindbeck, "Theological Revolutions and the Present Crisis," *Theology Digest* 23 (1975), pp. 315, 318.
[90] Ibid., pp. 319, 313.
[91] Boff, *Theology and Praxis*, p. 79. For a historical theological discussion of how liberation theology emerges but diverges from modern Western theology, see Gustavo Gutiérrez, "Theology from the Underside of History" and "The Limitations of Modern Theology: On a Letter of Dietrich Bonhoeffer" in his *Power of the Poor*, pp. 169–221 and 222–34.

"renounces definite conclusions and eternal truths" and "burst[s] the conceptual frames that imprison the mind." He sounds almost a/theological when he calls for dialectical theology as "perpetual commencement, transgression of limits, journey through the desert endlessly" and "play."[92] However, he is not advocating endless erring and play without profound concern for maintaining grammatical connection with the tradition and establishing a rich scriptural basis for the struggle for justice. He is as interested in the problem of the lack of regulative continuity as he is the problem of status quo theological rigidity in the dominant ecclesial tradition. Boff's hermeneutical mediation attempts to address both.

The production of theology's formal object in hermeneutical mediation takes place at the juncture of a number of complex dialectics in relation to scripture. Both the dominant-other dialectic (as I will call it) and the past-present dialectic are attempts to adhere to the hermeneutical maxim: "The norm of faith is scripture read *in the church*."[93] The dominant-other dialectic instantiates the impulse of plurality along with Boff's liberationist value of solidarity with the oppressed. Within a liberation hermeneutic, scripture read in the church involves the commitment to "interrogate the totality of scripture from the viewpoint of the oppressed."[94] The underlying dynamism for recasting theology's code of faith comes from this dialectic. Recasting can happen when the traditional interpretive framework and plain sense (as postliberals would say) encounter new readings of scripture and their implicit interpretive frameworks (e.g., the reading practices of base Christian communities). Relating this to the notion of a hermeneutical circle, we might say that the hermeneutical circle of the status quo is set into helical motion from "outside the system" of dominant reading practices, from the perspective "of 'the other' – the oppressed person."[95] Concern for otherness is made methodologically central from the start, creating what I would call a *weighted* dialectic, in that it privileges the perspective of the marginalized when reading the Bible. Without this oppositional perspective, the issue of recasting

---

92 Boff, *Theology and Praxis*, p. 206.
93 Ibid., p. 136.
94 Clodovis Boff, "Epistemology and Method of the Theology of Liberation," tr. Robert R. Barr, in *Mysterium Liberationis: Fundamental Concepts of Liberation Theology*, ed. Ignacio Ellacuría, S.J., and Jon Sobrino, S.J. (Maryknoll: Orbis, 1993), p. 79.
95 Boff, *Theology and Praxis*, p. 328 n. 3.

theology's formal object might never be broached (or broached only within the framework of the mainstream status quo).

The past-present dialectic also adheres to the maxim about scripture read in the church. This dialectical hermeneutical process indicates that doctrinal recasting is always a *re*casting, not a casting from scratch, because scripture is read in light of the church's *regula fidei*. There is no unmediated access to the text; it is "necessary to go by way of Christian tradition."[96] The primary purpose of the past-present dialectic can be viewed as instantiating the impulse of continuity (understood regulatively) in this recasting process. Boff explains that Christian communities have always sought to interpret the scriptures for their particular historical situations with "creative fidelity" to the internal logic of the message of Jesus "just as the primitive community sought to do." Even for the early Christian communities, this procedure was a dialectical interpretive interplay between each community's context and the gospel. Present communities should strive not to copy the literal content of the early churches' "labor of reading" (which ultimately became formalized in the canonical scriptures) but to establish a "correspondence of relationships" between their current contextualized interpretations and the contextualized readings of the early churches.[97] The patterns of reading encoded in scripture are what is paradigmatically normative.

Boff, as much as Lindbeck, is concerned with extratextual reading practices: "'selling cat for rabbit,'" as Boff colorfully puts it. To offset this danger, he specifies that the "thrust of this dialectic-hermeneutic comes from *scripture*" as the "*dominant term*."[98] I interpret this as another *weighted* dialectic in which the patterns of the early churches' readings are given a certain privilege of place in relation to the present community's patterns of reading. By weighting the dialectic toward scripture, one prioritizes a continuity with the past grammatical tradition of Christianity's founding witness without discounting the importance

---

[96] Ibid., p. 139.

[97] Ibid., pp. 148, 147. When Boff refers to a "labor of reading," he is speaking in part metaphorically, since the primitive communities were working with oral traditions along with Hebrew scriptures and possibly various "apostolic" writings. Boff considers a correspondence of relationships approach to be important for theologies of the political for which there is the danger of making "parallels between the Bible and politics that are too obvious and too facile" and of extracting from scripture the direct proof one needs for immediate political action (p. 152). See his discussion of "unacceptable" hermeneutical models in this regard, pp. 142–46.

[98] Ibid., pp. 267 n. 9, 149–50; see Boff, "Epistemology and Method," p. 80.

of contextualizing the gospel message pluralistically at other times and places. Weighting the past-present dialectic in this way makes it analogous to the postliberal method of intratextuality (which emphasizes how the Bible absorbs the world); however, Boff's emphasis on the dominant-other dialectic specifies the importance of keeping one's hermeneutic open to what is outside the traditional interpretive framework and plain sense. Recasting theology's interpretive framework is thus set in motion by the (weighted) dominant-other dialectic yet also disciplined by the (weighted) past-present dialectic. As a result, dominant interpretive frameworks and plain senses may be challenged by new, contextualized readings from the perspective of the oppressed. On the other hand, weighting the hermeneutic toward the canonical labor of reading of the early churches keeps this dynamic hermeneutical helix from becoming a spiral out of control, unaccountable to the tradition (grammatically understood).

Viewed in terms of the conceptuality of a wide reflective equilibrium dogmatics (where communal beliefs, doctrinal principles and background theories continually interact), doctrinal recasting is an example of one type of revision that can occur so that a new equilibrium is achieved. To the extent that the background theories or mediations employed in wide reflective equilibrium are diverse and to some extent independent from the other two elements, then the dogmatic reflective equilibrium can be critically widened even further. This brings us to the last aspect of the regulative-dialectical model: the critical component. The critical mediations or background theories I have in mind include the methods of biblical criticism which can be utilized for purposes of both a hermeneutics of retrieval and suspicion in theological interpretations of scripture. On this point, we can draw fruitfully from Tracy's emphasis on the many textual explanatory methods (e.g., historical- and literary-critical, structuralist, social scientific, etc.) which can enrich the church's retrieval of meaning in biblical texts as well as challenge and correct the parochialism of theological reading practices. Beyond these uses, I suggest that these explanatory methods can help us identify often-elided theological grammars embedded in Christianity's founding canonical and non-canonical texts. Although Tracy does not put it in quite this way, identifying units of tradition or the hand of the redactor can attune the reader of scripture to grammatical plurality and continuity in the text (think of the various christological grammars in the New Testament). One can read Tracy's particularly effective use of genre analysis in a similar way. For example, he presents apocalyptic as a literary genre entailing notions of "the eschatological 'not-yet' in every incarnational 'always-already' and even every 'but-even-now' resurrectional transformation." He focuses on the "*corrective*" aspect of this genre,[99] which I suggest can also be construed via rule theory as part of an interpretive framework, guiding the reader to certain grammars for speaking correctly about God. (That is, always speak of divine presence as eschatologically coming but also incarnationally having come as well as tranformationally active now.) Sensitivity to the literary plurality and historical complexity of the Bible can have ecumenical theological benefits as well. It is not at all surprising, in this regard, that Tracy can envision drawing from Ogden's Jesus-kerygma, Frei's realistic narrative and Gutiérrez's mystical and prophetic reading practices.

Notably absent from most liberation and postliberal hermeneutics is any use of ideology critique on the Bible itself. Given Boff's methodological weighting of scripture and Lindbeck's intratextual approach, there would seem to be an understandable tendency to apply a hermeneutic of suspicion only to interpretations of scripture and not to the Bible itself. I agree with Tracy's maxim for interpretation (which is put into practice by Ogden's method of deideologization): "If any interpreter so much as suspects that illusions, or repressed systematic distortions, may be present in any particular tradition, the need to develop [a] sense of suspicion becomes imperative."[100] Postliberal and liberation theologians often seem reticent about developing a sense of suspicion toward the text. However, if we have learned anything from the critical work of especially feminist theologians and exegetes in past years, it is that ideology (particularly androcentric gender bias) imbues the biblical text. Hence, a weighted past-present dialectical hermeneutic or an intratextual method needs to be mediated with critical background theories that include various ideology critiques. This will help ensure that the doctrinal recasting is wide and not ideologically narrow. Furthermore, this hermeneutics of suspicion can in turn aid in the process of retrieving new meaning from the Bible. The spirit of what Lindbeck says about the use of historical criticism applies to all critical

99 Tracy, *Analogical Imagination*, pp. 266, 265.
100 Tracy, "Hermeneutical Reflections," p. 45; original in italics.

textual therapies: "exegetical findings do make a difference. For one thing, they block eisegesis." Furthermore, and more to the point when using the Bible as the church's book, "[p]ossibilities that were once excluded because of theologically biased readings of what the scripture meant once again become options"[101] and scripture can be used anew to form appropriate Christian communal identity.

We have been exploring the task of construing a scripture–tradition relationship resistant to deconstruction and open to ecclesial plurality, especially the scriptural readings of the oppressed. The regulative-dialectical model I have proposed tries to make good on the impulses of continuity, plurality and critique through a synthesis of elements: a functionalist approach to scripture, rule theory of doctrine, dialectical recasting of doctrine, and critical exegetical and hermeneutical correctives. To the extent that the model succeeds in doing so, it sustains, I would argue, the focal values associated with these three movements. A well-rounded hermeneutic thus contributes to a theology attempting to nurture the values of solidarity, normative redescription and fully critical reflection.

Theologically reading the Bible as the church's book requires a method which is designed to cultivate continuity within and among Christian communities as well as with the tradition's past, especially its founding witnesses in scripture. A contextually flexible continuity within or among communities becomes intelligible when construing the doctrinal interpretive framework regulatively so that diverse reading practices can be seen as unified under compatible grammars. Continuity with the past is fostered with a dialectical hermeneutic between present and past readings that weights the contextual reading practices encoded in scripture. This weighted past-present dialectic privileges Christianity's canonical text without downplaying contextual appropriations of the gospel by present-day communities. Because this approach requires the theologian to attend to how grammars are encoded in contextually different communal uses of scripture, it endorses the postliberal focal value of normative (thick) description.

A regulative approach requires an impulse of plurality to prevent the interpretive framework (that informs how scripture is read) from

---

[101] George Lindbeck, "The Story-Shaped Church: Critical Exegesis and Theological Interpretation" in Green, ed., *Scriptural Authority*, p. 174.

becoming rigid or narrow. Dialectically recasting theology's regulative framework prevents the theologian's doctrinal approximations of the deep grammar from becoming rigidly entrenched when eschatological provisoes prove insufficient. A weighted dialectical method, which sets marginalized readings preferentially in opposition to dominant mainstream readings, widens the potential *consensus fidelium* and works against tendencies to overlook difference and otherness. This nurtures the liberationist focal value of solidarity with the oppressed. A functionalist approach also works to instantiate the impulse of plurality because grounding the plain sense of scripture in communal use allows for diverse, contextually determined normativity throughout the global church.

The impulse of critique is instantiated by the comprehensive use of nontheological critical tools (historical criticism, hermeneutics of suspicion, etc.) as mediations in the process of doctrinal recasting and as correctives for scriptural reading practices. Using these critical tools reenforces the value of theology as fully critical reflection. But like any critical background theory, these tools themselves must be subject to scrutiny, because even a corrective theory is grounded in its own ideological historicity. When interpreting scripture, critical tools are used but not in an uncritical or frivolously deconstructive way.

Reading the Bible theologically as the church's book involves entering a hermeneutical circle in which reading practices are informed by the community's regulative framework, and the framework itself is reinforced by communal readings of scripture. This circle should not be kept hermetically closed any more than a reflective equilibrium should be kept narrow. (Moreover, Taylor's point about books and texts is apropos here: like the book, the hermeneutical circle always includes the other that it struggles to exclude.) When all the above-mentioned impulses and methodological elements are synthesized into a single hermeneutical approach, one can envision productive, critical, dialectical interplay between regulative framework and plain sense, professional theologian and competent lay speaker, past and present, dominant tradition and marginalized voices. This dynamism prevents the hermeneutical helix of scriptural interpretation from collapsing into a vicious, closed circle. Without this synthesis, the impulse of plurality can become a hermeneutical spiral out of control; continuity can be reduced to shoring up the walls of dominant theology; and critique can become nothing more than intellectual play for those who have the leisure and power to find fault with a book countless believers live by.

What I believe is a strength of this model may appear to some as a weakness: as a heuristic model, it does not assert a transcommunal Christian norm for appropriateness. It privileges no historically reconstructed canon within the canon, no hermeneutically constructed working canon, no historically dominant plain sense – but only specifies impulses and weighted dialectics. Any full-bodied constructive theology requires a relatively adequate material norm for appropriateness, but it is also important to situate that material norm within the ongoing traditioning process, as envisioned, for example, by this regulative-dialectical model. Some theologians will also object to what may be perceived as an accommodation to the poststructuralist milieu of open texts, and they may conclude that this model promotes an unduly relativistic hermeneutical approach. It is true that I wish to take seriously the concerns of poststructuralism – but only as a critical background theory (among others) which unmasks potentially hegemonic appeals to definitive material norms – whether based on historical-criticism, theories of textual meaning, or ecclesial precedent. I do not see this model as causing debilitating relativism but as opening up opportunities to cultivate creative contextualized fidelity to scripture and tradition. This open-endedness is not a playful postmodern luxury but a necessity. Even Tracy, for all his advocacy of the foundational realistic reading of the passion concedes that "[e]very Christian theological hermeneutic today – no matter how powerful and believable its retrievals of its authoritative passion narratives . . . must now endure as not merely unfinished but as broken."[102]

In a time of brokenness (in the biblical sense of the seed needing to die in order to bear fruit and the deconstructive sense of breaking open and disseminating), we will need to be clear about our values and be open to the helical traditioning process. It may turn out that the traditional plain sense will, after all is said and done, stretch (to use Frei's metaphor) and not break. Whatever the case may be, we need to limn changes in the *sensus fidelium* which requires something more than well-oiled theory and method. All the theologians I have drawn from in this chapter would agree that an adequate theology today needs

---

[102] Tracy, *Dialogue*, p. 121.

what Boff calls a "hermeneutical *habitus*," in the Aristotelian sense of a character-forming "art."[103] Lindbeck calls for "a complex set of un-formalizable skills" and Tracy speaks of the "natural hermeneutical competence" of those willing to risk being confronted by the biblical classic – especially its prophetic word.[104] For the theologian, this *habitus* or set of skills or competence is a disciplined art, to be sure. It entails among other things: "the toil of exegesis, the inquiries of history, and the investigations of Christian fonts"; the use of the often "clumsy directives" of regulative doctrines which, nonetheless, are "preferable to uninspired and unreflected prejudices"; a relentless "hermeneutics of trust" in, as well as suspicion toward, the tradition.[105]

When interpretation is seen in these terms, the goal of reading scrip-ture becomes pedagogical. Boff speaks for all these theologians when he takes this notion of hermeneutical pedagogy in a christological direction. He states that acquiring a hermeneutical habitus has "the purpose of forming in the community the *nous Christou* (1 Cor. 2:16)."[106] A Christian dogmatics would explicate the wide reflective equilibrium nature of this christological pedagogy. For my purposes here, however, I have made a more modest proposal for an approach to scripture and tradition which endeavors to cultivate a hermeneutical *habitus* by implementing the impulses of plurality, continuity and critique when reading scripture theologically as the church's book. For the theologian, cultivating a hermeneutical *habitus* is one thing; hammering out a con-sensus in a diverse and often contentious global Christian community of discourse is another. In the chapter which follows, I will test my belief that rule theory can be used to adjudicate between differing plain senses and that voices from the margins can fruitfully be brought into dialectical conversation with first-world theology.

103 Boff, *Theology and Praxis*, pp. 152, 303 n. 86.
104 Lindbeck, *Nature of Doctrine*, p. 123; Tracy, *Plurality and Ambiguity*, p. 103.
105 Boff, *Theology and Praxis*, p. 152; Lindbeck, *Nature of Doctrine*, p. 79; Tracy, *Plurality and Ambiguity*, p. 112.
106 Boff, *Theology and Praxis*, p. 152. See Lindbeck's emphasis on christological "connatural knowl-edge" and the pedagogy of catechesis (*Nature of Doctrine*, pp. 36, 132ff.) and Tracy's discussion of Christian "training of the soul" ("Can Virtue Be Taught? Education, Character, and the Soul," *Theological Education*, suppl. 1 [1988], p. 51). It is beyond the scope of this essay to expli-cate the possible christological connections or underpinnings of the hermeneutical model I am proposing. Suffice it to say that I believe the theological focal values I am endeavoring to pro-mote throughout this text and in this hermeneutical model would also be vital components of a christology for our contemporary culture.

CHAPTER FIVE

Pursuing doctrinal common ground

The previous chapter proposes that a regulative approach to doctrine provides an effective way of identifying Christian intercommunal continuity. In this chapter, I will test that proposal by using rule theory to adjudicate between two specific constructive theological proposals which are apparently at a doctrinal impasse. This issue brings us to the perimeter of the methodological territory within which I have been moving in this book. Traversing those borders is highly appropriate because it allows us to get a sense of how the kinds of methodological issues discussed so far can have a positive impact on clarifying actual doctrinal disputes. Specifically, I will focus on Stanley Hauerwas's criticisms of Gutiérrez's concept of liberation. There are two reasons why it is illuminating to recast this postliberal–liberation theological debate. First, his critique of Gutiérrez seems to have left the impression that there are few points of significant doctrinal common ground between the two movements. This impression merits serious review in light of the way postliberal theology has evolved in the years following the publication of Lindbeck's *The Nature of Doctrine* and in light of the intermovement methodological compatibilities we have seen in previous chapters.[1] It is not a stretch of the imagination to envision constructive theological exchange between postliberals and liberationists holding promise for both – even assuming that materially different theological formulations will arise due, in part, to their involvement with such different socio-religious contexts. Second, since liberation theology's widening

---

[1] Stanley Hauerwas, "Some Theological Reflections on Gutierrez's Use of 'Liberation' as a Theological Concept," *Modern Theology* 3 (1986), pp. 67–76. George A. Lindbeck, *The Nature of Doctrine: Religion and Theology in a Postliberal Age* (Philadelphia: Westminster, 1984). An earlier version of this chapter appears in David G. Kamitsuka, "Salvation, Liberation and Christian Character Formation: Postliberal and Liberation Theologians in Dialogue," *Modern Theology* 13 (1997), pp. 171–89.

dissemination in North Atlantic theological and ecclesial circles in the past decade, it has been the subject of numerous critical evaluations, which Hauerwas's views to some extent reflect. These critiques range from collegial correction (I would place Hauerwas here) to thoroughgoing indictment of liberation theology on the relationship between salvation and socio-political liberation. Hence, addressing a postliberal version of this critique responds to a large segment of North Atlantic opinion of liberation theology, generally, and Gutiérrez, specifically.

An underlying concern of *The Nature of Doctrine* (as noted in chapter four) is to promote ecumenical dialogue, and this concern often marks the work of those theologians who associate themselves with Lindbeck's book. A case in point is Hauerwas who writes that he wants "to be the kind of performer Lindbeck describes" in *The Nature of Doctrine.*[2] Hauerwas makes good on his commitment to intra-Christian theological dialogue in his essay on Gutiérrez. This North American postliberal theological entree into conversation with a Latin American liberation theologian is noteworthy on two grounds. It is noteworthy because it marks a promising turn in what previously had been noticeably sparse in-depth postliberal–liberation theological interchange. (The important exception would be George Hunsinger's 1983 essay, "Karl Barth and Liberation Theology," which I will discuss below.)[3] Less promising, however, is that Hauerwas's robustly critical reflection on Gutiérrez's theological project lacks attention to a regulative doctrinal perspective – which is at the heart of Lindbeck's methodological proposal. Lindbeck argues that ecumenical discussions have been hindered by the lack of "adequate categories" to account for "doctrinal reconciliation without doctrinal change" and rule theory is designed to supply that lack.[4] By attending to the regulative principles informing Gutiérrez's writings, I believe we can go far in establishing a firm theological basis for ecumenical dialogue between liberation theologians such as Gutiérrez and postliberals such as Hauerwas. Moreover, reading Gutiérrez in light of a rule theory of doctrine would allow Hauerwas to voice his theological criticisms without obscuring

[2] Stanley Hauerwas, *Against the Nations: War and Survival in a Liberal Society* (Minneapolis: Winston, 1985), p. 1.

[3] *Journal of Religion* 63 (1983), pp. 247–63.

[4] Lindbeck, *Nature of Doctrine*, pp. 7, 15. For Hauerwas's more recent approving remarks on Lindbeck's rule theory, see Stanley Hauerwas, *In Good Company: The Church as Polis* (University of Notre Dame Press, 1995), p. 220 n. 19.

the grammatical compatibilities he might find with Gutiérrez (and the same applies to any other critic). To make my case, I will argue that Hauerwas's objections, although implicitly informed by some valid regulative principles and perhaps even partially justified at the time, nevertheless, are largely misplaced vis-à-vis Gutiérrez's writings as a whole today. Certainly, real and substantive theological differences exist between postliberal and liberation theologians; however, I will offer a reading of Gutiérrez that militates against Hauerwas's charge that Gutiérrez may have, "perhaps unwittingly, underwritten a sense of liberation at odds with the Gospel."[5] Once a regulative doctrinal basis for discussion of theological differences and compatibilities is established, further conversation can more easily proceed on any number of intermovement subjects. To illustrate, this chapter will include discussion of a closely related issue of vital concern to both postliberals and liberationists – the cultivation of appropriate Christian character. I wish to suggest that despite contextual differences, one can identify a doctrinal continuity and even pastoral complementarity in Hauerwas's and Gutiérrez's theological proposals for how to resist the spiritual and practical deformations that can occur in the Christian life. This is only one possible topic for postliberal–liberation theological dialogue, but it represents well how productive conversation could unfold not only between these two movements but in any intercommunal setting where rule theory is used.

While I will focus on Hauerwas's criticisms of Gutiérrez in his 1986 article, my intention is not to assess the status of that conversation alone. A more far-sighted procedure would be to begin with this essay and then to draw from other writings by Hauerwas and Gutiérrez (as well as Hunsinger's essay on Gutiérrez). This will allow me to demonstrate more definitively how Gutiérrez may currently be read in terms of rule theory and to provide a fuller picture of how some of Hauerwas's and Gutiérrez's pastorally oriented theological insights are related to the specific issue of Christian character formation. This procedure seems all the more appropriate since it might further productive theological dialogue not only between postliberal and liberation theologians but between the latter and their broader North Atlantic theological readership.

[5] Hauerwas, "Gutierrez's Use," p. 69.

A REGULATIVE ANALYSIS OF LIBERATION

One of Hauerwas's charges is that Gutiérrez's "account of liberation sounds far more like that of Kant and the Enlightenment than it does of the Kingdom established by Christ."[6] He hears in Gutiérrez's call for freedom "'from all servitude'" and for becoming "'artisans of our own destiny,'"[7] echoes of Kant's motto "'Have courage to use your own reason!'" Hauerwas questions whether Gutiérrez, "in the name of the salvation offered by Christ," has not thereby "underwritten an account of liberation that is profoundly anti-Christian."[8] If Hauerwas's language is unusually strong, it may be noted that this sort of criticism is neither new to him nor restricted to liberation theology. This criticism must be understood in light of a larger general argument he has sustained over the years against what he judges to be a Kantianism in which morality is freed from its historical communal moorings and universalized into a kind of "secularized version of Christian hope."[9] In his essay on Gutiérrez, Hauerwas quotes Iris Murdoch's critique of Enlightenment understandings of freedom exemplified by the "'Kantian man-God ... free, independent, lonely, powerful, rational ...'" He then asserts that Gutiérrez's liberation "rhetoric does not sufficiently guard against" Enlightenment understandings such as these. When a possibly Kantian-influenced "metaphor of liberation determines and controls all other ways of understanding the Christian life," then, Hauerwas fears, Christian life "can be distorted."[10]

---

[6] Ibid.

[7] Ibid.; Hauerwas is quoting the original 1973 edition of Gustavo Gutiérrez's *A Theology of Liberation: History, Politics and Salvation*, tr. and ed. Sister Caridad Inda and John Eagleson (Maryknoll: Orbis, 1973), p. 91. All my citations will be from the revised 1988 edition unless otherwise noted.

[8] Hauerwas, "Gutierrez's Use," p. 69. Elsewhere Hauerwas softens this by saying "underwritten an account of liberation that is oddly individualistic." Stanley Hauerwas, *After Christendom? How the Church Is to Behave If Freedom, Justice, and a Christian Nation Are Bad Ideas* (Nashville: Abingdon, 1991), p. 52. Despite this change, however, Hauerwas does not indicate whether he now wishes to retract his earlier charge. He clarifies that his concentration in *After Christendom?* on the first edition of *A Theology of Liberation* is not meant "to suggest [that] this is still the same position Gutiérrez holds"; nonetheless, he does not believe that Gutiérrez's later work "necessarily solves the problems" he finds in the 1973 text (Hauerwas, *After Christendom*, pp. 50–51; 173 n. 14). Hopefully this essay can put some of those "problems" into a new (regulative doctrinal) light.

[9] Stanley Hauerwas, *A Community of Character: Toward a Constructive Christian Social Ethic* (University of Notre Dame Press, 1981), p. 100.

[10] Hauerwas, "Gutierrez's Use," p. 70. In *After Christendom?* Hauerwas states that "Gutiérrez's rhetoric invites just that [Kantian] kind of interpretation ... Why rely on the church when you can depend on the courage of Kant?" (p. 55).

While Hauerwas agrees with Gutiérrez's emphasis on the "close relation between liberation as a theological concept and liberation as a social and political concept," he questions the appropriateness of Gutiérrez's description of the three levels of liberation. Hauerwas quotes a passage from *A Theology of Liberation* which describes these three levels: "'political liberation, the liberation of man throughout history, liberation from sin and admission to communion with God. These three levels mutually effect each other, but they are not the same.'"[11] He is troubled by the implication that the theological meaning of liberation from sin will be "translated into or identified with the liberation desired and sought" in the political sphere, with the result of "simply underwriting or approving of such [political] struggles in the name of 'liberation.'" Such a strategy, he argues, is unsuitable for instilling Christian-specific social relations because it places the hermeneutical locus for meaning outside the church and its scripture. The implication is that under the tutelage of Gutiérrez's three-level view of liberation, Christians will lose their "necessary [ecclesially and biblically rooted] paradigm" for Christian freedom.[12]

Hauerwas's presentation is a mix of various other criticisms, but I will focus on what I take to be his primary theological worries regarding Gutiérrez and suggest the extent to which I think Gutiérrez's theology, when read regulatively, has the resources to offset those worries.[13] Although Hauerwas exhibits a great concern about the Kantian overtones in Gutiérrez's rhetoric of persons as artisans of their own destiny, I do not think this need be a serious ongoing concern for postliberals for two reasons: first, in Gutiérrez's theology, the primary interlocutor is not the secular "Kantian man-God" but the

---

11 Hauerwas, "Gutierrez's Use," pp. 75, 68. Hauerwas's citation, of which I have reproduced part, is not strictly accurate and does not flag the error in Gutiérrez's original. See Gutiérrez, *Theology of Liberation* (1973), pp. 176–77. Gutiérrez's 1988 revised edition corrects the noninclusive language and other infelicities of the original 1973 edition. Hauerwas's *After Christendom?* reproduces Hauerwas's citation as it appears in his 1986 article (p. 51).

12 Hauerwas, "Gutierrez's Use," pp. 75, 76. See also Stanley Hauerwas, "The Church as God's New Language" in *Scriptural Authority and Narrative Interpretation*, ed. Garrett Green (Philadelphia: Fortress, 1987), pp. 179–98.

13 Hauerwas includes in his theological assessment of Gutiérrez's concept of liberation a critique of how that concept is used as a "single term of social analysis" ("Gutierrez's Use," p. 72). I only touched on Gutiérrez's much more nuanced view on this subject in ch. 1. In all fairness, however, Gutiérrez's most detailed exposition in English postdates Hauerwas's article. See Gustavo Gutiérrez, "Theology and the Social Sciences" in his *The Truth Shall Make You Free: Confrontations*, tr. Matthew J. O'Connell (Maryknoll: Orbis, 1990), pp. 53–84.

pious, oppressed "nonperson"; not the Enlightenment subject but sub-jugated populations.[14] In this context, the language of artisan of one's own destiny probably does not entail the kind of secularized self-sufficiency which Hauerwas associates with Kant. Second, while Gutiérrez stands by his concern for the oppressed, he has largely abandoned the rhetoric of artisan of one's destiny in his more recent writings.[15]

Hauerwas nonetheless raises a valid question when he states that part of the theological task "must be to try to find other images as com-pelling as liberation to depict the salvation we believe accomplished in Christ."[16] In this remark he may be read as expressing an important theological concern about privileging a single metaphor to describe Christian salvation. Historically theologians have endeavored to include a variety of metaphors for salvation – not always harmonizing them, but finding it theologically and pastorally valuable to retain a cluster of metaphors to describe what overcomes the ills of the human predica-ment. For example, metaphors of ransom or liberation have been used to address human captivity to evil. Metaphors of reconciliation or sat-isfaction have been used to address guilt for evils undertaken. Metaphors of moral influence have been used to address culpability due to sloth. A host of contemporary christological and soteriological formulations complement, reject or revise these classic families of metaphorical depictions of salvation. But whether the christology and soteriology are classic or contemporary, theological wisdom seems to suggest that appealing to a single metaphor to the exclusion of all others cannot adequately address the full spectrum of human sin and how it is over-come.[17] Hence, the question to which Hauerwas alludes remains. Is

---

[14] Gustavo Gutiérrez, "Theology from the Underside of History" in his *The Power of the Poor in History*, tr. Robert R. Barr (Maryknoll: Orbis, 1983), p. 193.

[15] A recent passing reference Gutiérrez makes to the poor gradually becoming "active agents of their own destiny" is the only exception of which I am aware. However, it is clear in this con-text that Gutiérrez has the "nonperson" not the "Kantian man-God" in mind. Gustavo Gutiérrez, "Option for the Poor," tr. Robert R. Barr, *Mysterium Liberationis: Fundamental Concepts of Liberation Theology*, ed. Ignacio Ellacuría, S.J., and Jon Sobrino, S.J. (Maryknoll: Orbis, 1993), p. 236.

[16] Hauerwas, "Gutierrez's Use," p. 71.

[17] For further comments on how to think theologically about evil, see David H. Kelsey, "Struggling Collegially to Think about Evil: An Interpretive Essay," *Occasional Papers*, The Institute for Ecumenical and Cultural Research, no. 16 (Sept. 1981). Two articles by Michael Root address these issues as well: "Images of Liberation: Justin, Jesus and the Jews," *Thomist* 48 (1984), pp. 512–34 and "Dying He Lives: Biblical Image, Biblical Narrative and the Redemptive Jesus," *Semeia* 30 (1985), pp. 155–69.

"liberation," as a central organizing theological concept, supple and inclusive enough to address adequately the range of ways in which the Christian tradition has wanted and would continue to want to speak of the evil that marks the human condition? In works subsequent to *A Theology of Liberation*, Gutiérrez has made preliminary inroads into the nuances of how the metaphor of liberation addresses the human condition of evil undergone and undertaken. I would suspect that for any fully developed soteriological and christological discussion he may undertake in the future, he would eventually wish to reach beyond the liberation metaphor to include others as well.[18]

The theological issue which I take to be at the heart of Hauerwas's concerns about Gutiérrez's theology has to do with the structure through which Gutiérrez makes the concept of liberation doctrinally central – that is, the three-level view of integral liberation. My surmise is that Hauerwas considers that Gutiérrez is unsuccessful in his attempt to depict the levels of liberation as a "'unity, without confusion.'"[19] He prefaces his discussion of Gutiérrez with a reference to those who assert "that liberation is equivalent to the notion of salvation," and he wonders whether the metaphor of "levels" adequately distinguishes between the forms of liberation.[20] He elsewhere also criticizes liberation theology for its tendency "to confuse political freedom with that offered by Christ."[21] The gist of Hauerwas's theological concerns about the levels of liberation seems to be that salvation and socio-political liberation will be conflated.

This worry is shared by other postliberal theologians, even those who have voiced an appreciation of Gutiérrez's contributions to theology. In his comparative essay on Gutiérrez and Karl Barth, Hunsinger illustrates in a more doctrinally specific manner the general concern to which Hauerwas alludes in his essay on Gutiérrez.[22] Noting some of

18 See Gustavo Gutiérrez, *We Drink from Our Own Wells: The Spiritual Journey of a People*, tr. Matthew J. O'Connell (Maryknoll: Orbis, 1984), ch. 4.
19 Hauerwas, "Gutierrez's Use," p. 71; in italics in the text. Hauerwas is quoting from Gutiérrez, *Theology of Liberation* (1973), p. x.
20 Hauerwas, "Gutierrez's Use," pp. 67, 75.
21 Stanley Hauerwas, *Truthfulness and Tragedy: Further Investigations into Christian Ethics* (University of Notre Dame Press, 1977), p. 233 n. 1.
22 I think Hunsinger is right in suggesting that Gutiérrez and Barth (along with those postliberals who are sympathetic with aspects of Barth's theological vision) "share too much common ground and have too much to learn from one another to allow them each to go unchanged their separate ways" ("Karl Barth and Liberation," pp. 259–60).

the particular doctrinal weaknesses Hunsinger observes in Gutiérrez's theology will help concretize our discussion of whether or not Gutiérrez risks confusing or conflating socio-political liberation and salvation. One doctrinal weakness he notes is that Gutiérrez does not ground the praxis of liberation in "the fact that God alone in divine righteousness procures right for us." The implication is that Gutiérrez's theology is marked by a confusion over priorities: the priority proper to "the divine indicative" about God's saving grace in relation to "the human imperative" to liberate the oppressed.[23] Second, there is a tendency "to define love for God almost exclusively in terms of neighbor-love." Hunsinger remarks that José Míguez Bonino faults some liberation theology for a kind of "monism" which results "when love for God collapses into neighbor-love." What can ensue is a third problem: "deifying history or humanity."[24] Although these problematic tendencies stem from a biblically valid passion to combat injustice and liberate the oppressed, there is the risk (to which Hunsinger judges Gutiérrez may at times succumb) of losing "sight of the great and decisive dialectic between God's grace and human sin" which in the Bible is "comprehensive and all-encompassing," embracing within it the "lesser dialectic of liberation and oppression." Put succinctly, Gutiérrez risks losing the ability "to differentiate liberation from salvation."[25]

I would argue that this critique is misplaced regarding Gutiérrez, but postliberals are not alone in raising this concern. Indeed, North Atlantic theological opinion regarding Latin American liberation theological views on salvation and liberation tends significantly to the same conclusion: liberation theology to some degree conflates salvation and liberation. It is beyond the scope of this chapter to survey comprehensively this opinion, but it puts this postliberal–liberation theological conversation into perspective to see where postliberal concerns fall in the spectrum of North Atlantic critiques of liberation theology on this issue. The critiques fall into roughly two kinds. Some theologians fault Latin American liberation theology (often in reference to

---

[23] Ibid., p. 259. Hunsinger's point is that Barth's theology exemplifies the first aspect and Gutiérrez's the second. I have reservations about this characterization of Gutiérrez's theology which would require too long an excursus on the development of his theology to explain. What follows will hopefully give some sense of how I read Gutiérrez as giving proper priority to "the divine indicative."

[24] Ibid., p. 261.

[25] Ibid., pp. 258–59, 261.

Gutiérrez specifically) for failing to clarify adequately the relationship between liberation and salvation. For Arthur McGovern, it is an issue of the need to give equal time to each topic.[26] Ogden claims that "liberation theologies typically tend to confuse – or do not adequately distinguish – two essentially different, though closely related forms of liberation": redemption from sin and emancipation from bondage.[27] Many others echo the idea that while liberation theology contributes positively to unmasking politically complacent theology, liberationists tend to conflate or risk confusing political projects of liberation and God's project of liberating humankind from sin.[28] I would include Hauerwas's and Hunsinger's concerns in this group.

The second type of North Atlantic critique entails a much more thoroughgoing indictment of the claims or implications of Latin American liberation theology. Most prominent among this type of critique have been the official observations made by the Vatican's Congregation for the Doctrine of the Faith against the supposed Marxist "seductiveness of the theology of Gustavo Gutiérrez," who is seen by certain officials in Rome as promoting the views that "liberation means political liberation" and "there is no sin except 'social sin.'"[29] Dennis McCann sees this problem as having deep structural roots: Gutiérrez's "failure to clarify the theological relationship between 'liberation' and 'salvation'" stems from the fact that his theology "possesses no theoretical resources for distinguishing religious transcendence from political enthusiasm."[30] John Milbank's more recent version of this critique is succinct but scathing: "in making the

---

26 "For example, Gutiérrez speaks of three levels of liberation but the first half of *A Theology of Liberation* deals almost exclusively with the issue of socio-political emancipation and most of the discussion about liberation from sin deals with eliminating unjust structures caused by sin." Arthur F. McGovern, *Liberation Theology and Its Critics: Toward an Assessment* (Maryknoll: Orbis, 1989), p. 82.

27 Schubert M. Ogden, *Faith and Freedom: Toward a Theology of Liberation*, rev. ed. (Nashville: Abingdon, 1989), p. 33. Ogden adds the qualification that any treatment of emancipation should also address any overt or implicit anthropocentrism (see pp. 106ff.). Latin American liberation theologians are only beginning to address this issue. See Leonardo Boff, *Ecology and Liberation: A New Paradigm*, tr. John Cumming (Maryknoll: Orbis, 1995).

28 See, for example, Craig L. Nessan's overview in his *Orthopraxis or Heresy: The North American Theological Response to Latin American Liberation Theology* (Atlanta: Scholars, 1989), esp. pp. 276ff., 303ff., 398ff.

29 The Congregation for the Doctrine of the Faith, "Ten Observations on the Theology of Gustavo Gutiérrez" (March 1983) in *Liberation Theology: A Documentary History*, ed. and tr. Alfred T. Hennelly, S.J. (Maryknoll: Orbis, 1990), p. 349.

30 Dennis P. McCann, *Christian Realism and Liberation Theology* (Maryknoll: Orbis, 1981), p. 4.

merely algebraic equation, liberation = salvation, they [political and liberation theologians] still celebrate a hidden working of divine design through purely immanent processes."[31] Many of the criticisms in this category have been challenged by liberation theology's defenders. Karl Rahner, just shortly before his death, vigorously defended Gutiérrez's orthodoxy and protested any condemnation of his theology.[32] Matthew Lamb argues that McCann distorts Gutiérrez's "dynamic distinctions between liberation and salvation."[33] Nicholas Lash finds the above quote by Milbank to be "not only false but tasteless" in light of "so many deaths, of such bereavement and imprisonment, and of so much patient suffering generously sustained in peaceful struggle."[34] In what follows, I add a very particular defense of Gutiérrez against the postliberal concerns described above. I will argue that one can find in Gutiérrez's writings responses to the worry that his liberation theology may, in the various ways articulated by Hunsinger, tend to conflate salvation and liberation.[35] By implication, this argument addresses indirectly the widespread North Atlantic mood of dissatisfaction with and even, occasionally, incrimination of liberation theology on this point.

Gutiérrez would agree that distinguishing between the forms of liberation is a crucial pastoral and theological concern. He has recently explained that, in his original presentation of the levels of liberation, he was invoking the classic theological principle which emerged from the Council of Chalcedon's resolution of the debates about Christ's two natures. He retrieved from Chalcedon's creedal formulation the principle "unity without confusion" or "distinct but neither confused nor separated" which he used to rule his own construal of the levels of liberation.[36] What holds together the levels of liberation theologically

[31] John Milbank, *Theology and Social Theory: Beyond Secular Reason* (Oxford and Cambridge, Mass.: Blackwell, 1993), p. 245; cf. p. 248.
[32] See Karl Rahner, S.J., "Letter to Cardinal Juan Landázuri Ricketts of Lima, Peru" (March 16, 1984) in Hennelly, ed., *Liberation Theology*, pp. 351–52.
[33] Matthew L. Lamb, "A Distorted Interpretation of Latin American Liberation Theology," *Horizons* 8 (1981), p. 358. McCann seems to have changed some of his previous critical opinions of Gutiérrez, based on what he finds in the new introduction to the 15th-anniversary edition of *A Theology of Liberation* (1988). See Dennis P. McCann, "The Developing Gutiérrez," *Commonweal* (Nov. 4, 1988), pp. 594–95. However, Lamb's critique of McCann's reading of liberation theology still stands.
[34] Nicholas Lash, "Not Exactly Politics or Power," *Modern Theology* 8 (1992), p. 357.
[35] In addressing this question, I will make reference to texts by Gutiérrez which postdate Hunsinger's essay since, it should be again noted, my intention is to investigate how postliberals and others should read Gutiérrez today.
[36] Gutiérrez, *Truth*, p. 122.

is that they share the same, ultimately eschatological, goal: "complete communion of human beings with God and among themselves." What distinguishes the levels of liberation is that they do not follow "parallel" or "convergent" roads in history.[37] Gutiérrez describes the first level, "political liberation," as comprising the socio-economic structural transformations needed for equitable collective human activity. Although structural social change is imperative, he emphasizes that it is not enough for human flourishing. Change on the personal, human level is needed as well. Liberation at the second level entails the transformation of human consciousness – specifically, awareness of one's freedom and responsibility to participate in the historical process of building a just society. Gutiérrez calls this level "human liberation throughout history." If the first level addresses external structural pressures upon the human person, the second level addresses the ideological and psychological factors contributing to human alienation. The third and deepest level of liberation is expressed traditionally as the radical "transition from sin to grace, from death to life" which Christ effects. Christ's "liberating gift" of redemption is the "ultimate precondition" for liberation at the other levels.[38] As Gutiérrez has written more recently, this "soteriological liberation" is the "dominant theme in liberation theology" because sin is "the ultimate root of all disruption of friendship and of all injustice and oppression." Any meaningful understanding of liberation must address sin as the willful rejection of God and neighbor and not just in its "derived and secondary sense" of the structures of "social sin."[39] Hence, genuine political and historical liberation may never be characterized as "all of salvation" or even as eventually convergent with salvation.[40] An adequate liberation theology must insist that salvation involves more than events of human emancipation on either a political or personal plane; it requires the gift of communion with God.

But while it is one thing to state a distinction between salvation and socio-political liberation, it is another thing to have in place a web of

[37] Gutiérrez, *Theology of Liberation*, p. 104. For a particularly insightful discussion of how Gutiérrez's treatment of the levels of liberation compares and contrasts with other influential modern Roman Catholic positions (especially Jacques Maritain and Karl Rahner), see Dean Brackley, *Divine Revolution: Salvation and Liberation in Catholic Thought* (Maryknoll: Orbis, 1996).

[38] Gutiérrez, *Theology of Liberation*, p. 103; cf. pp. 24, 25.

[39] Gutiérrez, *Truth*, pp. 135, 136, 137. See also *Theology of Liberation*, p. 226 n. 101.

[40] Gutiérrez, *Theology of Liberation*, p. 104.

regulative principles which can adequately reenforce that stated distinction. Discerning whether Gutiérrez employs regulative principles with this effect takes hermeneutical effort, since he does not couch his theology in terms of that conceptuality. Nevertheless, three of his core theological themes – namely, the church's preferential option for the poor, love of God and neighbor, and God's redemptive activity in history – can be read regulatively as preventing theological reductionism. Lingering concerns that Gutiérrez unwittingly conflates salvation with social and political liberation can be dispelled, I would argue, by demonstrating that the grammar or web of regulative principles informing his theological treatment of these themes serves to reenforce his portrayal of the various aspects of liberation as a unity without confusion.

The theme of the church's preferential option for the poor is one which might lead many readers of Gutiérrez to conclude that he has made himself vulnerable to the charge of not grounding the human imperative of liberating praxis in the divine indicative of God's saving righteousness (the first of Hunsinger's worries mentioned above).[41] However, upon closer examination, one finds in his explication of the theme of the preferential option for the poor, not a tendency toward a liberation–salvation conflation, but one of his most explicit regulative principles regarding the prevenience of God's grace – a principle which reenforces the priority proper to what Hunsinger calls the divine indicative. Gutiérrez does understand the preferential option for the poor as a statement about the church's responsibility to respond to the plight of the poor. More basically, however, it is a statement about how to think theologically in a context of oppression. Specifically, the church's preferential concern for the poor expressed in liberating praxis must be grounded in God's prevenient and gratuitous love for the poor. There is nothing in the poor spiritually or morally which merits preferential favor by God. God's special love for the poor is "not because the poor are good, or better than others, but just because they are poor." A biblical warrant, Gutiérrez suggests, for this view may be found in the beatitudes which "have in the first instance a *theological* character:

---

[41] The formula "preferential option for the poor" emerged into prominence in contemporary Roman Catholic circles especially at the Puebla Latin American Episcopal Conference (1979). See Gutiérrez, *Theology of Liberation*, p. xxvi. For Gutiérrez's most extensive discussion of the Puebla documents, see Gustavo Gutiérrez, "Liberation and the Poor: The Puebla Perspective" in his *Power of the Poor*, pp. 125–65.

they tell us who God is. Secondly, they are *anthropological*. That is, they emphasize the importance of spiritual dispositions in those who hear the word. These two aspects are ... complementary. But the theological aspect – the emphasis on God and his goodness toward the poor – is the primary."[42] The perspective Gutiérrez hopes to offset is one that follows from reading the Lukan blessing of the poor in an unnuanced manner via the Matthean blessing of the poor in spirit – a reading that could imply that God's preference shown to the poor will be based on their supposed ability to develop certain spiritual dispositions loved by God.[43]

God's goodness toward the poor is revealed in many ways but definitively in Christ who is *"God become poor."*[44] Christ's poverty should not be seen as a spiritual glorification of poverty but rather as a sign of God's "solidarity *with the poor* and ... a protest *against poverty*."[45] For this reason, Gutiérrez stresses that the church's commitment to work from the perspective of and in solidarity with the exploited and marginalized in Latin America must be first and foremost an expression of the desire to be faithful to "the mystery of God's revelation and the gratuitous gift of his kingdom of love and justice."[46] In other words, Gutiérrez certainly advocates the human imperative of the preferential option for the poor because of a concern for the liberation of the oppressed; however, he first theologically regulates that liberating praxis in terms of God's prevenient gratuitousness. The regulative principle one can glean from his views on the preferential option is that God's grace, not human needs or merit, has priority as the determining factor for the church's activity in the world. Hence the attempts Christians make to

---

[42] Gutiérrez, *Power of the Poor*, p. 140. See Gustavo Gutiérrez, *The God of Life*, tr. Matthew J. O'Connell (Maryknoll: Orbis, 1991), chs. 6, 7.

[43] See Gutiérrez, *Theology of Liberation*, pp. 170ff; *God of Life*, p. 132. Hauerwas seems to promote the very viewpoint Gutiérrez is opposing when he writes: "Among God's people the poor ... play a particularly prominent role ... Yet, it is not their poverty, not their oppression, nor their earthly powerlessness that make these persons paradigmatic citizens of God's kingdom; rather, their unencumbered reception of God's forgiveness and grace sets them apart as God's people" (*Against the Nations*, p. 116).

[44] Gustavo Gutiérrez, "God's Revelation and Proclamation in History" in his *Power of the Poor*, p. 13.

[45] Gutiérrez, *Theology of Liberation*, p. 172.

[46] Gutiérrez, *Power of the Poor*, p. 141. Gutiérrez details how the principle of the preferential option for the poor was advocated by Bartolomé de las Casas, the sixteenth-century Sevillian Dominican theologian and missionary, who championed the religious and political rights of the Indians against oppressive colonial attitudes and practices. Gustavo Gutiérrez, *Las Casas: In Search of the Poor of Jesus Christ*, tr. Robert R. Barr (Maryknoll: Orbis, 1993).

be in solidarity with the poor are meant to reflect (though always incompletely) the gratuitous solidarity with the poor of God in Christ. Thus, far from tending toward a liberation–salvation conflation, the notion of the preferential option for the poor may be read regulatively as instantiating the principle of the priority proper to God's saving grace.

A second doctrinal weakness Hunsinger identifies which could be a sign of a liberation–salvation conflation is the tendency to define love for God too exclusively in terms of neighbor love. Indeed, Gutiérrez stresses that love for God must not be spoken of as separate from solidarity with one's oppressed neighbor. Gutiérrez may be read as pushing the notion of "human mediation" of love for God to its limit, stretching the application of the Chalcedonian principle as well: "It is not enough to say that love of God is inseparable from the love of one's neighbor. It must be added that love for God is unavoidably expressed *through* love of one's neighbor."[47] Does this formulation represent a conflation of the two loves? I think not, especially when Gutiérrez's later writings are taken into account. However emphatic he is about the human mediation of love for God, he is equally emphatic that the two loves must be distinguished. He establishes the distinction by designating the correct ordering of their relation: a "true," "full" and "disinterested" love of neighbor "requires that we first experience the gratuitousness of God's love ... [O]ur relationship with God is a pre-condition for encounter and true communion with the other." The love of God in Christ, whose "free gift ... abounded for many" (Rom. 5:15), is the decisive, gratuitous condition for the possibility of the Christian's love for neighbor.[48] The regulative principle instantiated here is that one's relationship with God and one's relationship with one's neighbor must be distinguished but not separated – with the former being the condition for the latter and the latter being the unavoidable expression of the former. When Gutiérrez is read regulatively in this way, his theme of love for God and neighbor functions to prevent the conflation of God's salvific love for humanity in Christ and socio-political liberation. This rule establishes an orientation for seeing the Christian

[47] Gutiérrez, *Theology of Liberation*, pp. 114–15.
[48] Gutiérrez, *Our Own Wells*, pp. 112, 109. By "disinterested," Gutiérrez means a love that does not try to "impose an alien will" and which is "respectful" of the neighbor's own "needs and aspirations" (p. 112). This is vital because the neighbor is not to be seen as "an occasion, an instrument, for becoming closer to God" (*Theology of Liberation*, p. 116).

life not as simply a vertical relationship with God detached from a horizontal relationship with one's neighbor; rather the Christian life entails a cultivation of both relationships with a clear understanding of the nature of how they are related but distinct.

Another sign of a salvation–liberation conflation is the tendency to identify God's redemptive activity with some particular historical praxis of liberation. Does Gutiérrez speak of God as present in historical struggles for liberation in a way that (as Hunsinger worries) appears simply to identify divine action with those struggles, thus "deifying" some particular historical activity? If so, the risk of conflating salvation and liberation would seem unavoidable. Gutiérrez recognizes that God's relationship to history is an important issue for Latin American Christian communities actively involved in the process of social transformation. In order to address the issue of God's participation in and distinction from history, he appropriates regulative doctrinal resources found in classic treatments of divine transcendence and immanence. Gutiérrez has emphasized God's transcendence since early in his career, writing that the "God who reveals himself in history is a God irreducible to our manner of understanding him."[49] In a later publication, he strongly warns against any theological construction which "presumes to pigeonhole the divine action in history" and he is emphatic that "the mystery of God is not exhausted by its historical embodiment."[50] Although the Christian may trust that God will effectively bring to fulfillment the liberating activity God has begun, the doctrine of God's transcendence requires that one plead ignorance of how what happens historically will actually lead to that fulfillment.

Presumably, it is the way Gutiérrez speaks of God encountered in history, rather than simply some supposed insufficiency in his statements about God's transcendence, which might precipitate concerns about a possible deifying of history. He writes that "concrete history, is the place where God reveals the mystery of God's personhood," and the human struggle for liberation is seen as "a history in which the liberation of Christ is at work." These are the kinds of statements seemingly ripe for the charge of what Gutiérrez himself would call a "political

[49] Gutiérrez, *Power of the Poor*, p. 19.
[50] Gustavo Gutiérrez, *On Job: God-Talk and the Suffering of the Innocent*, tr. Matthew J. O'Connell (Maryknoll: Orbis, 1998), pp. 72, 17.

reductionism of the gospel."[51] He stands by these early statements but, aware of the kinds of reactions they have provoked in certain ecclesial and theological circles, has recently urged that formulations such as these "must not be taken out of their context" – the context being precisely "the irreducibility of God to history." Gutiérrez's recent discussions of the notion of God encountered in history have also endeavored to bring to light a dimension which was not emphasized in his earlier writings – that is, the hiddenness of God's immanence or presence in history. When he appeals to the biblical theme of "God as a hidden God" or when he characterizes "God's kingdom as inchoately present in history," he is not essentially deviating from his earlier formulations cited above about history as "the place where God reveals [Godself]." He is, however, emphasizing that even to the eyes of faith, God's presence in history is difficult to discern and probably most evident in the places where the church looks not often enough. Gutiérrez comments that the hiddenness of God was even in effect during the lifetime of Jesus, who made "himself present precisely through those who are 'absent' from history, those who are not invited to the banquet (see Lk. 14:15–24)."[52] The regulative principle undergirding these comments on transcendence and immanence is that the proper way to speak about God and history is that God's saving will cannot be identified with any particular historical praxis of liberation, but neither can the kingdom of God be spiritualized and relegated to a nonhistorical plane. One must instead speak of God as both acting immanently in history where liberating events unfold and as leading "this same history out beyond itself, to a fulness that transcends the scope of all human doing or telling."[53]

Taken together, the regulative principles at work in these three core themes (the preferential option for the poor, love for God and neighbor, and God's redemptive activity in history) bring a certain "joint logical pressure" (to use Lindbeck's phrase[54]) which guards against any

[51] Gustavo Gutiérrez, "Liberation Praxis and Christian Faith" in his *Power of the Poor*, pp. 52, 63, 68.

[52] Gutiérrez, *Truth*, pp. 180 n. 33, 157.

[53] Gutiérrez, *Power of the Poor*, p. 69. While I am discussing these theological notions in terms of rule theory, one cannot ignore the possible metaphysical implications entailed – especially regarding God and history. This is not the place to pursue this complex aspect of Gutiérrez's theology. For a brief discussion of Gutiérrez in this regard, see Peter C. Hodgson, *God in History: Shapes of Freedom* (Nashville: Abingdon, 1989), pp. 195–97.

[54] Lindbeck, *Nature of Doctrine*, p. 95.

conflation of God's salvific activity and human efforts for socio-political liberation. Indeed, Gutiérrez evinces as much concern as Hauerwas and Hunsinger on this point. Hence the worry that Gutiérrez unwittingly may tend to conflate liberation and salvation in a way that is at odds with the gospel appears unwarranted, especially when one takes into account a more expansive reading of his work in light of a rule theory of doctrine. If my identification of these regulative principles at work in Gutiérrez's theology is at all on the mark, then a significant obstacle to establishing productive, mutually critical dialogue between Gutiérrez and postliberal (and other) theologians on constructive theological issues has been removed. Moreover, ground will have been cleared to proceed with more clarity and theological subtlety to mutually beneficial contributions from liberation and postliberal theologians on issues such as Christian character formation.

CHRISTIAN CHARACTER FORMATION

Hauerwas's pastorally oriented theological concerns that Latin American liberation theology may be inadequate in fostering appropriate Christian character have been in evidence since the 1970s.[55] In his article on Gutiérrez (as noted above), Hauerwas worries that Christian communal life may be "distorted" by an "overriding" emphasis on an Enlightenment-influenced, secular concept of liberation. Hauerwas leaves the impression that those formed by such a view of liberation might make attaining socio-political liberation the norm of the Christian life, thus overlooking a more properly Christian type of freedom. In Pauline fashion, he stresses that freedom "is not an end in itself" but rather a "means in which it is made possible for us to serve one another." Freedom in Christ is freedom from being enslaved by "presuppositions and powers of the old world" and freedom for others which "comes by having our self-absorption challenged by the needs of others." Without a properly biblical understanding of this notion, there is a risk that liberation will be understood "not as a means to serve but as a means to dominate."[56] Hauerwas does not interpret Christian freedom in a privatistic way but approves of the connection liberation theology establishes between freedom in Christ and social justice. He writes that

[55] See Stanley Hauerwas, "The Politics of Charity" in his *Truthfulness and Tragedy*, pp. 132–43.
[56] Hauerwas, "Gutierrez's Use," pp. 70, 75.

Gutiérrez "is exactly right" in claiming that "the Kingdom brought by and through the ministry of Jesus fundamentally entails the establishment of a new order which ... is our salvation." Thus, his critique is not that liberation theology is wrong because it sees political aspects entailed in Jesus' preaching of the kingdom of God. Rather, Hauerwas seems to fear that Gutiérrez emphasizes aspects of political freedom in a way that distorts the biblical notion of "the freedom that we have as a gift from Christ [which] is of a very distinct kind."[57]

Gutiérrez is in accord with Hauerwas's Pauline point about Christian freedom being freedom from and freedom for. Gutiérrez explains that the biblical message of liberation is "not only that Christ liberated us" but that "he did it in order that we might be free ... to love." He has consistently promoted this biblically based view of freedom.[58] This general point of agreement notwithstanding, I suspect that Hauerwas is looking for and not finding in Gutiérrez's theology a pastorally oriented theological vision which would provide an overarching structure to combat actual distortions within the Christian life. For example, when Hauerwas advocates freedom from self-absorption and freedom for service to others, he has in mind the real temptations impinging on the church in a permissive, liberal capitalist society obsessed with the acquisition of power, material possessions and an understanding of freedom as self-actualization. He sees a direct connection between sin and this distorted understanding of freedom. Any "claim of freedom as a possession, as our achievement, is but a manifestation of our sin ... [which] is the assumption that we are the creators of the history through which we acquire and possess our character."[59] Furthermore, Hauerwas is also trying to counteract the pervasive mentality that just because a country like the United States has the power to use coercion to achieve a relative good, it is justified in doing so.[60] His principal focus is on getting first-world Christians to evaluate the self-deception that lies beneath their obsession with control: "When we say we want peace,

---

[57] Ibid., pp. 71, 75.

[58] Gutiérrez, *Theology of Liberation*, pp. 23–24; see *Truth*, p. 195 n. 124; *Our Own Wells*, p. 159 n. 1. For an extended discussion of the spiritual features which Gutiérrez associates with being "free to love," see *Our Own Wells*, esp. pt. 3.

[59] Stanley Hauerwas, *The Peaceable Kingdom: A Primer in Christian Ethics* (University of Notre Dame Press, 1983), p. 47.

[60] Ibid., p. 141. Hauerwas cites H. Richard Niebuhr's article "The Grace to Do Nothing" which addressed what he thought the US response should be to the 1932 Japanese invasion of Manchuria (see ch. 8).

we mean we want order," and we want to avoid any societal instability that might threaten an upwardly mobile American way of life. Instead of always striving for control, Hauerwas suggests (partly metaphorically and partly literally) an attitude of "[l]iving out of control."[61]

Here we arrive at a central feature of Hauerwas's pastorally oriented theological vision. His vision for a church free to live "out of control" is that it be a community able to live patiently with hope in what God will accomplish, not what humans can accomplish through the use of coercive power. What is needed to do this is schooling in virtues within the Christian communal setting. Two virtues he especially emphasizes are patience and hope. What I take Hauerwas to be suggesting is that these two virtues work together as mutual correctives to form an over-arching regulative framework for Christian character formation. The virtue of "hope must be schooled by . . . patience. Otherwise our hope too easily turns to fanaticism or cynicism" when confronted with "the inexorable tragedies" of our existence.[62] The virtue of patience "equally requires hope, for without hope patience too easily accepts the world . . . for what it is rather than what it can or should be."[63] The enthusiasm of hope is tempered with patience to prevent fanaticism. Longsuffering patience is imbued with hope to prevent a self-indulgent cynicism. Together, interactive virtues such as these function as practically oriented theological grammars which both are inspired by and help cultivate the character necessary for "remembering and telling the story of God we find in Jesus."[64]

Is there any comparable pastorally oriented vision in Gutiérrez's theology? I would argue that Gutiérrez has such a vision with elements which function to form Christian character in a manner similar to Hauerwas's proposal. Furthermore, when viewed in terms of their regulative frameworks, Gutiérrez's and Hauerwas's pastorally oriented visions may be to an important extent complementary, especially if one takes into account the way in which those visions are shaped by differing contexts. Unlike Hauerwas who addresses those tempted by

[61] Ibid., pp. 144, 105.
[62] Ibid., pp. 103, 145.
[63] Hauerwas, *Community of Character*, pp. 127–28. Hauerwas speaks of other virtues as well. For example, see his discussion of the virtue of courage in relation to patience and hope in Stanley Hauerwas, "The Difference of Virtue and the Difference It Makes: Courage Exemplified," *Modern Theology* 9 (1993), esp. pp. 256ff.
[64] Hauerwas, *Peaceable Kingdom*, p. 100.

ready access to power, Gutiérrez addresses those who have been subjugated by the misuse of power. In the context of the Latin American
church of the poor, fanaticism and cynicism on the whole present a
different face than what Hauerwas describes in the first-world context.
Gutiérrez notes a temptation to fanaticism, which he calls "immediatism."[65] This temptation is a reality for those grassroots pastoral
workers who become so "absorbed by the political demands of the
liberation commitment" that they lose the endurance and farsighted-
ness needed to work for long-term societal betterment.[66] More pervasive, however, than the temptation to immediatism is the temptation to
cynicism, or more accurately, resignation emerging from despair.
Gutiérrez notes the debilitating "combination of bitterness and dis-
couragement" felt by the poor (as well as by pastoral workers living
with the poor) overwhelmed by the "intermeshing afflictions that form
a chain and turn the life of the poor into a prison existence." Gutiérrez
suggests that the spirituality necessary to resist these temptations "is
germinating in this universe of unmerited afflictions."[67]

In recent works, he has given extensive attention to the spirituality
developing within the church of the poor. His study *On Job* is one
attempt, via a reading of this theological and literary classic from the
Bible, to assess and order certain forms of God-talk in the emergent
spirituality among Latin America's poor. In so doing, Gutiérrez addresses
pastoral concerns analogous to Hauerwas's about the hazards of
fanaticism and cynicism or despair which must be offset by the virtues
of patience and hope. I see no reason why Hauerwas could not agree
that his own approach to cultivating Christian virtues in resistance to
the prevailing North American culture of narcissism and power is
formally compatible and even complementary with Gutiérrez's
approach to cultivating a spirituality in resistance to the deformations
endemic to the Latin American context of poverty and suffering.

In *On Job* Gutiérrez focuses on two kinds of first-order Christian
communal languages, "contemplative" and "prophetic," which together
suggest the correct overarching grammar or regulative framework for
speaking of God and for being Christian. He calls one of these languages
contemplative or mystical because it predominantly articulates God's

---

[65] Gutiérrez, *Theology of Liberation*, p. 10.
[66] Gutiérrez, *Power of the Poor*, p. 51.
[67] Gutiérrez, *Our Own Wells*, pp. 118, 114, 115.

transcendence and mystery. Contemplative language gives voice to the awe Christians experience before the "mysterious horizon of God's gratuitous love."[68] However, in the midst of massive and unrelenting suffering, the transcendent God is sometimes spoken of (as Job does) as silent, remote, absent. In this context, contemplative language often takes the form of a lament, articulating an experience of abandonment by God.[69] Prophetic language predominantly articulates God's righteous presence – that is, God as the "defender or avenger" of the poor who are victims of oppression. Prophetic language most fully annunciates God's call for solidarity with the poor and opposition to injustice. However, in the midst of massive and unrelenting suffering, one might speak of being afflicted under "the rod" of God's "wrath" (Lam. 3:1), so that one is "enveloped . . . with bitterness and tribulation" (Lam. 3:5). In this context, prophetic language (again after the example of Job) sometimes takes the form of a righteous complaint or a "lawsuit" directed against God and on behalf of those who are suffering.[70] Such unabashed, heartfelt language seems to result in an apparent "splitting of God" into enemy and friend. Gutiérrez explains that this seeming bifurcation of God need not be taken as theological error or spiritual confusion but rather as "a sign that any approach to the mystery of God must be complex" – especially in light of great human suffering.[71]

These sorts of spontaneous first-order religious expressions of contemplative awe and lament as well as prophetic annunciation and complaint are all part of the community's grassroots piety. That piety only becomes distorted if one of these languages predominates to the point that the community is open to being manipulated either in the direction of political reductionism or otherworldly spiritualism. For example, when the oppressed are incited by political opportunists to call prophet-

---

[68] Gutiérrez, *On Job*, p. 96.

[69] Gutiérrez quotes, among others, these words of Job (23:2–3) about God (p. 54):
   My lament is still rebellious;
      despite my groans, his hand is just as heavy.
   Will no one help me to know
      how to travel to his dwelling? . . .
   If I go to the east, he is not there;
      or to the west, I still cannot find him.

[70] Ibid., pp. 64, 58. Job 13:3: "My words are intended for Shaddai; I mean to remonstrate with God" (p. 59).

[71] Ibid., pp. 65, 66.

ically for liberation by an historical "avenger," without recalling the mystery of God's gratuitous ways, there is the danger of a political reductionism of the gospel and immediatism. In this case, historical events of political struggle may be assumed to be coordinate with God's redemptive activity. Or, when the poor who feel abandoned by God are pacified by religious authorities with otherworldly images, without recalling the divine mandate of justice for the oppressed, then there is the danger of resignation and despair. The danger here has a different societal instantiation. Resignation does not typically irrupt into social conflict but rather can be easily manipulated to maintain the status quo of repressive political arrangements (as has been a pervasive socio-political reality in Latin American history).[72]

How can these dangers be averted? Gutiérrez argues that the "space" created by the "integrated" use of contemplative and prophetic languages can help cultivate the spiritual resources to resist political or religious manipulation of genuine popular piety in the church of the poor. According to Gutiérrez, these two languages "feed and correct" each other: "Without the prophetic dimension the language of contemplation is in danger of having no grip on the history in which God acts and in which we meet God. Without the mystical dimension the language of prophecy can narrow its vision and weaken its perception of the God who makes all things new."[73] When, for example, the communal language of prophetic complaint privileges the experience of the bitterness of God's presence, then the community will need the pastoral reminder that God should also be spoken of as the "Wholly Other," whose ways are unfathomable and free.[74] The contemplative language of divine mystery would thus counterbalance the image of God as one who enters human history to smite (Job 13:15). This is

---

[72] One commentator has noted that Gutiérrez's efforts to encourage the conscientization process within base Christian communities is a concrete attempt to prevent irruptions of desperate acts of violence from the poor sectors of Peruvian society. Without doing their own theological and political analysis, these communities will be prime targets for recruitment by violent extremist groups such as Peru's *Sendero Luminoso* (The Shining Path). See Curt Cadorette, *From the Heart of the People: The Theology of Gustavo Gutiérrez* (Oak Park, Ill.: Meyer-Stone, 1988), p. 63. The issue of violence, nonviolence and the Christian community is of import to both Gutiérrez and Hauerwas. (Hauerwas's principled stance on Christian pacifism has not been echoed, to my knowledge, by other postliberals.) Theologians from both movements need to converse fairly and subtly on complex issues such as this.

[73] Gutiérrez, *On Job*, pp. 94, 95, 96. See *Truth*, pp. 56f.; *God of Life*, ch. 8.

[74] Gutiérrez, *Truth*, p. 96. Gutiérrez identifies this as Barth's expression.

the lesson Job learns when he brings his complaint to God (Job 7:11) and receives, not an answer to his accusation (nor, for that matter, a repudiation of his bold act of complaint), but instead he encounters God's proclamation that God's actions are beyond human comprehension. Conversely, when the communal language of contemplative lament privileges the experience of God's silence or absence, then the community will need the pastoral reminder that God should also be spoken of as the defender of humanity's downtrodden. The prophetic language of divine presence would thus counterbalance the image of God as silent or absent. This is again how Gutiérrez understands Job's experience. The confidence Job gains by faith in his "living Avenger" sustains him in his debate with his so-called sorry comforters.[75]

Gutiérrez is suggesting, I would argue, a kind of cross-referencing regulative structure between these two biblical languages about God which can enable the church of the poor to develop a grammatically balanced way of speaking of God. Or, one might say, by living in the space created by the interconnection of these two languages, Christians can form the proper character for living faithfully in the midst of oppression.[76] The formal similarity between Gutiérrez's and Hauerwas's pastoral theological proposals is evident. Each addresses how to avoid the spiritual and practical deformations of fanaticism and cynicism by identifying the tensive space in which Christian fidelity lies. For

[75] Gutiérrez, *On Job*, p. 64. While Terrence Tilley ("God and the Silencing of Job," *Modern Theology* 5 [1989]) raises some important exegetical and literary points about the Book of Job which Gutiérrez overlooks, I disagree with his contention that Gutiérrez (in his interpretation of Job 42:6) "blames the victim of suffering for complaining" and hence "Gutiérrez has joined the torturers in silencing their victim" (p. 265). This strikes me as an unfair charge. Gutiérrez's point is that when Job, at a certain moment in the story, abandons his accusers' view of retributive justice, he ceases to engage in a certain kind of "complaining" about God. Job (or any victim of suffering) is by no means silenced, however. Gutiérrez argues that "the meaning of Job's final answer or, more accurately, of the book as a whole," is the discovery of interwoven prophetic and contemplative God-talk. Gutiérrez, *On Job*, p. 87.

[76] David Tracy sees in Gutiérrez's *On Job* an almost postmodern view of a "hidden-revealed God of hope" in the experiences of oppressed people whom "the grand narrative of modernity has set aside as . . . non-history" ("The Return of God in Contemporary Theology" in his *On Naming the Present: Reflections on God, Hermeneutics, and Church* [Maryknoll: Orbis; London: SCM, 1994], p. 43). He also recognizes in this text the kind of mystical-prophetic hermeneutic which he has long attributed to Gutiérrez. In a move no doubt influenced by Gutiérrez, Tracy develops his own cross-referencing dialectic of prophetic and mystical outlooks: "Without the prophetic core, the struggle for justice and freedom . . . can too soon be lost in mere privacy. Without the mystical insistence on love, the spiritual power of the righteous struggle for justice is always in danger of lapsing into mere self-righteousness and spiritual exhaustion" (*Dialogue with the Other: The Inter-Religious Dialogue* [Louvain: Peeters; Grand Rapids, Mich.: William B. Eerdmans, 1990], p. 118).

Hauerwas, it is the space created by the interactive grammatically .
informed virtues of patience and hope; for Gutiérrez, it is the space
created by interactive grammatically informed contemplative and
prophetic languages. The fact that Gutiérrez is primarily addressing a
third-world church afflicted by poverty and disempowerment, and
Hauerwas is primarily addressing a first-world church marked by
affluence and tempted to misuse power, does not obscure the regulative compatibility of their pastorally oriented insights. Neither do these
contextual differences mean that these two visions cannot be complementary; each one's pastorally oriented proposals may even be applicable in the other's general social context. For example, Hauerwas's
perspective on the virtues needed to counteract the self-interest and
self-protectiveness of those in power might be more to the point for
certain upper-class sectors of the Latin American church than
Gutiérrez's message about the spirituality of the church of the poor.
Likewise, Gutiérrez's perspective on the needs of the disempowered
might be a more appropriate message for the growing underclasses of
North American society than Hauerwas's message to those who need
to learn more about living out of control.

There is really no way of judging in the abstract whether Gutiérrez's
exposition on the languages of contemplation and prophecy or
Hauerwas's exposition on the virtues of patience and hope offers
the "better" way of averting the dangers of fanaticism and despair
and of forming Christian character embued with gratitude to God and
the freedom to serve one's neighbor. Indeed I have just suggested that
there may be reasons to synthesize aspects of both, as contextually
warranted. Whatever the case may be, this comparison of some of
their insights on Christian character formation, along with the regulative doctrinal analysis in the preceding section, should provide
sufficient impetus for postliberal and liberation theologians (and
others as well) to pursue further conversations on a great range of constructive theological issues.[77] With the guidance of rule theory and
with sensitivity to the particular contextual challenges which any
theological movement must face, mutually beneficial exchanges such

[77] Indeed, Tracy (with his prophetic-mystical dialectical hermeneutic) is well underway in his pursuit of this sort of intermovement conversation with liberation theology. See n. 76 above. See
Tracy, *Dialogue*, p. 118 n. 32; *On Naming*, p. 24 n. 11; "On Reading The Scriptures Theologically"
in *Theology and Dialogue: Essays in Conversation with George Lindbeck*, ed. Bruce D. Marshall
(University of Notre Dame Press, 1990), p. 66 n. 70.

as this could readily take place. There should be no insuperable impediment to productive dialogue other than the belief, which Lindbeck considers unwarranted, that any theological formulation which materially differs from one's own must therefore be "unwittingly heretical."[78]

[78] Lindbeck, *Nature of Doctrine*, p. 107.

CHAPTER SIX

Virtues and vices in theological practice

Although there are many differences among liberation, postliberal and revisionary perspectives on a spectrum of methodological and constructive issues, I have suggested some ways in which to recast those differences so as to open trajectories for fruitful future intermovement engagement. Each movement's approach has its strengths and weaknesses, its insights and oversights. I have tried to draw from what I believe are the strengths and insights of each in order to formulate proposals for theological practice better able to respond to contemporary culture's ecclesial, intellectual and social challenges. Wide reflective equilibrium apologetics, while not the only workable mode of theological engagement in the pluralistic public realm, forecasts necessary elements of an approach that is postmodernly sensitive, ideologically vigilant and Christian-specific: wide coherence, overlapping consensus and assimilative power tested by critical background theories. Other models for theologically reading the Bible as the church's book may exhibit hermeneutical impulses more diverse than the three to which I attended (pluralism, continuity, and critique); however, the regulative-dialectical conceptuality is a workable way for instantiating all three. The anticipated result is a sufficiently stable scripture and tradition relationship which remains open to change and otherness in an age of textual deconstruction, Christian communal plurality and creativity from history's underside.

These approaches to apologetics and hermeneutics, I argued, sustain the three movements' focal values. In the future, these values may be revised or new ones may be added but, for our current era, I believe theology is well served by being accountable to these values: fully critical reflection in the public realm, thick description of the habitable scriptural world which forms Christian communal character, solidarity with the struggles and spiritualities of the oppressed. Liberation, revisionary and postliberal theologians may well differ on the configuration of these values (as focal or less focused), but I am confident that they maintain the importance of all of them because of their indispensability for, among other things, sustaining the vitality and fidelity of Christian communities. If there is anything that is underlying common ground among the theologians from these movements it is their commitment to Christian theology as a form of ecclesial service. Although how these theologians decide to instantiate these values may differ, their decisions are not willy nilly or unduly relativistic because they wish to tailor their theological approaches to what is in the best interest of the life of the church. For these theologians at least, when one thinks about even highly theoretical questions regarding good theological practice, it involves very practical judgments related to the well-being of Christian communities. This practical ecclesial consideration is a central element in the logic informing decisions regarding good theological practice.

In the preceding chapters, some basic (though by no means exhaustive) paradigm-shaping questions about good theological practice were raised or implied. Should theological practice be conceptualized as a mutually critical correlation, as intratextuality, or some other way? Given theological plurality and the need for continuity, who has the burden of proof when negotiating intra-Christian disputes – the mainstream or the margins? Should one go with a broad or strict definition of theology? Since I too see good theological practice as involving very practical judgments related to serving Christian communities, my judgments on these questions are shaped by this practical end. I tend more toward a position somewhere between intratextual and correlational approaches, because I think doing so enhances the church's ability to form biblically shaped, grammatically competent practitioners who must relate to a rapidly changing pluralistic "host" culture.[1] I endorse widening the normative Christian consensus to include preferentially the oppressed at society's margins, but I advocate having the burden of proof regarding revising doctrinal positions rest with both the mainstream defenders of tradition as well as those theologians speaking with marginalized voices of change because such debate goes to the

---

[1] By "host" culture, I have in mind the use of this term in David H. Kelsey, "Church Discourse and Public Realm" in *Theology and Dialogue: Essays in Conversation with George Lindbeck*, ed. Bruce D. Marshall (University of Notre Dame Press, 1990), pp. 7–33.

heart of the life and fidelity of Christian communities. I favor a
broad rather than a strict definition of theology because theology
needs a stronger and wider engagement with Christian communities –
especially the fecund aspects of its plain sense and its grassroots
struggles.

My positions on these questions can be viewed as lodging somewhere between three sets of extremes. The first question has to do with
how the Christian theologian relates the scriptural world to the pluralistic host culture. At one end, you have extreme "external accommodation" to the extratextual perspectives of the host culture. At the
other end you have extreme "internal self-sufficiency" of scripture and
tradition taken as a self-contained world. Mutually critical correlational and intratextual orientations can be found at different places
between these two extreme positions. The second question has to do
with how the theologian is disposed to respond to theological changes
within the diverse Christian community. At one extreme you have
"preservation" which exclusively privileges guarding the mainstream
tradition; at the other extreme you have "innovation" which exclusively
privileges change (doctrinal, liturgical, institutional, etc.) in response to
marginalized or other experiences. The burden of proof can be placed
on the shoulders of theologians situated at different places between
these two extreme positions. The third question has to do with how the
theologian is disposed to view theology's relationship to the discourse
and practice of Christian communities. At one extreme you have
"detachment" where theology strives for complete independence from
Christian communal life; at the other extreme you have "connection"
where theology subjects itself to complete dependence on Christian
communal discourse, practice and institutional commitments. Broad
and strict definitions of theology can be found at different places
between these two extreme positions.

Although this schema overlooks some important nuances, it is helpful in giving us a sense of the extreme positions or poles the theologian
would probably want to avoid. With very few exceptions, it would not
be appropriate or expedient to pursue anything near these extreme
positions. One can locate a theologian's answers to the three questions
posed above by placing them on a continuum between these sets of
polar extremes: at the most balanced – that is, the middle – position
between the two poles or off to one side or the other, resulting in a more

unbalanced position, but one that may very well be warranted for particular reasons in particular contexts.

When trying in this way to map and evaluate the relative balance of theological positions, we can take a timely lesson from some ancient and medieval voices. Aristotle (and two of his renowned medieval interpreters, Maimonides and Aquinas) argued that in ethics, virtue is the mean between two extremes (e.g., courage is the mean between foolhardiness and cowardice). There is the strict, arithmetic mean and the virtuous mean, and they may or may not be the same. In fact, the virtuous mean for human behavior is most often not the strict, arithmethic mean. To attain the virtuous mean, one must tend slightly away from the vice to which one is more inclined in order to provide a margin of resistance given one's propensities. As Aristotle puts it, the virtuous mean is "some intermediate between excess and deficiency" which is "relative to us."[2] Since I am talking about a theologian's methodological decisions and not ethical behavior, my sets of poles are more accurately spoken of as extreme positions not vices, but I retain the language of vice and virtue because it articulates how the decision a theologian makes is not just a scientific calculation but is an attempt at prudent and, hopefully, even wise judgment. One is trying to make a decision that is not only warranted in the moment but a decision that looks toward long-term good ends for theological practice in service to the church and society at large.

External accommodation and internal self-sufficiency

The poles which characterize the issues entailed in the relationship between the extratextual host culture and scriptural world are external accommodation and internal self-sufficiency. To accommodate, at the extreme, is to privilege exclusively the claim to attention (to borrow Tracy's notion) of extratextual perspectives over that of a Christian ethos and worldview. Call it extreme *aggiornamento* or extreme cultural Christianity (in the sense of Niebuhr's "Christ of culture"[3]); the pull is toward contextualized accommodation to contemporary culture. Internal self-sufficiency, at the extreme, would mean an attempt exclu-

---

[2] Aristotle, *Nicomachean Ethics*, tr. Terence Irwin (Indianapolis: Hackett, 1985), 1106a26–33, p. 43. See also *Rambam: Readings in the Philosophy of Moses Maimonides*, tr. Lenn Evan Goodman (New York: Viking, 1976), pp. 226ff and Thomas Aquinas, *Commentary on the Nicomachean Ethics*, tr. C. I. Litzinger, O.P., vol. I (Chicago: Henry Regnary, 1964), II. L.XI:C 369–381, pp. 166–68.

[3] See H. Richard Niebuhr, *Christ and Culture* (New York: Harper & Row, 1951), ch. 3.

sively to work out of a scriptural framework and to rely solely on Christian categories. I want to revisit for a moment how revisionists and postliberals (as I read them) may be placed in relation to the "vices" of these two extremes in order to situate my position which splits the difference between their correlational or intratextual methods (along the lines of an approach like Boff's).

Revisionists and postliberals consider each others' methods as tending toward one or the other of these extremes. On the subject of hermeneutics, the gist of the postliberal concern with revisionary correlational method is the risk of an extratextualism that is systematic and controlling. The aptness of this charge regarding Tracy depends on whether one reads his description of mutually critical correlation between interpretations of the situation and interpretations of the Bible as always and systematically entailing an experiential-expressive theory of religion and a general phenomenological hermeneutics (which, for postliberals, would signal the danger of a distorting extratextualism), or whether one reads mutually critical correlation in a less philosophically loaded way. I believe the latter is possible, which would mean that mutually critical correlation, in theory, is not an extreme external accommodationist position but the arithmetic mean between the "vices" of sectarian internal self-sufficiency and rampant extratextualist accommodation.

While some of Tracy's work raises concern about the risk of extratextualism (e.g., in *Blessed Rage for Order* and some of *The Analogical Imagination*), he also describes the mutually critical correlating process in a more commonplace, low-key way as well. He rightly makes the descriptive point that mutually critical correlation is simply what happens when one converses with the text from a particular situation. Mutually critical correlation is to be thought of as "a general heuristic guide" which describes the process of textual interpretation as involving the equal interaction of "the inevitable presence of the interpreter's own preunderstanding (situation)" and "the claim to attention of the text itself." Tracy even stresses that this mutually critical correlating conversation with the biblical classic involves what Barth describes as entering "into the 'strange new world' of the Bible."[4] Hence, when mutually critical correlation is viewed formally as a heuristic model, it need not be taken as the polar opposite of intratextualism; rather, it

---

[4] Robert Grant, with David Tracy, *A Short History of the Interpretation of the Bible*, 2nd edn. (n.p.: Fortress, 1984), pp. 171, 158.

should be seen as the arithmetic mean between external accommodation and internal self-sufficiency. Materially, any mutually critical correlation may in fact turn out to be unduly extratextually accommodationist in ways that postliberals fear will distort the biblical world. However, in theory, this need not be the case.

Postliberals, nonetheless, raise an important point about what we might call the temptation or "vice" of extratextualism. Although extratextualism is not exclusively a problem of the modern period, postliberals emphasize how it is particularly rampant in liberal theology which makes translating Christian faith (into conceptualities attractive to modern, secular people) theology's paramount responsibility. In this secularized "user-friendly" climate, there is the real temptation to impose uninterrogated cultural assumptions onto one's conversation with the Bible to the point of eclipsing the habitable scriptural world which theology strives to redescribe. One might say that Lindbeck's call for intratextuality is a recognition of this temptation, which is not emphasized to the same extent by the mutually critical correlational model. Hence, while mutually critical correlation may in theory be perfectly neutral regarding extratextualism, it may not always be the prudent or wise model to follow if one is concerned with the focal value of thick description of Christian communal forms of life. This is an issue of finding the virtuous mean.

On the issue of scriptural hermeneutics, I advocate a weighted dialectical hermeneutic similar to Boff's. This method of dialectically relating the present community's contextualized reading of scripture to the internal logic of the New Testament communities' readings of the gospel message is weighted toward the latter as a dominant term. As a mediating position between intratextually absorbing the world and correlating interpretations of scripture and of the situation equally, this method allows the reader both to render a relevant, habitable biblical world and to use scripture in a contextually responsive way. Standing alone, however, this approach does not yet constitute the methodologically virtuous mean between host culture and scriptural world, even if it addresses the hermeneutical dilemmas involved in relating the two poles more effectively than either mutually critical correlation or intratextuality does. Since this hermeneutic operates out of a perspective weighted toward scripture (hence its placement slightly to the right of the arithmetic mean), it risks being pulled toward the extreme self-sufficiency pole (which would cause it to converge with intratextuality on the way). We therefore need to specify methodologically how to keep extratextual cultural realities vitally a part of theological practice which weights scripture as a dominant term. This is where the use of background theories becomes critically important. How background theories are brought into play in theological practice makes all the difference for finding a virtuous mean between the various discourses of host cultures and Christian discourse. Boff's method for a mediational use of non-theological theories (in combination with his cultural-linguistic and rule theory oriented approach to religion and theology) maintains the proper priority. When Boff insists that Christian theology "receives its text from" a background theory and "practices upon it a reading in conformity with its own proper code," he is not simply correlating non-theological and theological discourses.[5] They are related mediation-ally. The nontheological theory mediates the (so-called raw) material object which in turn is read by theology, whose grammar is constituted in relation to a weighted dialectical interpretation of scripture.

Boff and other liberationists emphasize the methodical use of the social sciences as background theories. They share this insistence with Tracy and Ogden.[6] This leaves the postliberals to be won over. A more integral and regulated use of the social sciences may be of increasing interest to postliberal theologians should they begin to perceive the situation as warranting such a strategy. At the moment, many post-liberals may see no need formally to advocate anything other than a very *ad hoc* use of the social sciences, guided by an intuitive sense of how extrabiblical and intratextual concepts should be related in a faithful, relevant and intelligible way. Nevertheless, should they decide that Christian social practices have become ineffective responses to contemporary culture, they might be persuaded that not only does the church need a story cohesive enough "to encode successfully the vicissitudes and contradictions of history,"[7] but the church also needs

---

[5] Clodovis Boff, O.S.M., *Theology and Praxis: Epistemological Foundations*, tr. Robert R. Barr (Maryknoll: Orbis, 1987), p. 31.

[6] See David Tracy, "The Foundations of Practical Theology" in *Practical Theology: The Emerging Field in Theology, Church and World*, ed. Don S. Browning (San Francisco: Harper & Row, 1983) and Schubert M. Ogden, *On Theology* (San Francisco: Harper & Row, 1986), p. 14.

[7] George Lindbeck, "The Story-Shaped Church: Critical Exegesis and Theological Interpretation" in *Scriptural Authority and Narrative Interpretation*, ed. Garrett Green (Philadelphia: Fortress, 1987), p. 175.

a method equipped with the nontheological tools necessary for rigorously analyzing those vicissitudes and historical contradictions.[8] Furthermore, if one were to grant that one's reflective equilibrium of Christian beliefs and regulative doctrines could succumb to ideological interests (as the history of Christian theology suggests), then critical social scientific background theories may come to be seen by postliberal theologians as indispensable for credible theological practice. If so, postliberals would join liberationists and revisionists in making the social sciences methodologically integral to theological practice.

While I believe that postliberals are poised for a methodological commitment to the explicit use of the social sciences as background theories, they are (in many cases) not there yet. No doubt, partly because postliberals have not emphasized this methodological issue, other theologians have stepped into the breach to comment on whether intratextual theology would be enhanced by proposals such as Boff's regarding social scientific mediation. One argument that has been forwarded repudiating Boff's position comes from John Milbank. An agenda of his *Theology and Social Theory* is to ensure "that the 'redescription' of Christianity advocated by Lindbeck and the Yale school [i.e., postliberals] will now have a fully social and political dimension."[9] Milbank believes this can only be accomplished by firmly diverting postliberalism away from methodological proposals such as Boff's. I take just the opposite position: the postliberal intratextual project will be strengthened by the kind of methodical use of social scientific background theories outlined by Boff. I think Milbank is mistaken both in his estimation of Boff and, correlatively, in his view that intratextual theology would benefit from relying almost exclusively on the development of its own "socio-historical gaze" apart from secular social sciences.[10]

Milbank makes two charges regarding Boff which are misleading:

---

[8] Kelsey has already made an observation to this effect in an essay in conversation with Lindbeck, writing that "[f]ruitful *theological* analysis...of the best modes of churchly engagement in a host society requires attention to the organization and dynamics of power in both the host society . . . and in [the] church." Kelsey goes on to suggest that "for its own cogency a cultural-linguistic theory of doctrine requires just such attention to power analysis precisely because the theory partly rests on the assumption that a church is constantly engaged with a constantly changing host society" ("Church Discourse and Public Realm," pp. 24–25).

[9] John Milbank, *Theology and Social Theory: Beyond Secular Reason* (Oxford and Cambridge, Mass.: Blackwell, 1993), p. 388.

[10] Ibid., p. 247.

(1) the "wooden theoreticism" of his method leaves the theologian with a "vacuous" task of simply announcing "that God (as he cannot but) agrees" with the analysis provided by secular "social science [which] presents theology with the social object perfectly described and perfectly explained";[11] and (2) Boff, like other liberation theologians, makes praxis the criterion of theology. There is no doubt that Boff's rather unorthodox synthesis of Althusser and Aquinas may seem a bit stiffly orchestrated at points, but it would be unfair to characterize it as leaving the theologian with a vacuous task. This viewpoint ignores the creative and dynamic nature of the work of the theological "second generality" (the code of faith) in the theoretical process. The social sciences provide theology with its object which is reworked theologically under the gaze of theology's own grammar. Boff is emphatic on this point: "Theology must hear [the social sciences] . . . but hear them in order to make *its* own voice resound, and say what *it* has to say."[12]

I suspect that what Milbank may object to is not the notion that the social sciences can sometimes aid the theologian who is trying to understand complex economic and political processes (in fact he affirms at one point that theology would "be foolish to forego such aid"). Rather, he is critical of the way theology historically has "sought to borrow from elsewhere *a fundamental* account of society or history" and then correlate the Christian tradition with it.[13] In other words, he fears an extratextual metanarrative in competition with the intratextual Christian metanarrative. Any *de facto* correlationist project runs this risk, and only an extreme internal self-sufficiency position completely avoids it (at least in theory). I believe that my description of Boff's method in chapters three and four sufficiently demonstrates that his theological approach is firmly enough grounded in the Christian grammar so as not to be subsumed by the mediations he uses. Even when the background theory used is linked to a social science like Marxism which also promotes a powerful *Weltanschauung*, Boff retains both his intratextual rootedness and his critical perspective. In a telling but somewhat tongue in cheek remark, Boff observes that "properly theological practice would consist . . . in practicing a 'Markan reading of Marx' . . . not a reading of Mark

---

[11] Ibid., pp. 248, 249.
[12] Boff, *Theology and Praxis*, p. 54.
[13] Milbank, *Theology and Social Theory*, pp. 247, 380; emphasis added.

by Marx."[14] Hence, I find no evidence that Boff proposes relying uncritically on a single, fundamental, secular socio-political account which
would dominate the Christian story.

A second criticism Milbank raises in relation to Boff is a version of
the prevalent North Atlantic critique of liberation theology noted in
chapter three: liberation theology's "'priority of praxis.'" While Milbank
admits that Boff has a more complicated spin on the theory–praxis
relationship – that is, he emphasizes strongly that theology as theory
is separate from praxis – he still places Boff among other liberation
theologians who affirm that "the pronouncements of theology must be
judged by whether or not they promote ... [liberating] action."[15] I
believe the presentation of Boff's views on the relation of theory and
praxis in chapter three sufficiently counters this charge. Having thus
dispensed with what is misleading in Milbank's critique of Boff, we can
get down to the crux of how they disagree and who proposes the better
methodological course of action for postliberals (or any theologian) to
take.

While Milbank tips his hat once or twice to the notion that theology
could justifiably seek some aid from the social sciences, the thrust of
his project is to "replace theology mediated by social science" with
"theology as itself a social science." His test case is Lindbeck's intratextual theology which he finds apparently vulnerable to making the
wrong methodological move in this regard. Milbank seems to urge
Lindbeckians to follow him in developing theology as its own "Christian
sociology."[16] Boff would have strong reservations. While Boff's interest
in the use of socio-political mediations for theological reflection was
originally sparked by concerns particular to the situation of politically
engaged Latin American liberation theologies, nevertheless, he also
directs his comments to North Atlantic theologies with "'traditionalist'"
or even putatively nonpolitical orientations.[17] Any theology which
ignores or improperly uses social scientific tools for analyzing the political realities which affect Christian communities will be hard pressed
to bring a critically relevant theological assessment to bear upon the
praxis of those communities, and, correlatively, it will be difficult to

---

[14] Boff, *Theology and Praxis*, p. 266 n. 8. Boff's remark is directed critically to Fernando Belo's *A Materialist Reading of the Gospel of Mark*.

[15] Milbank, *Theology and Social Theory*, pp. 249, 250.

[16] Ibid., pp. 251, 380.

[17] Boff, *Theology and Praxis*, p. 160.

bring the value of solidarity with the oppressed into focus. Boff has developed categories of methodologically improper ways of relating theology and the social sciences which range from completely excluding social scientific tools from theological practice to simply juxtaposing social scientific and theological discourses.[18] Lindbeck and Milbank fall into different categories in this regard.

Lindbeck's intratextual method of absorbing the world is so thoroughly metaphorical that it risks becoming what Boff calls "semantic mix."[19] In this approach, extratextual concepts are made acceptable and included – or, we might say, *absorbed* – into theology. An irony of Lindbeck's method is that these concepts can be uncritically assimilated (potentially distorting the Christian grammar) instead of being reworked grammatically, as Boff's mediational method proposes. This is clearly not the result Lindbeck intends, but his metaphors of intratextuality and absorbing the world are not accompanied by specific directives for how to relate nontheological and theological discourses. Methods, of course, cannot guarantee success, but they are preferable to potentially unreflected assimilation of extratextual concepts. Being classified as a semantic mix type would mean, however, that one has at least avoided the much more problematic way of relating theology and the social sciences which Boff calls "theologism." This approach either claims that the political realm is "self-evident" or that theology can "find everything it needs ... within its own walls" for addressing socio-political realities.[20] Milbank would seem to be promoting a kind of internally self-sufficient theologism – whether in modulated tones ("theology is just another socio-historical gaze ... alongside other gazes") or in more triumphalist tones ("theology as itself a social science, and the queen of the sciences for the inhabitants of the *altera civitas*").[21] For Boff, unless one clearly specifies a mediational use of the social sciences in theological practice, semantic mix or some other skewed use of these theories will surreptitiously slip in. One might even be lulled into thinking that theology can itself read the political. In light of Boff's warnings, it is difficult not to find Milbank's proposal for "a directly theological discourse about the socio-historical"

[18] Ibid., pp. 20–29.
[19] Ibid., pp. 27–28.
[20] Ibid., p. 26.
[21] Milbank, *Theology and Social Theory*, pp. 247, 380.

tinged with overconfidence about the capacities of theology to offer "the ultimate 'social science.'"[22]

Boff and Milbank can thus be seen as standing on either side of postliberal intratextuality. Both would argue (though differently) that the intratextual approach is currently insufficient methodologically on the issue of relating (to use Barth's metaphor) the Bible and the newspaper. I take Milbank as attempting to move intratextuality toward the pole of internal self-sufficiency. Boff would want to move it in the other direction toward his mediational method, situated slightly closer to the arithmetic mean. My sympathies are with Boff's move. Over and above the points made in this regard in chapter three, intratextuality (ironically) risks uncritically absorbing the host culture's dominant ideology – unless the theologian heads matters off at the pass, so to speak, by appropriately employing social scientific mediations in theological practice. A second irony of an intratextual theology that tries to be too internally self-sufficient by neglecting the use of critical mediational theories is that it leaves itself open to being manipulated by shrewd operators in the host culture to reinforce the socio-political status quo. To the extent that Christian communities have an intratextual message to bring to the world, whether it be in relation to the contradictions between wage labor and corporate profits or systemic racism or sexism, theology needs critical background theories to make best use of its particular, grammatically ruled Christian gaze.

Preservation and innovation

I have described the extremes associated with the second question – Who has the burden of proof when negotiating intra-Christian disputes? – "preservation" and "innovation." These terms indicate that the burden of proof can fall either on the preservers of the mainstream tradition or its marginalized challengers who advocate innovation. This issue was implicit in chapter five's exploration of doctrinal commonalities between Gutiérrez and Hauerwas. As it turned out, Gutiérrez and Hauerwas were seen as having largely compatible

---

[22] Ibid., pp. 249, 6. For another critical perspective on Milbank, see Robert H. Roberts, "Transcendental Sociology? A Critique of John Milbank's *Theology and Social Theory: Beyond Secular Reason,*" *Scottish Journal of Theology* 46 (1993). See also the appreciative and critical discussions of Milbank's text in *Modern Theology* 8, no. 4 (1992).

doctrinal positions, grammatically understood. Gutiérrez speaks from the perspective of the oppressed and their right to reclaim the Bible and effect socio-political change, but his theological views are quite doctrinally mainstream. That is, he believes that the orthodox tradition has the doctrinal and scriptural resources to speak a saving word to those who suffer.[23] Hence, his advocacy on behalf of the marginalized community of the poor does not translate into a push for doctrinal change beyond what Lindbeck would call the mainstream *consensus fidelium*.

For other communities of people marginalized from the mainstream, however, doctrinal innovation is a central platform of their program to reform the Christian tradition. In such cases, how does the theologian adjudicate between the voices of preservation and those of innovation? Lindbeck (who, as we saw in chapter four, tends toward traditionalism in biblical hermeneutics and doctrinal conservatism out of concern for ecumenicity) argues that "all mainstream Christian traditions have always taken the literal sense to be . . . realistic narrative" and that "the burden of proof rests on those who deny that the Christian mainstream has . . . rightly discerned God's word in Scripture." In order to safeguard this classic ecclesial reading practice (and the deep grammar that rules it), Lindbeck moves the virtuous mean toward the pole of preservation. (On this issue, Tracy currently might be taken as doing the same, since he too has been arguing for the primacy of the traditional realistic narrative sense of the passion.) I do not wish to disagree with the general, pious rule that "the Holy Spirit guides the church into the truth"; however, as Lindbeck himself notes, doctrines rooted in the traditional plain sense have often been dreadfully misused (e.g., appealing to "atonement motifs to tell battered women or members of oppressed races that they should go like Jesus as lambs to the slaughter").[24] It is no wonder that some elements of the mainstream tradition have not been heard by all as a saving word.

---

[23] See his argument for how Medellín and Puebla, and Latin American liberation theology in general, stand firmly within the tradition of Vatican II as attempts "to interpret the great themes of the Council." Gustavo Gutiérrez, "The Church and the Poor: A Latin American Perspective," tr. Matthew J. O'Connell, in *The Reception of Vatican II*, ed. Guiseppe Alberigo, et al. (Wash., D.C.: Catholic University of America Press, 1987), p. 193.

[24] George A. Lindbeck, "Atonement and the Hermeneutics of Intratextual Social Embodiment" in *The Nature of Confession: Evangelicals and Postliberals in Conversation*, ed. Timothy R. Phillips and Dennis L. Okholm (Downer Grove, Ill.: Intervarsity, 1996), pp. 229, 223, 236.

When discussing Tracy's views on scriptural interpretation in chapter four, I mentioned in passing the work of feminist theologian Rita Nakashima Brock as an example of a theology that does not appear to cohere with the tradition's historically normative realistic narrative plain sense of the passion.[25] Indeed, Brock's reading of the Gospel of Mark is meant to warrant a radically revisionary feminist theological proposal regarding christology and soteriology (among other doctrinal loci). In an instance such as this, in which the mainstream doctrinal consensus is being challenged by a voice from a marginalized group (i.e., women, especially those injured by dysfunctional, patriarchal family settings), the question arises: where should the burden of proof lie? According to Lindbeck's principle, the burden would lie predominantly with the innovator who is departing from the realistic, narrative reading (though I am sure Lindbeck would add that such a reading should no more be used to justify the battering of women than "*Christus est Dominus*" should have been used by crusaders to justify "cleaving the skull of the infidel"[26]). Brock might well argue that the burden lies predominantly with the tradition which must take responsibility for having provided explicit and implicit religious underpinnings for the psychic-emotional-physical damage inflicted on children in patriarchal family structures.

In the spirit of Tracy's notion of "conversation" or a Habermasian "communicative action," I would argue that the burden of proof lies equally with both preservers and innovators who must defend the validity of their claims. Tracy envisions conversation as embodying "some hard rules" such as: "listen to and respect what the other says, however different or other; be willing to correct or defend your opinions if challenged by the conversation partner; be willing to argue if necessary, to confront if demanded, to endure necessary conflict, to change your mind if the evidence suggests it."[27] There are important clarifications to this position. First, I am talking about equal burden of

---

[25] See Rita Nakashima Brock, *Journeys by Heart: A Christology of Erotic Power* (New York: Crossroad, 1988).

[26] George A. Lindbeck, *The Nature of Doctrine: Religion and Theology in a Postliberal Age* (Philadelphia: Westminster, 1984), p. 64.

[27] David Tracy, *Plurality and Ambiguity: Hermeneutics, Religion, Hope* (San Francisco: Harper & Row, 1987), p. 19; cf. p. 118 n. 28. For a discussion of the relation between Tracy's concept of conversation and Jürgen Habermas's concept of communicative action and their usefulness for the church's ethical discourse, see Paul Lakeland, *Theology and Critical Theory: The Discourse of the Church* (Nashville: Abingdon, 1990), esp. pp. 49ff. and ch. 6.

proof placed on theologians with effectively equal institutional access to a fair hearing.[28] The rules change when you have a situation with a significant imbalance of power among interlocutors (it goes without saying that a situation of systematic suppression of marginal voices would nullify or call for serious revision of the burden of proof requirement).[29] Second, equalizing the burden of proof requires each proponent not only to present their own doctrinal position but to address related social and ecclesial effects of either maintaining the doctrinal status quo or changing it. My point is twofold. Too much is at stake for Christian forms of life to say that everything in the tradition which cannot be vindicated of charges of deleterious effects should be jettisoned. Too much is also at stake to say that every grievance that marginalized groups have against the tradition is illegitimate until overwhelmingly proven otherwise. Hence, for the mainstream preservers to meet their burden of proof, they must address in a fully critical manner why the tradition should be upheld after having been implicated in systemic oppression. For the marginalized innovators to meet their burden of proof, they must address how their doctrinal alternatives are less problematic and at least equally beneficial as the tradition they propose revising.

To see the sense of this approach, consider, for example, the challenge of Brock's reading of the Gospel of Mark in relation to the traditional plain sense of the passion narratives as found, for example, in Frei's *The Identity of Jesus Christ*. I have already discussed Frei's text briefly in chapter three, pointing out how it can be read as a kind of wide reflective

28 In stressing this point about what Thomas McCarthy calls "effective equality," I am presupposing that judgments drawn from conversation can be "the result . . . of the force of the better argument and not of accidental or systematic constraints on communication," even though "this supposition is usually (and perhaps even always) counterfactual." Thomas McCarthy, *The Critical Theory of Jürgen Habermas* (Cambridge, Mass. and London: MIT Press, 1978), pp. 306, 309. I agree with Paul Lakeland who suggests that this Habermasian "ideal speech situation" can appropriately be taken as an "eschatological vision" or "transcendent hope in a future realization" (*Theology and Critical Theory*, pp. 241–42).

29 A situation such as this recalls Michel Foucault's notion of insurrectional "subjugated knowledges." If, as Foucault argues, power is not just hegemonically repressive but permeates "the social body" with differing local effects, then power must be seen as also productive at many levels. It "traverses and produces things, it induces pleasure, forms knowledge" – including subjugated knowledges. Michel Foucault, *Power/Knowledge: Selected Interviews and Other Writings, 1972–1977*, ed. and tr. Colin Gordon, et al. (New York: Pantheon, 1980), pp. 81ff., 93, 119. Nevertheless, for those affected inordinately by repressive power, it would not be appropriate to call for equal burden of proof which is more proper to the "effective equality" conditions of communicative discourse discussed above (see previous note).

equilibrium dogmatics – combining Christian beliefs, regulative principles and background theories to promote the notion of Jesus' unsubstitutable identity in the story of his death and resurrection. According to Frei, Jesus' identity is exemplified most intensively in a realistic narrative reading of the passion accounts: "The focus of the story remains on ... Jesus himself as the unsubstitutable person he is."[30] The theological grammar implicit in this reading specifies that there can be no other subject for the actions he enacts, no "other hero, human or divine, nor that 'everyman' for whom he might mistakenly be thought to be a symbol." Moreover, those who follow him find their "own specific and unsubstitutable identity" in relation to the Jesus story realistically understood. According to this construal of Jesus, our humanity is enriched by Jesus; whereas "[n]owhere in the Gospel story is Jesus' own humanity enriched by his relation with others."[31] This is the necessary condition for "Jesus' irreversible 'forness'" on our behalf, as Gene Outka puts it. Jesus is perfectly and redemptively for us; this empowers us with the freedom to be for our neighbor, even if our neighborly activity is "nonredemptive" and inevitably "shot through with vulnerability and loss and wasted opportunities."[32]

Brock would claim that this traditional emphasis on Jesus' unique redemptiveness promotes the notion of a male hero figure and, correlatively, a psychologically unhealthy passivity (especially for women). The destructive behaviors that can ensue include the "inability to assert oneself against abusive treatment" or to resist demands for inordinate and damaging self-sacrifice.[33] Defenders of the mainstream tradition might argue that until a better doctrine comes along (i.e., one that can still fully account for human wasted opportunities and God's "forness"), the doctrine of Jesus' unique redemptiveness should hold – despite its past or potential for future misuse. My point is that this position should be fully argued and not simply asserted and promulgated. To argue this position, defenders of the traditional view of redemption would need

---

[30] Hans W. Frei, *The Identity of Jesus Christ: The Hermeneutical Bases of Dogmatic Theology* (Philadelphia: Fortress, 1975), p. 135. Unlike the earlier accounts of Jesus' ministry, Frei suggests that in the passion–resurrection accounts, "the storied Jesus is most of all himself" (pp. 142–43).

[31] Ibid., pp. 133, 81.

[32] Gene Outka, "Following at a Distance: Ethics and the Identity of Jesus" in Green, ed., *Scriptural Authority*, pp. 153, 158.

[33] Brock, *Journeys by Heart*, p. 32.

to address the troubling social and theological issues Brock raises in order fully to meet their burden of proof. Meeting this obligation would be part of practicing theology as fully critical (theoretical and practical) conversation.

Brock approaches the Gospel of Mark in light of the fact that we are all damaged in male-dominated social systems like the gender-biased family. From this perspective, she reads Mark as an account of the uneven but unmistakable breakthrough of healing relationships which can address our "brokenheartedness."[34] The gospels provide accounts of what she calls "erotic" power – that is, nondominating, relational wholeness which ultimately "leads us to a greater sense of the whole of life as sacred." The source of this power is not exclusively Jesus Christ but "Christa/Community," a term which synthesizes the concepts of Christ and *basileia*. Christa/Community is the erotic-power-driven community related to Jesus as "one historical part" of a much larger network of those who incarnate the spiritual "power which restores heart."[35] Although the gospel text Brock works with is, loosely defined, narrative, her plain sense is not realistic or history-like. She reads the story of the Gerasene demoniac (Mk. 5:1–20) allegorically as a "vivid metaphor of internalized oppression."[36] Her reading of the inter-calated stories of Jairus's daughter and the hemorrhaging woman (Mk. 5:21–43) is a sociologically oriented, feminist critical historical retrieval of submerged female agency. Jesus' tomb is given a structuralist analysis, and the resurrection is interpreted in an existentialist manner as the disciples' experience of a living Spirit.[37] According to Brock's reading, Mark does not render Jesus' unsubstitutable and, therefore, salvific identity in the passion–resurrection sequence (read narratively as Frei does). Even Jesus at times cannot heal (Mk. 6:6) but must use "helpers . . . to expand the field of erotic power" in order to do the heal-ing work "which he cannot do alone."[38] From a rule theory perspec-tive, she reads the Gospel of Mark as entailing theological grammars which promote Christa/Community as a co-creation of people who have confronted the demons of their "own pain and despair" (after the

---

[34] Ibid., pp. 87f.
[35] Ibid., pp. 46, 69, 103.
[36] Ibid., p. 78.
[37] Ibid., pp. 81ff. and 102f.
[38] Ibid., p. 87.

example of Jesus in the desert) and whose faith in their self-worth "empowers [them] . . . to be healed by each other."[39]

Some theologians might respond that Brock's christology of erotic relational power entails the loss of a transcendent divine savior (and appeals to God's transcendence are a needed avenue of social empowerment for those resisting dominance by their earthly masters[40]). Brock might argue that such appeals to a transcendent savior are too often turned against the powerless, and thus should be abandoned in favor of appeals to immanent, relational erotic power. My point, again, is that this doctrinal innovation should be argued fully, because to accept Brock's doctrinal revisions would mean massive changes in the tradition (theological, liturgical, ecclesial, etc.). To meet her burden of proof, she would need to address (in addition to the concerns already raised) how to fill the significant liturgical gap created by the loss of deep-seated symbols of a uniquely redemptive, transcendently powerful savior.

For the theological discussion to go forward, all parties would need to understand the tradition as "comprised of those voices of the past and present which *debate* the true nature of the Christian faith" (as Ronald Thiemann puts it).[41] When debating, the burden of proof must rest on both positions – with the above-mentioned provisoes in effect. (A regulative approach would be nearly indispensable for sharpening grammatical and vocabulary differences and compatibilities.) Since there is ample reason (i.e., the life and fidelity of Christian communities) to require theologians from the mainstream and the margins to defend the validity of their positions, the virtuous mean on the issue of burden of proof should be the arithmetic mean between preservation and innovation. This in no way would compromise a weighted dialectical hermeneutic (as discussed in chapter four) which privileges the scriptural readings of the "other." It goes without saying that dominant theology carries the moral responsibility continually to expose itself to marginalized voices within the global church. The maxim of equal burden of proof is not an excuse for privileged sectors of mainstream theology to close themselves off from what

---

[39] Ibid., pp. 81, 86.

[40] See Kathryn Tanner, *The Politics of God: Christian Theologies and Social Justice* (Minneapolis: Fortress, 1992).

[41] Ronald F. Thiemann, *Revelation and Theology: The Gospel as Narrated Promise* (University of Notre Dame Press, 1985), p. 73; emphasis added. Thiemann is drawing from Alasdair MacIntyre's definition of tradition as "an historically extended, socially embodied argument" (p. 72).

Gutiérrez calls the militant readings of the Bible of the church of the poor.

Detachment and connection

The final set of poles has to do with theology's detachment from and connection to Christian communal discourse and praxis. This issue brings us back around to chapter one's discussion of strict and broad definitions of theology – strict definitions tending toward detachment and broad definitions tending toward connection. I argued already that there is nothing in principle wrong with defining theology either broadly or strictly, so long as all three of the theological values I have been promoting are formally acknowledged in not too unfocused a way. Each definition of theology reenforces certain risks in relation to the hazards associated with the pole of connection or detachment. For example, the closer one moves toward the pole of detachment (which characterizes Ogden's strict definition), the more one risks losing focus on the value of normative redescription which entails reflecting with the Christian community. The closer one moves toward the pole of connection (which characterizes Frei's and Gutiérrez's broad definitions), the more one risks losing focus on the value of fully critical and independent theological reflection on the Christian witness.

What then would the arithmetic mean look like on this issue? While no definition of theology ever is perfectly and statically balanced between these two poles, I would argue that Boff's definition in *Theology and Praxis* approximates fairly well the arithmetic mean on this issue. As discussed in chapter three, Boff defines theology strictly, reserving the term for critical, discursive theory on faith as distinguished from performative, self-involving religious discourse in faith. He understands that theology can sometimes become "a charism in the church" and a "genuine expression of faith and *agape*"; however, theology must practice autonomy from religious discourse by "interposing" between that discourse and itself "the tools of [its] method."[42] Boff's valuing of theology's critical independence does not cause his theology to inch down the line toward the pole of detachment, as is the case with Ogden. I attribute this to the fact that Boff's view of how theology and

---

[42] Boff, *Theology and Praxis*, p. 113.

religious discourse are related differs from Ogden's in a significant way. Ogden simply states that the two discourses are related by virtue of the prior existence of the Christian religion on which theology reflects. Boff, on the other hand, specifies an organic, somewhat cultural-linguistic, linkage between religious and theological discourse. Although the form of the two discourses is different, they are both ruled by the same grammar (implicit in religious discourse, explicit in theology). This shared grammar makes the breach between them only a "quasi breach."[43] One cannot characterize Ogden's norm of appropriateness as a shared organic element between theology and witness, since the Jesus-kerygma is not a connatural norm embedded in beliefs and practices of Christians but is a canon before the canon imposed by the theologian. Boff's notion of the regulative grammar shared by theological and religious discourse, combined with a liberation theological sensibility for the grassroots church's struggle for justice, allow him to value theology's critical independence without moving toward the extreme of detachment. Ogden's strict conception of theology, when combined with a methodologically unspecified sense of how the connatural sense of the Christian witness might critically bear upon theology, may not be able to ward off the "vice" of too much detachment.

I fully recognize that Ogden's strict definition of theology can, in some contexts, itself be a virtuous mean. There are situations where a strict use would be not only appropriate but very needful, for example, a theological school so tightly controlled by a governing religious institution that doing theology consisted of handing on a hierarchically promulgated dogma. Theologians might have difficulty calling this activity "theology as fully critical reflection" and might be impelled to apply the term theology more strictly in that setting in order to reinforce the idea of theology's freedom to reflect critically on any Christian claim. As a result of his tenure on the Special Committee on Academic Freedom in Church-Related Colleges and Universities of the American Association of University Professors, Ogden makes a strong case for a scholarly theology free from ecclesiastical censure, citing several recent instances of loss or restriction of the academic freedom of religion professors at university and nonuniversity schools of theology.[44] This

---

[43] Ibid., p. 116.
[44] See Schubert M. Ogden, "Theology in the University: The Question of Integrity" in his *Doing Theology Today* (Valley Forge, Pa.: Trinity, 1996), pp. 80–91.

problem is not just a North American phenomenon. In chapter five, I mentioned the criticism of Gutiérrez by the Congregation for the Doctrine of the Faith. Moreover, Clodovis Boff spoke out strongly against the Vatican's disciplinary "silence of obedience" that was placed upon his brother Leonardo in 1985.[45]

In light of Boff's personal experience with ecclesial disciplinary oversight, it may seem ironic that he has, in more recent years, changed in his thinking away from a strict definition of theology. In his discussions in *Theology and Praxis* regarding how theology should be related to the discourse of Christian communities, Boff is clear not to call the latter "theology." Following the completion of this text, which was originally his dissertation at the Catholic University of Louvain, Boff returned to Brazil where he has divided his time between teaching at the Pontifical Catholic University in Rio de Janeiro and pastoral work with base Christian communities in the Amazon jungle.[46] Given this new context, it is perhaps not surprising that he has retreated from defining theology strictly. In a recent article, he speaks of liberation theology as "a single comprehensive theological process" entailing three modes: popular (grassroots), pastoral and professional. This change to a broad definition of theology may reflect that Boff has concluded that a strict definition could not do justice to the role which the discourses of base Christian communities play in professional theological reflection. He seems to have developed more of an existential appreciation for how grassroots and pastoral theologies have their own nonacademic but still critically reflective sense to which theology should seriously attend in order to be both fully critical and in solidarity with the oppressed.[47]

This shift in Boff's thinking is instructive for helping us understand

---

[45] See Leonardo Boff, "Summons to Rome: A Personal Testimony" and Clodovis Boff, "The Value of Resistance" in their *Liberation Theology: From Dialogue to Confrontation*, tr. Robert R. Barr (San Francisco: Harper & Row, 1985). See also Paul E. Sigmund, *Liberation Theology at the Crossroads: Democracy or Revolution* (New York and Oxford: Oxford University Press, 1990), ch. 9.

[46] See Clodovis Boff, O.S.M., *Feet-On-The-Ground Theology: A Brazilian Journey*, tr. Phillip Berryman (Maryknoll: Orbis, 1987).

[47] Clodovis Boff, "Epistemology and Method of the Theology of Liberation," tr. Robert R. Barr, in *Mysterium Liberationis: Fundamental Concepts of Liberation Theology*, ed. Ignacio Ellacuría, S.J., and Jon Sobrino, S.J. (Maryknoll: Orbis, 1993), pp. 67, 70. Despite this change in terminology, Boff's major methodological commitments appear to be fairly continuous with his early work. For example, he remains unchanged in his insistence that praxis, while the indispensable "*material* starting point, that is, the raw material" for theology, is not its validating criterion (p. 59).

the notion of the virtuous mean. Boff's early position (a strict definition of theology) epitomizes the ideally balanced arithmetic mean between detachment and connection. However, theology does not take place in an ideal realm. Theology is an historical practice and the theologian must constantly adjust methodological elements in order to maximize the ability to enhance "virtues" and avoid "vices" in changing contexts. Boff's move from a strict to a broad definition can be viewed as an attempt to continue to focus on theology's critical task but in a different way – that is, slightly closer to the connection pole. He may have strategically deemphasized the value of theology's independence as a part of fully critical theoretical practice; however, he might argue that employing a broad definition has enhanced his ability to bring a more relevantly critical assessment to the actual communities with which he is currently concerned by acknowledging their own critically reflective theologizing potential. In other words, a virtuous mean requires prudent judgments for accepting some losses to maximize other goods which are pressing for a particular context.

An enduring legacy of the era of modern theology has been its ability to draw from the rich resources and challenges of academia's philosophical, historical and scientific consciousness. As a result, much of the theological guild today has comfortably settled into cultivating that scholarly consciousness. Some theologians, however, have discovered that the vitality of theology in the foreseeable future is not going to come simply from within the walls of the academy; rather, it is going to burst through the cracks in the walls which separate the professional theologian from the creativity, fidelity and plurality of Christian communities. Indeed, for all their differences, I believe this discovery is (implicit or explicit) common ground among revisionary, postliberal and liberation theologies. An attempt to listen to the church exudes from Gutiérrez's *We Drink from Our Own Wells*; it inspires the programmatic visions in Lindbeck's *The Nature of Doctrine* and Ogden's *Faith and Freedom,* and animates notions such as Tracy's prophetic-mystical dialectic, Frei's functional plain sense and Boff's hermeneutical *habitus.*

Theology in contemporary culture must be reconceived in order to make best use of the connatural critical insights from the grassroots church. It is for this reason that I identify the virtuous mean closer to the pole of connection than detachment and tend toward a broad rather than a strict definition of theology. The insights of the theologizing emerging from Christian communities must be allowed to inform and correct professional theology – all the more so when that theologizing is from those Christians who have been structurally excluded from theological conversation and material well being. Their contemplative and prophetic denunciation and annunciation, born out of suffering and hope, is not a perspective readily understood by the privileged. Academic theology can get by quite comfortably without this perspective. Will it thereby have maximized its possibility of realizing a good and fruitful end? Given the realities of today's world, I think not. Echoes from Aquinas continue to provide a timely lesson. Being oriented to the ultimate good requires nothing less than the charisms of wisdom guided by love.[48] Theological practice does not require such graces for its intellectual work to proceed, but theologians must therefore take care – especially in light of the world's despised and rejected – that we do not lose our "taste," as Gutiérrez says, for the kinds of charisms which give us a dim sense of knowing and loving as God knows and loves.[49]

[48] See Thomas Aquinas, *Summa Theologiae*, II–II, q. 45, a. 2.
[49] Gustavo Gutiérrez, *A Theology of Liberation: History, Politics, and Salvation*, tr. and ed. Sister Caridad Inda and John Eagleson; author's new introduction and revisions, tr. Matthew J. O'Connell (Maryknoll: Orbis, 1988), p. xxxii.

Select bibliography

Aquinas, Thomas. *Commentary on the Nicomachean Ethics.* Translated by C. I. Litzinger, O.P. Vol. I. Chicago: Henry Regnary, 1964.

Aristotle, *Nicomachean Ethics.* Translated by Terence Irwin. Indianapolis: Hackett, 1985.

Beardslee, William A. "Poststructuralist Criticism." In *To Each Its Own Meaning: An Introduction to Biblical Criticisms and Their Application,* edited by Steven McKenzie and Stephen Haynes. Louisville: Westminster/John Knox, 1993.

Bernstein, Richard J. *Beyond Objectivism and Relativism: Science, Hermeneutics, and Praxis.* Philadelphia: University of Pennsylvania Press, 1983.

"Radical Plurality, Fearful Ambiguity, and Engaged Hope." *Journal of Religion* 69 (1989): 85–91.

Boff, Clodovis, O.S.M. "Epistemology and Method of the Theology of Liberation." Translated by Robert R. Barr. In *Mysterium Liberationis: Fundamental Concepts of Liberation Theology,* edited by Ignacio Ellacuría, S.J., and Jon Sobrino, S.J., 57–85. Maryknoll: Orbis, 1993.

Feet-On-The-Ground Theology: A Brazilian Journey. Translated by Phillip Berryman. Maryknoll: Orbis, 1987.

"The Nature of Basic Christian Communities." Translated by Paul Burns. In *Tensions Between the Churches of the First World and the Third World,* edited by Virgil Elizondo and Norbert Greinacher, 53–58. Concilium 144. Edinburgh: T. & T. Clark; New York: Seabury, 1981.

Theology and Praxis: Epistemological Foundations. Translated by Robert R. Barr. Maryknoll: Orbis, 1987.

Boff, Leonardo. *Ecology and Liberation: A New Paradigm.* Translated by John Cumming. Maryknoll: Orbis, 1995.

Boff, Leonardo and Clodovis Boff. *Liberation Theology: From Dialogue to Confrontation.* Translated by Robert R. Barr. San Francisco: Harper & Row, 1985.

Brackley, Dean. *Divine Revolution: Salvation and Liberation in Catholic Thought.* Maryknoll: Orbis, 1996.

Brock, Rita Nakashima. *Journeys by Heart: A Christology of Erotic Power*. New York: Crossroad, 1988.

Brown, Delwin. *Boundaries of Our Habitations: Tradition and Theological Construction*. Albany: State University of New York Press, 1994.

"God's Reality and Life's Meaning." *Encounter* 28 (1967): 256–62.

Buckley, James J. "Revisionists and Liberals." In Ford, ed., *The Modern Theologians*, 327–42.

Cadorette, Curt. *From the Heart of the People: The Theology of Gustavo Gutiérrez*. Oak Park, Ill.: Meyer-Stone, 1988.

Chopp, Rebecca S. "Latin American Liberation Theology." In Ford, ed., *The Modern Theologians*, 409–25.

Cone, James H. *Black Theology and Black Power*. New York: Seabury, 1969.

The Congregation for the Doctrine of the Faith. "Ten Observations on the Theology of Gustavo Gutiérrez" (March 1983). In *Liberation Theology: A Documentary History*, edited and translated by Alfred T. Hennelly, S.J., 425–30. Maryknoll: Orbis, 1990.

Cunningham, David S. "Clodovis Boff on the Discipline of Theology." *Modern Theology* 6 (1990): 137–58.

Daniels, Norman. *Justice and Justification: Reflective Equilibrium in Theory and Practice*. Cambridge University Press, 1996.

"On Some Methods of Ethics and Linguistics." *Philosophical Studies* 37 (1980): 21–36.

"Wide Reflective Equilibrium and Theory Acceptance in Ethics." *Journal of Philosophy* 76 (1979): 256–82.

Davidson, Donald. "On the Very Idea of a Conceptual Scheme." In *Post-Analytic Philosophy*, edited by John Rajchman and Cornel West, 129–43. New York: Columbia University Press, 1985.

Dean, William. *History Making History: The New Historicism in American Religious Thought*. Albany: State University of New York, 1988.

Derrida, Jacques. *Of Grammatology*, Translated by Gayatri Chakravorty Spivak. Baltimore and London: Johns Hopkins University Press, 1976.

Fiorenza, Francis Schüssler. *Foundational Theology: Jesus and the Church*. New York: Crossroad, 1986.

"Systematic Theology: Task and Methods." In *Systematic Theology: Roman Catholic Perspectives*, edited by Francis Schüssler Fiorenza and John P. Galvin, 3–87. Vol. I. Minneapolis: Fortress, 1991.

"Theology as Responsible Valuation or Reflective Equilibrium: The Legacy of H. Richard Niebuhr." In *The Legacy of H. Richard Niebuhr*, edited by Ronald F. Thiemann, 33–71. Minneapolis: Fortress, 1991.

Ford, David F. "On Being Theologically Hospitable to Jesus Christ: Hans Frei's Achievement." *Journal of Theological Studies* 46 (1995): 532–46.

Ford, David F., ed. *The Modern Theologians: An Introduction to Christian Theology in the Twentieth Century*. 2nd edn. Cambridge, Mass. and Oxford: Blackwell, 1997.

Foster, Matthew. *Gadamer and Practical Philosophy: The Hermeneutics of Moral Confidence.* Atlanta: Scholars, 1991.

Foucault, Michel. *Power/Knowledge: Selected Interviews and Other Writings, 1972–1977.* Edited and translated by Colin Gordon, et al. New York: Pantheon, 1980.

Frei, Hans W. "An Afterword: Eberhard Busch's Biography of Karl Barth." In *Karl Barth in Re-View,* edited by H. Martin Rumscheidt, 95–116. Pittsburg: Pickwick, 1981.

"Barth and Schleiermacher: Divergence and Convergence." In *Barth and Schleiermacher: Beyond the Impasse,* edited by James O. Duke and Robert F. Streetman, 65–87. Philadelphia: Fortress, 1988.

The Eclipse of Biblical Narrative: A Study in Eighteenth and Nineteenth Century Hermeneutics. New Haven and London: Yale University Press, 1974.

"How It All Began: On the Resurrection of Christ." *Anglican and Episcopal History* 58 (1989): 139–45.

The Identity of Jesus Christ: The Hermeneutical Bases of Dogmatic Theology. Philadelphia: Fortress, 1975.

"The 'Literal Reading' of Biblical Narrative in the Christian Tradition: Does It Stretch or Will It Break?" In *The Bible and the Narrative Tradition,* edited by Frank McConnell, 36–77. New York and Oxford: Oxford University Press, 1986.

"Theological Reflections on the Accounts of Jesus' Death and Resurrection." *Christian Scholar* 49 (1966): 263–306.

Theology and Narrative: Selected Essays. Edited by George Hunsinger and William C. Placher. New York and Oxford: Oxford University Press, 1993.

Types of Christian Theology. Edited by George Hunsinger and William C. Placher. New Haven and London: Yale University Press, 1992.

Geertz, Clifford. *The Interpretation of Cultures.* New York: Basic, 1973.

Grant, Robert with David Tracy. *A Short History of the Interpretation of the Bible.* 2nd edn. N.p.: Fortress Press, 1984.

Green, Garrett, ed. *Scriptural Authority and Narrative Interpretation.* Philadelphia: Fortress, 1987.

Griffiths, A. Phillips. "Transcendental Arguments." *Proceedings of the Aristotelian Society* 43. Suppl. (1969).

Gutiérrez, Gustavo. "The Church and the Poor: A Latin American Perspective." Translated by Matthew J. O'Connell. In *The Reception of Vatican II,* edited by Guiseppe Alberigo, et al., 171–93. Wash., D.C.: Catholic University of America Press, 1987.

"Faith as Freedom: Solidarity with the Alienated and Confidence in the Future." In *Living with Change, Experience, Faith,* edited by Francis A. Eigo, O.S.A., 15–54. Villanova University Press, 1976.

The God of Life. Translated by Matthew J. O'Connell. Maryknoll: Orbis, 1991.

Las Casas: In Search of the Poor of Jesus Christ. Translated by Robert R. Barr. Maryknoll: Orbis, 1993.

"*Mirar lejos*." *Paginas* 93 (1988): 63–97.

On Job: God-Talk and the Suffering of the Innocent. Translated by Matthew J. O'Connell. Maryknoll: Orbis, 1988.

"Option for the Poor." Translated by Robert R. Barr. In *Mysterium Liberationis: Fundamental Concepts of Liberation Theology*, edited by Ignacio Ellacuría, S.J., and Jon Sobrino, S.J., 235–50. Maryknoll: Orbis, 1993.

The Power of the Poor in History. Translated by Robert R. Barr. Maryknoll: Orbis, 1983.

"Reflections from a Latin American Perspective: Finding Our Way to Talk about God." Translated by John Drury. In *Irruption of the Third World*, edited by Virginia Fabella and Sergio Torres, 222–34. Maryknoll: Orbis, 1983.

"The Task of Theology and Ecclesial Experience." Translated by Dinah Livingston. In *La Iglesia Popular: Between Fear and Hope*, edited by Leonardo Boff and Virgil Elizondo, 61–64. Concilium 176. Edinburgh: T. & T. Clark, 1984.

A Theology of Liberation: History, Politics and Salvation. Translated and edited by Sister Caridad Inda and John Eagleson. Maryknoll: Orbis, 1973.

A Theology of Liberation: History, Politics and Salvation. Translated and edited by Sister Caridad Inda and John Eagleson. Author's new introduction and revisions; translated by Matthew J. O'Connell. Maryknoll: Orbis, 1988.

"Theology, Spirituality, and Historical Praxis." Translated by Robert R. Barr. In *The Future of Theology: Essays in Honor of Jürgen Moltmann*, edited by Miroslav Volf, et al., 176–84. Grand Rapids, Mich.: William B. Eerdmans, 1996.

The Truth Shall Make You Free: Confrontations. Translated by Matthew J. O'Connell. Maryknoll: Orbis, 1990.

We Drink from Our Own Wells: The Spiritual Journey of a People. Translated by Matthew J. O'Connell. Maryknoll: Orbis, 1985.

Hauerwas, Stanley. *After Christendom? How the Church Is to Behave If Freedom, Justice, and a Christian Nation Are Bad Ideas*. Nashville: Abingdon, 1991.

Against the Nations: War and Survival in a Liberal Society. Minneapolis: Winston, 1985.

"The Church as God's New Language." In Green, ed., *Scriptural Authority*, 179–98.

A Community of Character: Toward a Constructive Christian Social Ethic. University of Notre Dame Press, 1981.

"The Difference of Virtue and the Difference It Makes: Courage Exemplified." *Modern Theology* 9 (1993): 249–64.

In Good Company: The Church as Polis. University of Notre Dame Press, 1995.

The Peaceable Kingdom: A Primer in Christian Ethics. University of Notre Dame Press, 1983.

"Some Theological Reflections on Gutierrez's Use of 'Liberation' as a Theological Concept." *Modern Theology* 3 (1986): 67–76.

Truthfulness and Tragedy: Further Investigations into Christian Ethics. University of Notre Dame Press, 1977.

Unleashing the Scripture: Freeing the Bible from Captivity to America. Nashville: Abingdon, 1993.

Hodgson, Peter C. *God in History: Shapes of Freedom.* Nashville: Abingdon, 1989.

Review of *Erring*, by Mark C. Taylor. *Religious Studies Review* 12 (1986): 256–61.

Hunsinger, George. "Afterword: Hans Frei as Theologian." In Frei, *Theology and Narrative*, 235–70.

"Hans Frei as Theologian: The Quest for a Generous Orthodoxy." *Modern Theology* 8 (1992): 103–28.

"Karl Barth and Liberation Theology." *Journal of Religion* 63 (1983): 247–63.

Kamitsuka, David G. "The Justification of Religious Belief in the Pluralistic Public Realm: Another Look at Postliberal Apologetics." *Journal of Religion* 79 (1996): 588–606.

"Salvation, Liberation and Christian Character Formation: Postliberal and Liberation Theologians in Dialogue." *Modern Theology* 13 (1997): 171–89.

Kelsey, David H. "Church Discourse and Public Realm." In Marshall, ed., *Theology and Dialogue*, 7–33.

"Method, Theological." In *The Westminster Dictionary of Christian Theology*, edited by Alan Richardson and John Bowden, 363–67. Philadelphia: Westminster, 1983.

"Struggling Collegially to Think about Evil: An Interpretive Essay." *Occasional Papers.* The Institute for Ecumenical and Cultural Research, no. 16 (Sept. 1981): 1–6.

The Uses of Scripture in Recent Theology. Philadelphia: Fortress, 1975.

Klemke, E. D., ed., *The Meaning of Life.* New York and Oxford: Oxford University Press, 1981.

Körner, Stephan. "The Impossibility of Transcendental Deductions." *Monist* 51 (1967): 317–31.

What Is Philosophy? One Philosopher's Answer. London: Penguin, 1969.

Kort, Wesley A. *Bound to Differ: The Dynamics of Theological Discourses.* University Park, Pa.: Pennsylvania State University Press, 1992.

Kuhn, Thomas S. *The Structures of Scientific Revolutions.* 2nd edn. University of Chicago Press, 1974.

Lakeland, Paul. *Theology and Critical Theory: The Discourse of the Church.* Abingdon, 1990.

Lamb, Matthew L. "A Distorted Interpretation of Latin American Liberation Theology." *Horizons* 8 (1981): 352–64.

Lash, Nicholas. "Not Exactly Politics or Power?" *Modern Theology* 8 (1992): 353–64.

Lindbeck, George A. "Atonement and the Hermeneutics of Intratextual Social Embodiment." In *The Nature of Confession: Evangelicals and Postliberals in Conversation*, edited by Timothy R. Phillips and Dennis L. Okholm, 221–40. Downer Grove, Ill.: Intervarsity, 1996.

"Barth and Textuality." *Theology Today* 43 (1986): 361–82.

"Discovering Thomas: The Classic Statement of Christian Theism." *Una Sancta* 24 (1967): 45–52.

The Nature of Doctrine: Religion and Theology in a Postliberal Age. Philadelphia: Westminster, 1984.

"Scripture, Consensus, and Community." *This World: A Journal of Religion and Public Life* 23 (1988): 5–24.

"The Story-Shaped Church: Critical Exegesis and Theological Interpretation." In Green, ed., *Scriptural Authority*, 161–78.

"Theological Revolutions and the Present Crisis." *Theology Digest* 23 (1975): 308–19.

Lints, Richard. "The Postpositivist Choice: Tracy or Lindbeck?" *Journal of the American Academy of Religion* 61 (1993): 655–77.

Maimonides, Moses. *Rambam: Readings in the Philosophy of Moses Maimonides.* Translated by Lenn Evan Goodman. New York: Viking, 1976.

Marshall, Bruce D. "Absorbing the World: Christianity and the Universe of Truths." In Marshall, ed., *Theology and Dialogue*, 69–102.

"Truth Claims and the Possibility of Jewish–Christian Dialogue." *Modern Theology* 8 (1992): 221–40.

Marshall, Bruce D., ed. *Theology and Dialogue: Essays in Conversation with George Lindbeck.* University of Notre Dame Press, 1990.

McCann, Dennis P. *Christian Realism and Liberation Theology.* Maryknoll: Orbis, 1981.

"The Developing Gutiérrez." *Commonweal* (Nov. 4, 1988): 594–95.

McCarthy, Gerald. "Meaning, Morals and the Existence of God." *Horizons* 9 (1982): 288–301.

McCarthy, Thomas. *The Critical Theory of Jürgen Habermas.* Cambridge, Mass. and London: MIT Press, 1978.

McGovern, Arthur F. *Liberation Theology and Its Critics: Toward an Assessment.* Maryknoll: Orbis, 1989.

McMullin, Ernan. "The Fertility of Theory and the Unit for Appraisal in Science." In *Essays in Memory of Imre Lakatos*, edited by R. S. Cohen, et al., 395–432. Dordrecht: D. Reidel, 1976.

Míguez Bonino, José. *Christians and Marxists: The Mutual Challenge to Revolution.* Grand Rapids, Mich.: William B. Eerdmans, 1976.

"Popular Piety in Latin America." Translated by J. P. Donnelly. In *The Mystical and Political Dimensions of the Christian Faith*, edited by Claude

Geffré and Gustavo Gutiérrez, 148–57. New York: Herder & Herder, 1974.

Toward a Christian Political Ethics. Philadelphia: Fortress, 1983.

Milbank, John. *Theology and Social Theory: Beyond Secular Reason*. Oxford and Cambridge, Mass.: Blackwell, 1993.

Murphy, Nancey and James Wm. McClendon, Jr. "Distinguishing Modern and Postmodern Theologies." *Modern Theology* 5 (1989): 191–214.

Nessan, Craig L. *Orthopraxis or Heresy: The North American Theological Response to Latin American Liberation Theology*. Atlanta: Scholars, 1989.

Nichols, Aidan, O.P. "The Story of *Praxis*: Liberation Theology's Philosophical Handmaid." *Religion in Communist Lands* 17 (1989): 45–58.

Niebuhr, H. Richard. *Christ and Culture*. New York: Harper & Row, 1951.

Nielsen, Kai. *After the Demise of the Tradition: Rorty, Critical Theory and the Fate of Philosophy*. Boulder, Co.: Westview, 1991.

Ogden, Schubert M. *Christ Without Myth: A Study Based on the Theology of Rudolf Bultmann*. Dallas: Southern Methodist University Press, 1961.

"Concerning Belief in God." In *Faith and Creativity: Essays in Honor of Eugene H. Peters*, edited by George Nordgulen and George W. Shields, 81–94. St. Louis: CBP, 1987.

Doing Theology Today. Valley Forge, Pa.: Trinity, 1996.

"The Enlightenment Is Not Over." In *Knowledge and Belief in America: Enlightenment Traditions and Modern Religious Thought*, edited by William M. Shea and Peter A. Huff, 321–27. Cambridge University Press, 1995.

"The Experience of God: Critical Reflections on Hartshorne's Theory of Analogy." In *Existence and Actuality: Conversations with Charles Hartshorne*," edited by John B. Cobb, Jr., and Franklin I. Gamwell, 16–42. University of Chicago Press, 1984.

Faith and Freedom: Toward a Theology of Liberation. Rev. edn. Nashville: Abingdon, 1989.

"*Fundamentum Fidei*: Critical Reflection on Willi Marxsen's Contribution to Systematic Theology." *Modern Theology* 6 (1989): 1–15.

Is There Only One True Religion or Are There Many? Dallas: Southern Methodist University Press, 1992.

"Karl Rahner: Theologian of Open Catholicism." *Christian Advocate* (Sept. 7, 1967): 11–13.

"Linguistic Analysis and Theology." *Theologische Zeitschrift* 33 (1977): 318–25.

"The Metaphysics of Faith and Justice." *Process Studies* 14 (1985): 87–101.

"The Nature and State of Theological Scholarship and Research." *Theological Education* 24 (1987–88): 120–31.

"On Teaching Theology." *Criterion* 25 (1986): 13–14.

On Theology. San Francisco: Harper & Row, 1986.

The Point of Christology. San Francisco: Harper & Row, 1982.

"Present Prospects for Empirical Theology." In *The Future of Empirical Theology*, edited by Bernard E. Meland, 65–88. University of Chicago Press, 1969.

"Process Theology and Wesleyan Witness." In *Wesleyan Theology Today*, edited by Theodore Runyan, 65–75. Nashville: Kingswood, 1985.

The Reality of God: And Other Essays. San Francisco: Harper & Row, 1963.

Review of *Types of Christian Theology*, by Hans W. Frei. *Modern Theology* 9 (1993): 211–14.

"The Service of Theology to the Servant Task of Pastoral Ministry." In *The Pastor as Servant*, edited by Earl E. Shelp and Ronald H. Sutherland, 81–101. New York: Pilgrim, 1986.

"Toward Doing Theology." *Journal of Religion* 75 (1995): 1–14.

Outka, Gene. "Following at a Distance: Ethics and the Identity of Jesus." In Green, ed., *Scriptural Authority*, 144–60.

Park, Andrew Sung. *The Wounded Heart of God: The Asian Concept of Han and the Christian Doctrine of Sin*. Nashville: Abingdon, 1993.

Phillips, Winfred G. "Schubert Ogden's Transcendental Strategy Against Secularism." *Harvard Theological Review* 82 (1989): 447–66.

Placher, William C. "Postliberal Theology." In Ford, ed., *The Modern Theologians*, 343–56.

"Revisionist and Postliberal Theologies and the Public Character of Theology." *Thomist* 49 (1985): 392–416.

Unapologetic Theology: A Christian Voice in a Pluralistic Conversation. Louisville: Westminster/John Knox, 1989.

Proudfoot, Wayne. *Religious Experience*. Berkeley: University of California Press, 1985.

Rahner, Karl, S.J. "Letter to Cardinal Juan Landázuri Ricketts of Lima, Peru" (March 16, 1984). In *Liberation Theology: A Documentary History*, edited and translated by Alfred T. Hennelly, S.J., 351–52. Maryknoll: Orbis, 1990.

Rawls, John. *Political Liberalism*. New York: Columbia University Press, 1993.

A Theory of Justice. Cambridge, Mass.: Harvard University Press, 1971.

Roberts, Robert H. "Transcendental Sociology? A Critique of John Milbank's *Theology and Social Theory: Beyond Secular Reason*." *Scottish Journal of Theology* 46 (1993): 527–35.

Root, Michael. "Dying He Lives: Biblical Image, Biblical Narrative and the Redemptive Jesus." *Semeia* 30 (1985): 155–69.

"Identity and Difference: The Ecumenical Problem." In Marshall, ed. *Theology and Dialogue*," 165–90.

"Images of Liberation: Justin, Jesus and the Jews." *Thomist* 48 (1984): 512–34.

Rorty, Richard. *Consequences of Pragmatism*. University of Minneapolis Press, 1982.

"Metaphilosophical Difficulties of Linguistic Philosophy." In *The Linguistic*

Turn: Recent Essays in Philosophical Method, edited by Richard Rorty, 1–39. University of Chicago Press, 1967.

Objectivity, Relativism and Truth: Philosophical Papers. Vol. 1. Cambridge University Press, 1991,

Philosophy and the Mirror of Nature. Princeton University Press, 1979.

"Transcendental Arguments, Self-Reference, and Pragmatism." In *Transcendental Arguments and Science: Essays in Epistemology*, edited by Peter Bieri, et al., 77–103. Dordrecht: D. Reidel, 1979.

Ruether, Rosemary Radford. *Sexism and God-Talk: Toward a Feminist Theology.* With new introduction. Boston: Beacon, 1993.

Sigmund, Paul E. *Liberation Theology at the Crossroads: Democracy or Revolution.* New York and Oxford: Oxford University Press, 1990.

Stout, Jeffrey. *Ethics After Babel: The Language of Morals and Their Discontents.* Boston: Beacon, 1988.

The Flight from Authority: Religion, Morality, and the Quest for Autonomy. University of Notre Dame Press, 1981.

Tanner, Kathryn E. *God and Creation in Christian Theology: Tyranny or Empowerment.* New York and Oxford: Blackwell, 1988.

The Politics of God: Christian Theologies and Social Justice. Minneapolis: Fortress, 1992.

"Public Theology and the Character of Public Debate." *The Annual of the Society of Christian Ethics* (1996): 79–101.

"Theology and the Plain Sense." In Green, ed., *Scriptural Authority*, 59–78.

Taylor, Mark C. *Erring: A Postmodern A/theology.* University of Chicago Press, 1984.

Thiemann, Ronald F. *Constructing a Public Theology: The Church in a Pluralistic Culture.* Louisville: Westminster/John Knox, 1991.

"Radiance and Obscurity in Biblical Narrative." In Green., ed., *Scriptural Authority*, 21–41.

Revelation and Theology: The Gospel as Narrated Promise. University of Notre Dame Press, 1985.

Tilley, Terrence W. "God and the Silencing of Job." *Modern Theology* 5 (1989): 257–70.

"Incommensurability, Intratextuality, and Fideism." *Modern Theology* 5 (1989): 87–111.

Tracy, David. *The Analogical Imagination: Christian Theology and the Culture of Pluralism.* New York: Crossroad, 1986.

"Approaching the Christian Understanding of God." In *Systematic Theology: Roman Catholic Perspectives*, edited by Francis Schüssler Fiorenza and John P. Galvin, 133–48. Vol. 1. Minneapolis: Fortress, 1991.

"Argument, Dialogue, and the Soul in Plato." In *Witness and Existence: Essays in Honor of Schubert Ogden*, edited by Philip E. Devenish and George L. Goodwin, 91–105. University of Chicago Press, 1989.

Blessed Rage for Order: The New Pluralism in Theology. New York: Seabury, 1978.
"Can Virtue Be Taught? Education, Character, and the Soul." *Theological Education.* Suppl. 1 (1988): 33–52.
Dialogue with the Other: The Inter-Religious Dialogue. Louvain: Peeters; Grand Rapids, Mich.: William B. Eerdmans, 1990.
"The Foundations of Practical Theology." In *Practical Theology: The Emerging Field in Theology, Church and World,* edited by Don S. Browning, 61–82. San Francisco: Harper & Row, 1983.
"Hermeneutical Reflections in the New Paradigm." In *Paradigm Change in Theology,* edited by Hans Küng and David Tracy, 34–62. New York: Crossroad, 1989.
"Lindbeck's New Program for Theology: A Reflection" *Thomist* 49 (1985): 460–72.
On Naming the Present: God, Hermeneutics, and Church. Maryknoll: Orbis; London: SCM, 1994.
"On Reading The Scriptures Theologically." In Marshall, ed., *Theology and Dialogue,* 35–68.
Plurality and Ambiguity: Hermeneutics, Religion, Hope. San Francisco: Harper & Row, 1987.
"Religious Studies and Its Community of Inquiry." *Criterion* 25 (1986): 21–24.
Response to the review symposium on his *The Analogical Imagination. Horizons* 8 (1981): 329–39.
Response to the review symposium on his *Plurality and Ambiguity. Theology Today* 44 (1987/88): 513–19.
"Theology, Critical Social Theory, and the Public Realm." In *Habermas, Modernity, and Public Theology,* edited by Don S. Browning and Francis Schüssler Fiorenza, 19–42. New York: Crossroad, 1992.
"The Uneasy Alliance Reconceived: Catholic Theological Method, Modernity, and Postmodernity." *Theological Studies* 50 (1989): 548–70.
Wallace, Mark I. *The Second Naiveté: Barth, Ricoeur, and the New Yale Theology.* Macon: Mercer University Press, 1990.
Werpehowski, William. "Ad Hoc Apologetics." *Journal of Religion* 66 (1986): 282–301.
West, Cornel. "Afterword: The Politics of American Neo-Pragmatism." In *Post-Analytic Philosophy,* edited by John Rajchman and Cornel West, 259–75. New York: Columbia University Press, 1985.
Prophesy Deliverance! An Afro-American Revolutionary Christianity. Philadelphia: Westminster Press, 1982.
Williams, Michael. "Coherence, Justification, and Truth." *Review of Metaphysics* 34 (1980): 243–72.
Wood, Charles. *The Formation of Christian Understanding: An Essay in Theological Hermeneutics.* Philadelphia: Westminster, 1981.

"The Knowledge Born of Obedience." *Anglican Theological Review* 61 (1979): 331–40.

Vision and Discernment: An Orientation in Theological Study. Atlanta: Scholars, 1985.

Young, Pamela Dickey. *Christ in a Post-Christian World.* Minneapolis: Fortress, 1995.

Index

Althusser, Louis, 89, 181

Anselm, 28, 88

apologetics, 53, 54, 55, 59, 60, 62, 63, 65, 67, 68, 72, 74, 83, 88, 92, 93, 103
  ad hoc, 2, 22, 23, 24, 41, 46, 88n47, 90, 91n53
  Christian-specific, 82, 85, 89, 90, 91, 95, 107
  and coherentist justification, 9, 50, 51, 52, 66, 78, 79, 80, 81, 87, 97, 108
  and consensus, 9, 50, 51–52, 66, 79, 81, 94–95, 97, 108
  as good dogmatics, 73, 86, 107
  liberationist, 75–76, 77n9, 101
  non-Christian-specific, 82, 83n29, 84, 85, 107
  postliberal, 8, 75, 76, 77n9
  revisionist, 8, 47, 48, 52, 66
  see also credibility; reflective equilibrium; transcendental arguments; truth

Aquinas, Thomas, 28–29, 82, 89, 96, 176, 181, 195

Aristotelianism, 96, 98

Aristotle, 11, 71n90, 176

assimilative power, 3, 76, 101–102, 173

atheism, 55n26, 57, 67–70, 72, 92–57

a/theology, 109–111, 140

background theories, 9, 78–79, 81–82, 86–90, 93, 100, 107–108, 142, 145, 173, 179–80

Barth, Karl, 1, 22–25, 72–73, 86, 103–104, 115, 116n17, 149, 154, 155n23, 169n74, 177, 184

Beardslee, William A., 111n6

Bernstein, Richard J., 9, 69–70, 71, 72, 96

Bible, 28, 62, 103, 109–147, 177, 178
  as church's book, 109, 113, 132, 135, 144, 145, 173
  and the poor, 113, 185, 191
  see also intratextuality; scripture

Boff, Clodovis, 5, 6, 7, 48, 76, 98, 106n112, 177
  and apologetics, 48, 84–85, 89–91, 92n57, 93, 103
  on Aquinas, 89, 181
  on Barth, 103–104
  on defining theology, 191–94
  on doctrinal recasting, 112, 125, 132–33, 139–42
  and experiential-expressivism, 85
  on hermeneutics, 124n41, 141n97, 147, 178, 194
  and Kuhn, Thomas, 98n80, 139
  and Milbank, 180–84
  on praxis, 104, 105, 106, 181, 182, 193n47
  and reflective equilibrium, 81–82
  and religious discourse, 81, 105n106, 133
  and rule theory or grammar, 80–81, 133, 181
  on social sciences, 90, 104–107, 179, 180–81, 183–84
  Theology and Praxis, 6, 93, 104, 191, 193

Boff, Leonardo, 156n27, 193

Brock, Rita Nakashima, 131, 186, 188–90

Brown, Delwin, 55n26, 111n6

Buckley, James J., 5n8

Cadorette, Curt, 169n72

Chalcedon, 137n86, 157, 161

Chopp, Rebecca S., 5n8

consensus fidelium, 137, 138, 145, 185

credibility,
  practical, 31, 32, 35, 45, 52–53, 75–76
  theoretical, 8, 9, 22, 23, 25, 31, 33, 34, 38, 45, 52–53, 75–76

cultural-linguistic, *see* religion, theory of

culture, 3, 4, 10, 19, 35, 174, 176, 178

Cunningham, David S., 80n21